AF479998

52 PICK UP

Life in Perfect Disorder

BY
DANI FORREST

52 Pick Up:
Life in Perfect Disorder
by Dani Forrest

Copyright © 2024 by Dani Forrest

All Rights Reserved. No part of this publication may be reproduced, stored in a retrieval system, or transmitted in any form or by any means, electronic, mechanical, photocopying, recording, scanning, or otherwise, without the prior written permission of the author.

ISBN (paperback) 979-8-8791-5522-8
ISBN (hardcover) 979-8-8691-7792-6
Also available as an ebook

Design by DTPerfect Book Design

Author Agent Contact: wilene@wcdenterprises.com

For Paul,
who gave me a reason,
a season and a love
like no other.

PROLOGUE

I stand in the shower washing the day away, an exhausting day of doctor's appointments, bloodwork, test results, and treatment plans. Looking down, I watch the water circle the drain. Just enough mental real estate remains for me to pull up the random fact that water drains clockwise in the northern hemisphere, counterclockwise south of the equator and straight down at the equator. I guess it's all a function of where you happen to be standing.

It occurs to my fatigued mind that memory is similar. Not at all linear, somewhat circular, and flowing in different directions, depending on perspective. And many times, not even flowing at all, but scattered here and there in unrelated fragments like snapshots fallen from a photo album—an awkward conversation, a loved one's final, liberating exhalation, a random car ride, an illicit kiss. Random flashes that, with effort, I manage to slide back into their proper chronological slots. Yet the sense of orderliness I've always craved eludes me. And I don't know whether I'm actually remembering the past or just telling myself stories about it.

From where I now stand, drenched and naked, the earliest memories emerge as those of an unnamed girl while later ones feel like letters from a separate, nameless self. Some seem to be the recollections of others, yet somehow, I am intimately familiar with them. Other stories, I know, are really and truly mine.

BEST LAID PLANS

Amy sits on the stiff, uncomfortable sofa in the little walk-up apartment. Her husband, Gabe, isn't home. It's New Year's Day, so he's watching the Rose Bowl over at Alan and Sheila's house. Amy isn't *bothered* by that, exactly. But she misses him, realizing with a tinge of melancholy that it won't be just the two of them ever again in a day or two or three. It would be nice to have him here with her, snuggling on the sofa under the big, crocheted afghan, his hand resting on her stomach. She's just too pregnant and uncomfortable to go anywhere. The baby is coming any day now, and it isn't as if their *alma mater* UCLA is playing—otherwise she of course would have made an effort and had their friends over for fondue and canapés.

Amy strokes her taut, ready-to-burst belly. She reaches for another chocolate from the large Whitman's Sampler box on the glass coffee table. She's already gone through her favorites—the truffles, nut clusters and toffees. But she can't stop. Even the disgusting ones—the molasses chews and nougats—taste *so* good today. She's going to demolish the entire box, a whole pound of chocolate which doesn't even taste that great. But today it feels like just about the best thing she's ever eaten.

She supposes it's just as well she watches the game alone today. Let Gabe have his fun. He'll be starting his last semester at UCLA Law School *and* becoming a new father, all in just a few days. She misses him but knows he needs a certain lightness that he doesn't always find with her. So serious, her Gabriel, with his worrisome thoughts about life and death, waking her up in the middle of the night with a desperate urgency, saying things like *we're all going to die someday*. It's all she can do to manage the house, prepare for the baby and worry about how they'll manage since she isn't working now, without having to think about dying on top of everything else. She and Gabe are young—twenty-three and twenty-four. For her, death is an abstract thing that happens mostly to older people—or politicians, like the dashing President John F. Kennedy, who just six weeks ago was tragically cut down right into the pink lap of his horrified wife.

Late that night, Amy lies awake and restless as Gabe sleeps soundly beside her. Maybe it was all that chocolate or the fact that there's no position that feels comfortable for her anymore. She finally winds up on her side, facing her husband's body and watching the contour of his back rise and fall with each breath. Even though they had planned for the baby to come during Gabe's last year of law school, Amy wonders, as she often does but only at night and only in secret, whether Gabe is truly happy about the baby, whether he even really wants it. He never actually said so, and she's never asked him. He makes jokes when other people are around. "It's perfect timing, really. Just when my student draft deferment ends, the parental one begins," he'll say. Or sometimes, "Perfect timing except for the due date. There goes the tax deduction for '63!"

Amy has longed to be a mother ever since she and Gabe were married three years ago. She'd wanted to have a baby right away like most of their high school friends, but postponed parenthood to help put Gabe through law school. There's a plan in place, and Amy likes plans. Law school, a baby, and then, if Gabe passes the bar right away and sets up a profitable practice, a house and hopefully another baby. There's really no reason it shouldn't all happen according to plan. She should just fall peacefully asleep, secure in the soothing knowledge that everything is on schedule.

ONE

The itsy, bitsy spider climbs up the waterspout…

Two cats that look the same, with creamy-colored warm bodies, brown tails, velvety black ears. The nice one is Koko and lives at Grama Lopez's house. Koko sits with the toddler outside and doesn't mind being hugged. The mean one is Sherlock, and he lives with Grandma May. Sherlock bites sometimes for no reason. Other times he approaches the toddler and skims his body against hers if she's silent when she sits up.

A playpen. She sits in it for hours, safe, enclosed and calm as long as she can see her mother or Grama Lopez through the netting. Her dolls sit with her—Chatty Cathy who talks and Pitiful Pearl who cries.

"Look at this, Gabe." Her mother puts a book in the playpen. No pictures, just lines of black things that look like something, but they don't seem right. She turns the book around so the things look right.

Her mother takes the book out of the playpen and puts another one in. No pictures but more black things that don't look right. She again turns the book around, so they do.

"Did you see that? She knows the book is upside down even though she can't read! Can you imagine?"

Her father towers over the playpen, peering down at her.

"A chip off the old block." He smiles before walking out the door.

A copper cup glinting in the sun as she learns to take the handle and drink from it, careful not to let the water drip from the sides of her mouth.

Down came the rain and washed the spider out…

Clanking at night while she lies in her crib. She crawls past the closet where the clanking, warm thing lives. When the thing gets very hot, it has a burning smell that she thinks is the smell of being scared.

She knows how to climb out of her crib. She toddles to her mother's room and watches her sleeping alone in bed. She lifts her mother's eyelid, and that wakes her up.

Her father, when he's home, stands over the sink in the tiny bathroom. She listens to the slick sound of metal moving over his face, taking with it the white foam and the tiny hairs that combine in a frothy soup in the basin. And then he is gone.

Her mother takes her to the bowling alley and drops her off at the nursery. She sits with blocks and crying babies, looking out the window at the cars rushing by, impatient for her mother to come back and rescue her.

She cries when her parents go out at night. They leave her with an old lady with bony hands who doesn't know what to do when the toddler falls and cuts her forehead on the corner of the glass coffee table. The lady holds a wet cloth against her head, rocking her and singing a nervous lullaby while the white cloth turns red.

Out came the sun and dried up all the rain...

Her mother pushes her on a swing at the park. Her insides feel gooey, like warm cookies. The swing moves to and fro as the sun plays hide and seek with her among the drying leaves of a giant tree.

Rhythm class. She and her mother jump and dance and run to music in a large room at the park recreation center. *Sugar pie, honey bunch, you know that I love you...* The music jumps out from a red record player in the corner, crackling and alive.

She crawls and stands and sways and falls and stands up again on the shiny linoleum floor, waving her arms and clapping her hands. She circles the room as best she can, sometimes moving, sometimes not, and sometimes just feeling the music expand inside the body that feels so new to her.

And the itsy-bitsy spider climbed up the spout again...

TWO

He takes a rare moment of stillness before he walks into the office, stopping to squint at the placard that bears his name. *Law Offices of Gabriel W. May.* Simple gold lettering on glossy black marble. Classy and professional, much more so, anyone could see, than the fake-brass plates below his that list the names of the other attorneys in the shared suite. Satisfied after a quick buff with the sleeve of his suit jacket, he bestows a dimpled grin on the receptionist and confidently strides into the corner office.

He stands for a moment at the window. He gazes down on La Cienega Boulevard, watching the cars rush the straight shot up to Sunset and the Hollywood Hills, the spiritual heart of the city. The soft light of late September casts a sad, moody glow over the buildings and landscaping; the days are getting shorter.

Gabe had moved into the building this past summer after he won his first big trial against an insurance company. He and Amy have started house-hunting in Cheviot Hills where all the well-to-do Jews live. They aren't Jewish, but all his clients think they are, which seems to be good for business, so he sees no need to correct anyone.

Checking his pile of messages, he settles down to a morning of phone calls, dictation and research for a summary judgment motion that has to be filed by the end of the week. He's good at what he does—a real Doberman when he wants to be. He likes the comparison to his boyhood dog, Bailey, who once pinned his best friend to the wooden gate, snarling until Gabe called him off.

Gabe works hard, but he knows in his heart that in a very short time he's going to be far beyond all this. The filings, court appearances and meetings with distraught clients, the humdrum workaday life of a sole practitioner sharing a suite with plodders lacking vision. All of it will soon be in his past. He's good at what he does, but it's not enough to slake his thirst for something else, something more.

At 4:00 pm, he hits the intercom button on the telephone unit and tells the receptionist he's heading to a meeting and won't be back. Instead of leaving via the main entrance, he walks out the back exit and down nine flights of stairs, where his black Corvette 427 gleams in its reserved parking space.

Amy was mad at him when he bought the Corvette. She wanted him to hang on to the VW bug he'd had since law school, because that would be the responsible thing to do. She wants them to save for the house and for the second child she's been talking about ever since the baby turned two in January.

Time. He feels the press of it, gnawing at him, propelling him forward toward a future that at once thrills and scares him. He's only twenty-seven, but he already knows there won't be—there will never be—enough of it. It's only when he slides into the driver's seat of his high-speed car that he feels he has a chance of keeping up, of catching time before it gets away from him altogether.

As happens most afternoons when he isn't in court, the car, of its own accord, seems to hang a left out of the parking lot onto La Cienega and up toward Sunset. By the time it passes Fountain Avenue, Gabe feels fully back in control as he upshifts and then guns the car up the steep incline to where the Hollywood Hills begin. He veers right, downshifts and speeds up as Sunset starts its long descent from Beverly Hills toward downtown.

Gabe loves driving The Strip every day, as he's done since he drove his new car off the lot in January. His destiny is here—he feels it. It's in the neon cursive splash of the large Schwab's sign just past Crescent Heights. It follows the seductive curves of the road that hugs the hills and lives in the clubs and the recording studios. His fate lies in this vibrant world galaxies away from the staid flats adjacent to Beverly Hills where Amy takes the baby on sedate walks in the stroller.

One August night when the apartment is too hot for sleep, he sneaks out of bed and makes the drive, parking at the top of La Cienega and walking down to Gazzarri's. It's 2:00 am, and the Strip throngs with people marinating in the sultry summer night. The mod, mop-topped boys in skinny suits and their girls in short skirts and pastel tights with matching patent leather Mary Janes. The Strip is one long, never-ending party, and he doesn't want to miss one minute of it.

He pulls up to the curb across the street from Whisky a Go Go. The marquee advertises The Byrds for tonight. Before that it was The Doors; Gabe snuck out to see them on one of his night wanders after telling Amy he couldn't sleep and was going to the office to prepare for an upcoming trial. He sat mesmerized while Jim Morrison inhabited *The End* with such primal love and lust and hate and rage that it was as if he were channeling the angst of an entire generation. Gabe stood that night in silent solidarity with everyone in the club, all of them at the edge of a gaping maw that felt awful and beautiful and raw and irresistible all at the same time. He sat alone in his car for a long time after the show, and then went home to an apartment, a wife and a toddler—a whole existence—that seemed to be slipping away.

"Well, hello, handsome."

The owner of the low, singsong voice slides into the passenger seat as Gabe's heart begins to hammer even before he looks at her—which he doesn't. He just closes his eyes and kisses her and breathes her in. Then, because he can't get too lost in her, he pulls back and starts the engine.

Gabe met Honey when he first started cruising Sunset, in the early days when he parked the car after a while and just walked. One day he passed a beauty salon, and through the window he saw an angel's face in profile with short, white-blonde curls framing it like a halo. He'd never had a manicure, but that day he did. Just so that angel would hold his hands for a few minutes while he looked into those gray eyes with the long, platinum lashes.

He went back every week for a while but eventually abandoned the pretense after Amy one day picked up his hand, looked at his buffed nails and then dropped it, saying nothing. So now he just picks Honey up every afternoon when her shift ends. Sometimes they just drive together up and down Sunset, to its end downtown and then to its other end at Pacific Coast Highway.

Mostly though, they just drive The Strip, from Sierra Drive at the Beverly Hills end to Havenhurst Avenue at the West Hollywood end, and back again. They talk about life, astrology (which Honey practices when she isn't doing nails) and Gabe's dreams.

He knows he can do what Gil Tanzini and Elmer Valentine did with their nightclub, the Whisky: create a hub for music and the people who make it happen. Not necessarily on Sunset, but somewhere close by because he already sees that the energy of The Strip can't be contained. It can't edge north into the residential neighborhoods of the hills, but it can spill south, and maybe even east, down Highland or La Brea. He started mingling with agents and managers in the music business and thinks he can get some decent headline acts, some up-and-comers, and of course go-go girls will be easy to find. The city is filled with long-legged, aspiring Twiggys who would love nothing more than to dance on elevated platforms above dozens of hungry male eyes, some of which could even make them stars. A huge, untapped market exists for those patrons beyond their twenties wanting to catch the magic—or just the underbelly of the magic—escorts and their pimps, low-level gangsters, general rounders.

Honey listens to every word with admiring eyes, taking them off him only to reach into her leather-fringed purse for a beaded cigar case where there is always a smoke at the ready for him. Nights when he can get away, when Amy thinks he's working late or at a client dinner, he and Honey head to Gazzarri's, or the Whisky, or sometimes just for hole-in-the-wall Mexican food on east Sunset. It doesn't matter as long as he's with her, gazing at her as she listens to him spin his future, her adoring eyes assuring him that yes, it can all happen and yes, it *will* all happen.

THREE

When she learns that a little brother or sister will soon arrive, she wonders if the baby will come via a knock at the front door, like the ladies who come to play Pan with her mother on Wednesdays. Or whether the man in blue who jogs up the porch steps every day will drop it through the slot in the front door where she leaves the letters her mother writes for her to Hobo Kelly on TV.

Every afternoon she lies on the beige sofa in the living room of the new house watching Hobo Kelly. She wants to jump through the television into Hobo Junction and hop onto Hobo Kelly's back when she flies far above the cities in search of fellow *mischief makers*. That way she'll be there when her name is called, when it's time for Hobo Kelly to crank the Magic Toy Box that spits out Lite Brites and ant farms for the kids who write her letters.

When she isn't watching Hobo Kelly, she's with Grama and Papa Lopez or Grandma and Zhido May, or sometimes with Auntie Di. Her mother is *busy,* and her father is *at the office.* Usually one of the grandmas comes to pick her up. Each has a big, white Cadillac with pointy tail fins like shark's teeth. Grama Lopez's car has plush turquoise on the inside, and Grandma May's has black shiny leather that sticks to the girl's legs when she sits in it.

Grama Lopez lives just down the street from where Auntie Di is a cheerleader at the high school. The little girl runs through the door and right away opens the third drawer down from the kitchen counter where Grama keeps the treats. Striped shortbread and chocolate grahams or donuts with the fine white powder that melts on her tongue. After that, she skips down into the den, where Grama will put a shiny disc onto her fancy record player. The big speakers crackle and then the music starts, Herb Alpert & The Tijuana Brass, The Ray Conniff Singers or Sing Along with Mitch. She lies on her tummy on the floor of the den, looking at the album covers, singing along when there are words and *la-la-la*-ing along when there aren't.

Papa putters in the yard or the cellar. He doesn't talk very much and when he does, it's mostly Spanish. *Chica Niña,* he calls her—vowelly-soft words that blur together. She doesn't know what they mean, but his voice envelops her with softness like the afghan quilts Grama crochets, zigzag stripes of brightly colored yarn. During summer, the luxurious scent from their fig tree wafts in through the screen door, and Grama brings in baskets of plump figs, pink, rich flesh bursting out from their bottoms. In winter, the smell comes from the kitchen, from flaky squares of flour, sugar and butter cradling dollops of hot apricot or berry jam. Grama takes her to the sofa and reads her favorite book, *Tootle,* about the naughty little train that refuses to stay on the rails after engineer Bill tells him to, and they both listen for the oven timer as the air grows heavy with the smell of cookies.

In the afternoons, Auntie Di pulls up to the house in her powder blue VW bug with the little dark blue pom pom on the top of its radio antenna. She loves to watch Auntie Di get out of the car, swinging her hair, long and straight and brown like chocolate with shiny red flecks in it, and then bounding up the path like a tan, long-legged Ferris wheel. She mostly wears her cheer uniform, a short blue and white pleated skirt, white shirt with a blue "H" on it, bobby socks and sneakers. Grama is making her a miniature outfit to match Auntie's. Sometimes when she sleeps over and Auntie is out with her boyfriend, she sneaks into the closet to shake the big blue and white pom poms. The colored strips of shiny plastic blur together when she shakes them really hard, and then she closes her eyes and listens to the pleasing *swish-swish* and imagines what it will be like when it's her turn to be a cheerleader.

If Auntie doesn't go out, they drive down to Baskin Robbins. Even though there are thirty-one flavors, she just orders whatever Auntie gets, rocky road or pistachio on a sugar cone. She doesn't really like pistachio because anything that's green should taste like either lime or mint. But she eats it anyway because she wants to do whatever Auntie does. And then she licks the sticky ice cream off her fingers as Auntie zooms her little car back to Grama's. Auntie wraps her in a big blanket and drags her really fast around the house after Grama and Papa go to bed. She has to promise not to laugh too loud so she just covers her mouth to tame the wild burst of joy that feels good and simple and clean as she tumbles around inside the blanket.

When her father's parents Grandma and Zhido May pick her up, they take her home to their little turquoise house. A long hedge runs on either side of the walkway, punctuated by twin cypress bushes next to the sidewalk. She pulls a few needles off one and hands them to Grandma May, as she does every visit. In return Grandma says, "Why, thank you." Every time Grandma laughs with amazed delight, as if no one had ever thought to do such an original and amusing thing as hand her a bunch of cypress needles.

Just like Grama Lopez, Grandma May reads the same book to her over and over again, except at her house it's *Butterball*, about a little chick who is a bother to his family until he can rescue the key to his mother's picnic basket and save the chicken family's day out. She memorized the words to both *Butterball* and *Tootle* so that she can mouth them along with each grandma.

You see, said Mother Hen, sometimes it's good to be small…

Or,

Then the Dreadful Thing happened. After all that Bill said about Staying on The Rails No Matter What, Tootle jumped off the tracks and raced alongside the Black Horse!

Sometimes a grandma will change the words, like say *you know* instead of *you see* or *awful* instead of *dreadful*. The girl always makes sure to correct them when they do that because they have to read the exact words.

Both grandmas offer to read her other books. Wouldn't she like to hear a different story?

No, she wouldn't.

She has to hear those stories over and over because those are the ones she's decided to learn to read by herself. She'll be starting school in two years, her mother says. So, she thinks she'd better learn to read *now* because two years might be happening very soon. She's three years old, almost four now, but she was two years old right before that, so really it seems that two years should have happened already or will happen very soon. She is eager to start kindergarten, which she imagines to be a pretty place where reading and writing happen. And where there are roses like the ones Grandma May names to her as they walk around the backyard, touching the velvety petals with gentle reverence and inhaling their dressy tea-party smell.

Sometimes while Grandma May hangs laundry on the line out in the yard behind the rose bushes, Zhido takes her out to lunch in the big Cadillac. They go to the Copper Penny where she orders a burger with fries and a Coke. She sits up all proper and quiet in the red leatherette booth they share, sensing that she must be especially quiet and good around Zhido. She hears him asking her mother all the time:

"When is my *grandson* coming?"

It sounds like she's done something wrong, that she is not *just right*, the way she feels she is with the grandmas and with Papa. Even though she learned to speak a few words in Arabic, which is what they speak in Lebanon where Zhido is from, and even though he's patient while she sits at his feet and unties and then re-ties his brown leather shoes over and over, she knows she shouldn't ask questions or ask him to read to her. She doesn't want to bother him while he sits in his recliner, intent on the latest episode of *Gunsmoke*.

Still, she feels content, cocooned in the collection of moments tumbling one after another like the colored blocks that fall from their plastic box onto the floor and lie there until she decides what she's going to make them do. In the moments when she's in the places where she feels most cherished. She likes being in the new house, too, even though she's still not used to it and will have to share it with the New Baby when it arrives.

She likes going to the supermarket with her mother because now she's old enough to go get the milk by herself, walking straight down the aisle to where all the cartons stand like soldiers in a line. She knows to pick up the big carton with the red letters, not the thin one with the blue letters or the tiny one with the yellow letters. Proud that she knows what to do, she returns to her mother and the shopping cart, holding the milk carton like a trophy and ready to learn to do another important and helpful thing.

One day, right after she brings the milk over, she feels especially good and helpful and happy to be with her mother as they gather ingredients for chocolate chip cookies. The joy of being a good helper combines with glad thoughts of cookie dough and how it will look later in the hazy yellow light of the oven, spreading and rising and glistening like the gladness inside her now. She thinks of herself and her mother in their matching checkered aprons, licking spoons and peering at the cookies as they spread out and puff up.

A man she doesn't know approaches her mother and begins a conversation. He wears a suit and tie and black-rimmed glasses like her father's. After a moment, her mother introduces the man to her as Mr. Arnold, a man from the school where her mother used to teach.

The girl's gladness can't be contained. It spreads out like gooey cookie dough in the oven to the people in the market and also to Mr. Arnold. She puts her arm around his leg because that is only as high as she can reach. She hugs his leg, leaning her head against him as she thrums with joy and with the wonder of just being alive.

But Mr. Arnold grows alarmed at her closeness; he recoils, crossing his arms and trying to rebuff her attempts at physical contact. She feels him doing that, but she clings anyway, hugging him harder, willing him to be happy with her, as the grandmas and Auntie Di always are. But Mr. Arnold remains stiff and uncomfortable. After he leaves, her mother grabs her roughly by the arm and, with punishing intensity, questions her.

"What on Earth were you doing, Martha? Couldn't you see that man didn't want you touching him? He doesn't know you. Why were you hugging him? You embarrassed him. You embarrassed me. Don't you EVER do that again!"

And then the vast well that a minute ago had been so filled with good feels suddenly empty. She puts her head down so that no one will see her tears and follows her mother, who resolutely marches toward the cashier line. She doesn't know what the word *embarrassed* means, but it involved something that she did that should never be done. And now the gladness and wonder are gone, replaced by something else that she has never felt before and that has no name.

FOUR

Her father is gone. Her mother's shiny black hair is short now. When the girl asks when he's coming back to see her, she sees the fleeting change in her mother's face, the little number eleven that appears on her forehead just above her nose, and the way her lips press together hard. And then her mother is gone, out through the olive-green front door that squeaks when it opens, and off to teach again like she did before she was a mom.

Wandering through the quiet morning, the girl is careful to avoid the laundry room that contains Sofia, the helper brought in to take care of her and Baby Greg when her mother had to go back to work. She likes the freshness of a new day, the sight of rotating spray from the sprinklers in the yard and the drops of water landing and glistening on the grass. The quiet of the house holds her, tight and safe and snug.

She walks into the room where her baby brother Greg sleeps, staring at him through the white slats of his crib until he opens his eyes. When he sees her, she crouches down beneath the crib and then rises again slowly, making the scariest face she can think of. But that doesn't make Greg cry. It makes him laugh, and suddenly, she laughs too, and then she thinks that maybe she'll stop wishing for him to be sent back to wherever he came from.

She sits at the kitchen table, looking at the picture cards that her nursery school classmates sent her after she had her tonsils out. She remembers being in the hospital and how thirsty she was when she woke up. The water there hurt her when she drank it. There was something wrong with it and she tried to make her mother find better water, but her mother laughed and said it wasn't the water, it was her throat that was sore from the operation.

Baby Greg is sick and screaming with the croup. Sofia holds him in her arms, rocking him back and forth as she paces the kitchen floor.

The girl looks at the cards, which are mostly scribbled crayon marks with some glue and glitter on top. She wishes her mother were there, but her mother is on a trip with her new friend, Mr. Hathaway. Sofia is nervous, and she's nervous too. She stacks the cards, and then cuts them into pieces, and then glues them to a large piece of construction paper, and still Greg screams.

Sofia calls Grama Lopez. After that, Sofia wraps Greg in his fuzzy blanket and says she has to take him outside. Sofia tells her to stare at the clock above the stove, and when the big hand moves from the one to the three, that will be ten minutes, and then to wave from the window. She stares at the clock, watching the big hand slowly move as the long skinny hand tick-ticks in circles. When the big hand reaches the three, she waves from the window, and then Sofia comes back in and says that the cold air finally put Baby Greg to sleep.

She hates nursery school. She wants to stay home with her books and her toys and the sprinklers and Hobo Kelly.

Her father tried to take her to school the first day, which was right before he went to live somewhere else. She held on to the doorknob with one hand, and then he pulled her other arm so hard that it hurt her shoulder. Her mother had to take her to the doctor, so she didn't start school until the next day.

"Moonie, you have to go. Mommy's working and Sofia has to take care of baby Greg. Don't you want to be a big girl now?" Only her mother and grandma call her Moon or Moonie, short for Moondrops, the name of her mother's Revlon lipstick she used to put on when no one was looking. And then when she got caught that became her nickname.

She *does* want to be a big girl, to read and to write. But there is no reading and writing where her mother drops her off. The other children are babyish and boring, content to water paint on the concrete playground, finger paint endless circles and blobs on construction paper, and then lie down on cots for daily nap time. She lies on her cot with her eyes open while the others sleep, thinking about the one thing she likes there which is the color wheel that sits in the art room next to the crayons and markers. She doesn't know why it's there. The other children ignore it in their everyday mad scramble for purple and pink and blue crayons. Tired-looking ladies with their lips pressed into tight straight lines dole out Ritz crackers in the afternoon, but she prefers to sit at the tiny art table. The order of colors on the wheel feels pleasing and right.

She sits on the playground staring through the metal squares of the chain-link fence, or slumps in a swing, listless. When she hops down, an odor of metal from the chains is on her hands and it turns her stomach.

All the children are herded in for lunch at noon.

"God is great, God is good, now we thank him for our food." She recites the prayer they've all been taught, bowing her head to look at her lunch of mashed potatoes spotted with tiny pieces of ham. They get mad if she doesn't clean her plate, so she eats even though she isn't hungry, thinking about how *good* doesn't rhyme with *food*.

Outside, she throws up the mashed potatoes and ham. Her mother picks her up and gives her Orange Crush to settle her tummy.

At home in the afternoons, she is free. She sits cross-legged on the floor next to her bed with *Tootles* and *Butterball*, looking at the groups of letters on each page as she says the words her grandmas read to her, willing herself to match what she's heard to what she still can't decipher on the pages.

Her mother buys her a spelling book, the kind that big kids use. She carries it around the house pretending to be in school. Sitting at the kitchen table, she makes marks in the book, frustrated because she knows it's all just babyish scribbling. She can't read and she can't write, so she doesn't know how to learn the way the book wants her to.

A tiny wooden bench sits in her room next to the bed. It was a birthday present from her mother's friend, Sheila. The top of it is shiny and shellacked, painted with flowers and her own name in large cursive letters.

Martha

When she gets tired of trying to read, she tries to write, tracing over the letters on the bench with her finger and then trying to make the same movements on a piece of paper with a blue crayon. But the marks she makes are just squiggles that look nothing like the pretty writing on the little bench.

Sometimes a big brown spider with long creeping legs crawls out from under her four-poster bed. She drops her books and her crayons and runs screaming into her mother's room where she flops down on her tummy on the king size bed to watch *Batman* and *Bozo.*

Her mother works every day now since her father left. In the morning, the girl sits and watches her mother get ready. A row of white Styrofoam heads sits on the vanity table. Her mother selects a wig of wavy long hair to place over her own pixie, or a fall to sweep into a bouffant. She picks out her skirt and jacket suit for the day, blue or black or gray, and a brightly patterned scarf to go with it. When her mother unscrews the gold cap from her lipstick tube and twists the bottom to reveal the pretty pink insides, the girl knows it is time to hop off the bed and wait by the front door. Together they will ride in the blue Mustang until her mother drops her off at nursery school. She stands at the window, waving as her mother drives away to teach other, bigger kids.

Sunday is the day her father comes to visit. She sits on the cement steps that lead down to the driveway, waiting for the black Cadillac to float up the street. Often, he doesn't come, but she sits on the porch anyway until her butt is cold and numb and her mother says she has to come inside. When he does come, he takes her to Kiddie Land, standing with his hands in his pockets while she goes on the pony ride and the boat ride and the bumper cars. He buys her cotton candy and sits with her while she pulls pink strands from the white paper cone and mashes them with her fingers until they are dark and grainy and chewy.

After a while, he starts bringing Miss Honey with him in the front seat of the Cadillac. She looks at the back of Miss Honey's head, the fine strands of teased, white-blond hair that remind her of the cotton candy at Kiddie Land. Miss Honey is always touching her or her father, with long nails that are a different color every week, hot pink or coral or fire engine red. Miss Honey doesn't wear suits and scarves like her mother; she wears fur and feathers and beads and leather. She talks in a sweet, whispery, cotton-candy voice that matches her hair.

They ride up the elevator to her father's apartment. Miss Honey reads playing cards that she fans out before her, staring at the faces and the numbers and the shapes as if they are speaking to her.

"Hmm," she says, in a voice different from her usual candied tone.

"Queen of Spades. Intelligent, but too much thinking. Many paths. No happiness until she masters that mind." Miss Honey sweeps the cards back into a neat, stacked deck, and the cotton candy returns when she laughs and looks at the girl's father. "Just like you said, Gabriel. A chip off the old block."

She's mostly at home with her mother and Greg, though. And because her mother works so much, it seems that Sofia has to stay.

She loves Sofia at first, the thick dark hair that is so like her mother's, the stories she tells about her home in Colombia where giant scorpions come out at night and can kill you with one bite. She makes fragrant platters of *bandeja paisa,* beans and rice and sausage and plantains that Sofia says helps to make her less homesick. Then Sofia snuggles with her in the little bedroom next to the kitchen, on the white coverlet-covered twin bed. Sofia sucks on salted orange quarters while they watch José Feliciano from the small black and white television on the dresser, and Sofia tells her the English words for what he sings in Spanish.

Then Sofia goes back home to Colombia to pick up the rest of her things so she can move in full time with the family. When she comes back, she's...*different.* Not mean—not at first. Just quiet. She spends most of her time now with Greg, playing with his tiny baby hands and wiggling his baby toes, rushing to his crib whenever he cries, whisper-singing melancholy Spanish songs to him as he dozes in his automatic swing. When she isn't cleaning or cooking or caring for Baby Greg, Sofia stays in her little room with the door closed. No more invitations to come in and snuggle.

One night after dinner, when her mother is out with Mr. Hathaway and Greg is asleep in his room, she stands outside the closed door to Sofia's room. She can hear sounds, the staccato talking coming from the Spanish television station. She knows she shouldn't, but she feels her hand on the shiny metal doorknob, turning it slowly. When the door opens, she sees Sofia standing in front of the mirror, holding her long, lustrous brown hair in a fist clenched tight at the nape of her neck. In the other hand, she holds a pair of scissors with blades that look like the beak of an ugly, metallic bird.

In one bite that shiny bird takes off all of Sofia's beautiful hair, leaving only sad, chewed up ends that lay upturned and confused-looking against her pale, exposed neck. Then Sofia turns, with brimming, desperate eyes that meet hers. The hideous bird clatters to the floor, and the eyes shift from red to black.

"Diabla!" Sofia lunges at the doorway where the girl stands shocked and exposed, like the jagged edges of Sofia's hair. She runs to her own room and scrambles under the bed, her thumb finding its way into her mouth, the terror of spiders momentarily forgotten as she listens for the sound of Sofia's Keds slap-slapping across the linoleum.

Suddenly there is the reassuring sound of the front door unlocking, and the low voices of her mother and Mr. Hathaway echoing from the hall. She slithers out from the dusty down-below and crawls under the yellow bedspread, pulling it up to her chin. She closes her eyes even though she knows her mother won't look in on her before the master bedroom door closes and muffles the sound of their voices.

Nothing is ever said about that night. Only Sofia's hostility remains, always there and always taking the little girl by surprise, when she wakes in the night frightened because the house is dark and her mother is gone, or when she leaves her toys in the living room. She is a *diabla*. Whatever that means, it's not good, and it's a secret. She is a *diabla* only when her mother is gone. Because she's a *diabla*, there may come a night when her mother never returns, and Sofia often reminds her of this in her querulous, accented voice.

At night she dreams of spiders, armies of hairy, spindly-legged creatures that emerge from under her bed and grow into giant monsters with legs like scissor blades.

FIVE

She finally starts Big Kid School, and she knows how to say it, too. *Kindergarten.* It isn't a garden with roses as she had imagined, but there's a pretty teacher with a shiny black bouffant like her mother's. She sits on the carpet in a circle with the other children while Miss Gunther reads from a big book about rocks and then holds the book up to show the pictures. The children all crane their necks to see. *Sedimentary rocks. Igneous rocks. Metamorphic rocks.* Big words for big kids. Miss Gunther says the words slowly and makes the children repeat them aloud.

On Friday morning the sixth-grade helpers come, girls with long, straight hair that swings as they walk and bright patterned skirts with white knee-high socks. They read with the kindergarteners and help them sound out lists of vocabulary words. She has learned to read well before this, by memorizing *Tootle* and *Butterball* as her grandmas read and then sitting with the books and finally matching the sounds to the letters. And then after that happens, she finds to her delight that suddenly she's able to read *everything.*

With nothing else to do, she just sits and admires her sixth-grader, Carol, who dutifully reads *Green Eggs and Ham* aloud slowly, using her index finger to point to each word as she reads and tapping the floor with her green-sneakered feet. Carol has long, red hair with eyelashes and freckles to match. She wears a Girl Scout uniform, and the badges on her green sash are what the little girl reads instead. *Community Safety. Drawing & Painting. Folklore. Health Aid.*

Carol has her read the list of vocabulary words. She can read everything now, so they're easy. This week the words are about eating.

Cup. Plate. Fork. Spoon. Knife. She feels bad that the words are so easy and that there's nothing for Carol to help her with, so she pretends to stumble, saying *kuh-nife* even though she knows better.

"Nooo", says Carol. "The k is silent. Nife." The girl smiles and says the word properly. She's happy, finally, to be in *real* school where she gets to learn things even though she already knows a lot of them. Not like preschool, where she quickly tired of babyish games and nap time and the impatient ladies in charge of snacks.

So much to find out here, and then playtime in the yard where she and the other children chase each other around and around. Troy chases her the most. She thinks one day she might let him catch her, and then she'll kiss him. Maybe.

Kindergarten ends by lunchtime, which is also what makes it better than the long, boring days at preschool. Her favorite days are when Grama Lopez picks her up and takes her to McDonalds or Jack in the Box. They sit at a table under an umbrella where she has a cheeseburger, fries and a Coke while Grama has a fish sandwich. They roll pieces of their buns into tiny balls to throw to the waiting sparrows. Then Grama takes her to a movie, *Cinderella* or *Snow White* or her favorite, *The Sound of Music,* where she knows all the songs because Grama plays the records for her at home.

Her mother marries Mr. Hathaway, who she now calls "Daddy Landon," because Landon is his first name. She gets to be the flower girl in their little wedding in the neat little white church. She wears a white cotton dress with white tights, white patent leather Mary Janes and a yellow headband decorated with white daisies. Her mother wears a yellow coat dress and styles her hair so that little black tendrils curl down in front of her ears. They carry matching big and little bouquets. And then afterward, everyone comes to the house, her family, Grama and Papa and Auntie Di, and Uncle Johnny, who comes home from college for the wedding. Her pretty new stepsister Linda is there, too, who's fifteen and has long, swinging hair like the sixth-grade helpers. Grandma May and Zhido are there, too, but they stand a bit stiffly and separately and they don't smile as much as everyone else.

Daddy Landon buys her mother a big station wagon with wood panels and comes to live with her and her mother and baby Greg and Sofia in the house where her father used to live.

She likes Daddy Landon. He's much older than her mother and father, tall and tanned with green eyes that crinkle at the corners when he smiles. He brings her a book from the Sierra Club that has pictures of rocks and streams and trees. She sits on his lap, and he explains all the pictures to her and is very happy that she knows the different kinds of rocks she learned about from Miss Gunther.

Her favorite picture is the one of the Big Black Cloud. It takes up the whole page. There's only a tiny bit of blue sky, and Daddy Landon says that it's an approaching thunderstorm. He explains to her what makes thunder and what makes lightning and how lightning runs faster than thunder, so thunder makes a lot of noise trying to catch up.

She's never known a thunderstorm, but then one night she does. Her mother and Daddy Landon have a party in the house. It's raining hard outside, harder than she's ever heard. She walks around drinking the bottoms out of everyone's martini glasses, which is fun because it makes her feel dizzy and happy at the same time—and her mother thinks it's funny.

She has a new toy, a slingshot thing that tumbled out of a cereal box one morning, and her mother put it together for her. She runs around the party, among all the pants and party dresses, running to the door every time a guest arrives so she can look at the rain hammering down just beyond the front porch.

And then she sees it—a great big flash of light followed by a deafening *crack.* The air rumbles and shakes the living room windows just as her mother pulls the last arriving guest into the warm house and shuts the door. The girl squeals and runs to her room, where she jumps in bed and pulls the bedspread over her head to make a fort. The fabric is thin, so she can still see through it. Every time the lightning flashes it illuminates the little cubby where she sits, shooting her little slingshot and counting the seconds to the thunder just as Daddy Landon taught her. And when the thunder comes, it mixes with the happy sounds of laughter, music, clinking glasses in the living room and with the rain drumming on the roof.

Right after her mother and Daddy Landon get married, her father marries Miss Honey at her father's nightclub. They show her a picture after, of her father smiling in his black suit and holding a cigar. His arm is around Honey, slender in a white lace jumpsuit with long bell sleeves and a high neck, her short, white-blonde hair teased big and high.

Her father picks her up on a Saturday afternoon to spend the night at their apartment. Sofia walks her to the door with her small pink suitcase; her mother stays in the master bedroom with the door closed. She climbs into the back seat of the cavernous black Cadillac, and her father lets her dial the giant telephone that is attached to the hump between the two front seats. She's never seen a phone in a car before; her father says it's one of the first ever made. She tries to call her mother, but all she hears is crackling and her father says that's because it's hard to get good reception.

Honey turns to her from the front seat.

"Hi, sweetie." Honey is wearing a hat made of colored beads. Some of them drop down from the bottom to frame her face and they move when she moves, like a dancing rainbow. Honey's hand stays on her father's leg while he drives, the long pink nails grazing the fabric of his pants.

They arrive at her father's nightclub, which is open in the daytime just for today, because there's a wedding reception there. She spins around and around on a red leather stool and drinks Shirley Temples with extra cherries. The bride is a pretty, brown-skinned lady who wears a white mini dress and a short veil that sits on top of her head like a netted cake-plate cover.

Soon her stomach starts to hurt. Nausea above combined with a gurgling below. It happens mostly when she's with her father and Honey but other times too, when she's among people she doesn't know and feels suddenly and inexplicably nervous. She wants to dash out the door, to go somewhere else, somewhere quiet and familiar. She feels like Grandma May's cat Sherlock, who panics when people he doesn't know come over and then jumps through his cat door and out into the night. Instead, she curls up on Honey's lap, letting her mouth once again find her thumb so that the rhythmic sucking can soothe her insides.

They take her shopping and buy her a purple dress and white patent leather knee boots. She gets to wear everything out of the store and lays her legs across the back seat of the Cadillac so she can admire the shiny whiteness and the little stacked heels as they drive home.

Her father's apartment is at the very top of a tall building at the top of a very big hill on Sunset Boulevard. She loves the name of that street. It makes her think of a giant orange sun casting its last light before night comes and the lights of the city begin their nightly show in the city beneath her father's window.

They pass a goldfish pond in the courtyard just outside the lobby. She loves to sit by its edge, watching the orange and white mottled shapes sway beneath the water's surface. Their gaping mouths open and close when she comes because they know she has the bread that Honey gives her to feed them. She reaches down close. They will take the bread from her hand if she keeps very still.

An elevator clanks up twelve floors, to a place with windows that go from the floor to the ceiling, revealing streets and buildings far below and the ocean far beyond.

We were talking about the space between us all
And the people, who hide themselves
behind a wall of illusion
Never glimpse the truth,
then it's far too late
when they pass away…

She lies on her tummy on the white shag carpet of her father's apartment, reading the lyrics on the back of the Beatles' Sgt. Pepper's Lonely Hearts Club Band record album and singing along as the music plays on her father's stereo. She knows every song, but her favorite is *Within You Without You* because the sound of the music and the sense that she gets from the words, although she's not quite sure what they mean, make her feel as if she might melt into the giant orange sun as it settles behind the ocean. She stands up and walks to the window and peers down just as the lights start to come on in the streets and buildings below. When the sun is totally gone, the blackness comes, covered by a twinkling blanket that delights her up here, far and away and above.

SIX

She holds on tight to Daddy Landon's hand. Her feet feel squishy and unnatural, swimming around in wet, white Keds. Her mother insists she wear sneakers onto the reef because the rocks are sharp.

Her mother watches them from the beach, one hand shading her eyes under a floppy yellow hat. Greg runs back and forth, jumping on the baby waves. The girl tried to explain to her little brother that jumping on the waves isn't what makes them crash, but he didn't seem to understand or care and so she gave up and left him to it.

The further they walk out onto the reef, the deeper the pools, the bluer the water. The neverending, whispering *waaaahhhh* sound of the big waves calls to her as they crash in the distance. Daddy Landon will keep walking with her as long as she wants to. He has taught her the names of all the fish that glide and wriggle underneath her. Clown fish. Parrot fish. Emperor angelfish. Triggerfish. Grouper.

This island place wraps her in the kindness of turquoise water, striped fish and cottony clouds. In a week, she'll be home in California again, but for the first time since she left, she isn't craving home as she did the whole time they lived in Sydney, Australia. Her mother says it's been a year; she knows only that she was six then and is almost seven now. Greg didn't know how to talk then, but he does now. There were opposite seasons in Australia; in June and July she wore a school uniform of gray wool with a gray felt hat, and then in December and January a gray and yellow cotton dress with a straw hat.

In Sydney, she spent rainy afternoons in a large living room in an odd house with many levels, overlooking a strange ocean. Large drops pummeling the window, hiding the view of a strange bridge glimmering across the harbor, and a strange new building called the Opera House that looked like a white, half-underwater sea monster. She imagined climbing on its back and riding under that bridge, all the way back home to California.

She learned to be satisfied with pop-up cards filled with sticks of Juicy Fruit gum in place of Grama Lopez and with letters smelling like rose petals instead of Grandma May. With her father's occasional page of inky scrawl in place of him. With Judy Collins in place of Auntie Di. With putting the record player arm over and over again at the beginning, setting the needle down gently at the beginning of *Both Sides Now*. Looking at the album cover for hours, at Judy's sun-streaked hair and dreamy blue eyes, until Judy morphed into Auntie Di and once again it was the inside of Grama Lopez's living room. Singing along and crying when she was sure her mother couldn't see, because she couldn't put a name to the deepening cavern inside of her, the one that suddenly appeared when she found herself in a different country and a new school with girls who spoke with strange accents and who, in turn, viewed her as equally odd.

Today, the cavern fills with brightly colored sea life and distant white clouds and the feel of Daddy Landon's hand holding hers as she names the fish. She feels full, as if she has eaten something delicious, like the *bandeja paisa* that Sofia used to make before she turned mean. She doesn't know where in California she will be living with Greg and her mother and Daddy Landon and Sofia. But it will be near her father and her grandparents, and so she hopes that she will feel full again there, too.

Walking across the reef, she spies cobalt blue starfish, dozens of them, clinging to the slick dark rock or in placid repose on the bleached sand in the clear shallows. She lets go of Daddy Landon, crouches low over the rock and plucks two of the creatures from the sand where they rest. One for each hand.

She steps with care on the long walk back to shore. The sea stars lie in her hands, hard and resistant. These blue creatures will come home to California with her, she decides. They will live in a tank next to her bed with sand and plants and colored rocks. They will have each other, so they won't be lonely. And she will have them, two living souvenirs of fullness.

SEVEN

She sits in the beige, windowless room today, as she does every Wednesday after her mother picks her up from school early to bring her here. She isn't sure why; her mother says it's to help her "adjust."

She doesn't tell the other kids in her class why she has to leave early and they don't ask. Every Wednesday at 2:00 pm, the office lady, Mrs. Rothman, comes to the classroom. The girl is always ready, with her Partridge Family homework folder in front of her. David Cassidy stares at her with his big brown eyes framed by soft feathered hair, his full, parted lips looking as if they're about to tell her something secret and sweet. She slips the folder into her backpack along with her math and spelling books and follows Mrs. Rothman to the office, where her mother waits to drive her to see Dr. Van Heusen.

"How are you today, Martha?"

Dr. Van Heusen crosses his legs and hunches forward slightly from across the table. She looks at him, at his oiled black hair edged with gray and the large square glasses. He squints at her, and she sees the wrinkles form at the corners of his eyes. And the eyebrows that should separate but don't because he just has one long black eyebrow that looks like a mustache but in the wrong place.

She says nothing. She doesn't feel like talking. She didn't understand today's math lesson and is nervous about being able to finish her homework. Her best friend Yuko ate lunch with Alicia today and not her, and that is worrisome as well. She hasn't been at her school long enough for that not to matter because she isn't at all sure about the other girls in her class. She wonders if Yuko is really her new best friend, after all.

Dr. Van Heusen removes two plastic puppets from the toy box that sits between them, a boy and a girl. He places one on each hand.

"Hi, Mary! How are you feeling?" Dr. Van Heusen uses a bright, chirpy voice to animate the boy puppet with the shiny yellow hair and round, vacant blue eyes.

"I'm kind of scared, John! Yesterday I got lost on the bus, and my mom couldn't find me!" Dr. Van Heusen uses a higher voice for the girl puppet, jerking his hand back and forth in an attempt to make the puppet act scared, but instead it just looks like it has that shaking disease that Grama Lopez's cousin has. Dr. Van Heusen then tilts his head and peers at her, waiting for a response.

She looks at him, at the gross wet spots under the armpits of his short-sleeved collared shirt, at his white arms with black hairs on them, at the brown tie speckled with a yellow knotted print. It reminds her of a long piece of poo with corn in it. If her little brother Greg were here, he would say that out loud, and she would laugh.

But she doesn't laugh. She just looks at Dr. Van Heusen.

"Fuck you," she finally says. "Bastard."

Dr. Van Heusen stares at her with his watery, impassive eyes and she thinks of her mother, brushing and braiding her hair every day before school, her fine, brown obedient hair that stays in place. Good-girl hair. A good girl wouldn't say those words or even know them. But she *does* know them because she borrows books from her mother's bedside table. *The Day of the Jackal. The Godfather.* She reads them while her mother is playing tennis at the park or out for the night with her stepfather, while Sofia watches Spanish television in her room behind the kitchen.

Fucking asshole Van Heusen with his goddam puppet shows. Her mother must have told him about the bus thing last week—which wasn't anything, but now they're all making it something. All that happened was that she got on the wrong bus after school.

There are three yellow buses in a row that all look the same. How is she supposed to remember which is the right one on her first day at the new school? She gets on the one she thinks is right and then watches through the window as the bus passes her house instead of stopping by the yellow fire hydrant on the corner, and continues all the way up the street, turning right on the boulevard. The bus doesn't stop again until after it has gone really far down the busy boulevard. When it does stop, she gets off and walks the long journey back home. The street is dark by the time she trudges through the wrought-iron front door.

"Where you been, Martha? Your mother is very upset. She been out looking for you for three hours!"

Sofia rises from the wood floor she is polishing, appearing to show concern rather than the rage which is her usual response when the girl does something wrong.

She walks by Sofia into her room and slides under the bed. Unsure whether her mother is going to punish her, she hides so as to have more time to prepare by listening for the tone of her mother's voice and the rhythm of her gait—slow and light, or frantic and thudding—before being found.

Her mother arrives back at the house a few minutes later, feet thudding hard and heavy into the bedroom, hands reaching under the bed to pull her out. She feels herself enveloped in her mother's arms rather than slapped and scolded, hearing relieved sobbing and feeling her mother's bothered breath against her still-tight braids.

Yet she feels nothing. Not remorse that she upset her mother nor regret that she hadn't paid proper attention when told which bus to take. Just tired from the long walk home, and from the thick, cloying fear that seems to have taken over the house in her absence.

"Shit," is what she says to herself after her mother finally leaves the room. It's a bad word, but the bad makes her feel good.

EIGHT

She and Greg ride in circles around the garage as they do whenever both cars are gone, Greg on his Big Wheel and she on her Schwinn. She stands up to pedal faster, rising off the pink flowered banana seat.

But then Greg stops. "Meow," he says.

"Shut up, idiot."

But then she hears it again, and it isn't coming from her little brother but from the wall. They jump off their bikes and crouch down to see two blinking yellow eyes in the tight space between a large cardboard box and the back of the garage. The box is too heavy for them to move, so they sit, taking turns stroking the gray striped head that eventually emerges.

The garage door opens, and Karen Carpenter's plaintive voice fills the driveway. The girl hears before she even sees the brown Audi pull in that her mother is home first. She smiles. They'll be allowed to keep the kitty. And when they all move the box together, they see a small gray kitten huddled next to the larger tabby cat. She names the kitten Nugget, and Greg names the mother cat Pippi Longstocking. Sofia places the two cats into a box and takes them into the house, and their mother tells Greg to go with Sofia to make sure the kitties don't get lonely.

Today is Sunday. Her father is supposed to pick her up at noon. But he doesn't always come. Sometimes she sits cross-legged in the living room in front of Daddy Landon's grandfather clock, waiting for both hands to align on the twelve when the bells play the longest song of the day. The song plays and the hands move on, and if they make it to 1:00 pm, which is the shortest song the clock plays, then she knows her father definitely isn't coming.

"Remember, Moon," her mother says, "Greg still doesn't know."

Her father had come calling one day and accidentally met Greg. He was introduced as *Our friend, Gabe.* And that's who Greg is supposed to think he is.

She feels important to have been given that responsibility, to be considered old enough to know what the adults know, which is that Greg wouldn't understand because he's only four. Greg thinks their stepdad, Daddy Landon, is his real dad because he was only two when Landon married their mother and then took them all to Australia. She also calls Landon "Dad" sometimes instead of "Daddy Landon" just like she calls their real father "Dad." It's no big deal. Unlike Greg, she's old enough to understand that you can have two dads. And she remembers the time before Daddy Landon.

What she doesn't understand is why she still has to spend Wednesday afternoons with Dr. Van Heusen, leaving school early so he can use his stupid puppets to try and trick her into talking.

When she and Greg and her mother and Daddy Landon first come home from their year in Australia, she gets scared at night alone in her room. She creeps up the stairs to her mother and Daddy Landon's room, falling asleep on the upstairs landing. She doesn't know why she does that, exactly, but it feels better to be closer to her mother at night than by herself in a dark room. Although, of course, she would never climb into her mother's bed. Only a baby would do that. Her mother says that it has to do with her father and coming back from Australia and that Dr. Van Heusen will make her feel better. For a while, her father isn't allowed to come visit. Her mother says Dr. Van Heusen thinks that's best. But it actually makes her feel worse, on top of the irritation she feels at having to be stared at, like an animal in a cage at the zoo, by Dr. Van Heusen every week.

But then, her father starts coming again, mostly, and she's been entrusted with a secret. That must mean she is "adjusting."

Today Grama Lopez takes Greg for the day so their father can pick her up at the house in his black Aston Martin sports car. They rush down Sunset Boulevard, windows rolled all the way down as she sings *American Pie* as it plays on the radio. She doesn't know if music can save her mortal soul, as the song asks, but she senses that it can and that it's happening right then and there. She's thrilled to be there in that sleek car, happy like when she sings with the Carpenters alongside her mother in the brown Audi. But here and now she is someone else. Someone prettier and more interesting. Someone all the girls at school would compete to sit with at the yellow lunch tables outside the cafeteria, that all the boys would like. She tells her father to go faster, and he does. His long black hair ripples, his diamond earring flashes in the sun and her brown ponytail whips in the wind.

Later, he takes her to Grandma and Zhido's house for dinner. Grandma May takes her outside to look at her roses. "Pretty ladies," she calls them. When they go back inside, the girl feels inspired to sit on the sofa all straight and grown-up and regal like the pretty lady flowers.

During dinner, Grama Lopez appears at the door with Greg. Grandma and Zhido and Grama Lopez and her father all look at each other. There is murmuring. They weren't all supposed to be here at the same time. Grama Lopez wanted to bring Greg for a visit but didn't know Gabe was coming.

Greg charges through the front door when he sees Gabe, so Grama Lopez has to follow.

"Hi, Gabe! Do you like go-karts?"

She watches her father turn away and wipe his eyes before getting up from the table to sit on the carpeted living room floor with Greg. Grama Lopez perches on the sofa and everyone else continues to eat in uneasy silence, forks and knives clattering.

Greg chatters on about go-karts and trains. Then, when there's a lull, Gabe takes a gentle grasp of Greg's chin and lifts it so that Greg has to look at him for a second.

"Greg. Do you know who I am?"

Greg meets his father's gaze and then returns to the business of sorting through a shoebox filled with small metal cars.

"You're my daddy," he replies, handing Gabe a green Hot Wheels Corvette.

The adults look at each other in confusion.

She looks down at her plate; although she can sit like a proper grown-up at the table, she realizes she isn't one at all on the inside. She can't keep a secret.

NINE

She flies down the street on a Sunday afternoon, from Yuko's house to her own. It's all downhill, so she hardly has to pedal the Schwinn. Pink tassels dance off the shiny metal handlebars as she sticks her legs out straight, sometimes zipping in and out of half-moon driveways. Except for the one in front of the elm-shaded house everyone thinks is haunted.

She had spent the night at Yuko's home, in the house with all the clocks that Yuko's dad collects. All the clocks chime, but Yuko's dad can never get them all to do it at the same time. Some of them chime on the hour, others on the half or quarter hour. The floors in the house are all made of shiny dark wood, so when the clocks chime—and they're always chiming—the sounds echo throughout the house. She likes the sound of time.

Yuko's father is American, and her mother is Japanese. At dinner time, they don't eat steak and macaroni and cheese. Yuko's mother deep-fries abalone and scallops for dinner and puts them over sticky steamed rice topped with a deep, brown, salty liquid called soy sauce. She wasn't too sure about all that when she first started sleeping over at Yuko's, but now she likes that food and its taste of ocean and earth and of places she has never been to, all mixed together.

Tiny pebbles crunch under her bike wheels as she veers off the street toward her house. She stops suddenly when she sees a tuft of gray fur sticking out from one of the low bushes that lines the driveway. Dropping her bike, she edges closer, somehow knowing what will be there.

It's Nugget, who had gone missing two weeks ago. The little gray kitten that she found in the garage a year ago with his mom, Pippi Longstocking. He now lies there, mouth gaping open. Little, gross, white things wriggle around in the spaces where his eyes used to be.

When Nugget disappeared, her mother said that he'd probably gone off to find a female cat. When Pippi Longstocking went away shortly after, her mother said she was sick and had to be put to sleep. And then there's Grama Lopez's friend, Conchita, with the pointy eyeglasses. Conchita got sick too, but she wasn't put to sleep. Conchita *passed away,* which sounds like she boarded a train which got smaller and smaller as it bore her off to some distant, unknown destination.

She stands for a long time, looking at the decomposing thing that used to be Nugget. She understands that whatever happened to him, he wasn't put to sleep and didn't just go to sleep. He didn't pass away either; even though she sees he's dead, there is still this thing here. While it doesn't seem to be Nugget, she isn't convinced that any part of him is somewhere else. She tries to cry because she thinks that's what she's supposed to do but finds she can't.

When she slips through the front door, Daddy Landon's grandfather clock is booming 4:00 pm through the empty house. Her parents must be playing tennis, and Greg is probably at the park with them. So there is no one she can tell about Nugget.

It was supposed to be her day with her father, but he canceled his visit. Honey has baby Christopher now and so they're busy with him. Which is a relief because the baby is fussy and cries all the time and makes a nauseating, disgusting mess when he eats. Everything about him makes her want to throw up.

She wanders upstairs to her parents' bedroom and turns on their radio. She looks at the books stacked on her mother's bedside table: *Fear of Flying. Rabbit, Run. The Other Side of Midnight.* Nothing new this week.

Being alone in the house feels good today. Sofia is there, but Sofia leaves her alone now that she is older. She now views Sofia as little more than a collection of sounds: the whine of the vacuum cleaner or the squeak of cloth against glass or the dramatic musings of Spanish soap opera characters distantly emanating from Sofia's room. Sounds that let her know which part of the house to avoid.

Her new favorite song starts to play. She loves Paul McCartney and is old enough to remember, or it could have been that Auntie Di told her he was a Beatle. She walks to the window and gazes down at the yard. She sees the swimming pool and the white Styrofoam floaties bobbing in aimless circles like giant, weightless half-moons. Last summer, she and Greg put their beagle, Deacon, in one of them, laughing as he gamely did his best to avoid capsizing. Beyond the pool and the lawn and the metal chain-link fence that marks the end of the yard, she can just see the top of the bell tower of her school peeking up between the eucalyptus trees on the hillside.

And when I go away, I know my heart can stay with my love, it's understood…

She feels the melancholy start to seep into her in tandem with the sad-sounding strains of the song, the late Sunday afternoon despair that lately has started to grip her. The gathering of another school week starts to press down upon her, another round of math lessons she will struggle with, the ever-shifting girl alliances that are at best unpredictable and at worst heartbreaking. The mean girl Yvette Cate and her followers always circling, always looking to strike when she is least prepared for their jibes.

And when the cupboard's bare, I'll still find something there with my love, it's understood…

She wonders whether this melancholy means that she is starting to grow up, to become like the people in her mother's books that she reads in secret. People who love and fight and cry and kill and fuck and create all sorts of varied miseries, it seems, merely by virtue of being alive. She feels herself in this room, in this house, where there are parents and a little brother and a beagle and a pool and a playhouse filled with Barbie dolls and stuffed animals. She occupies her girlhood uneasily, because as she is growing up, she is also feeling smaller.

On one side of this house lies Nugget, the once bright-eyed ball of plushy fur who is now lifeless and overrun by maggots. On the other side, just beyond the chain-link fence, is the schoolyard, the things she hears there, her friends' houses and all the whispered or sometimes shouted grownup conversations she hears when she isn't supposed to. Her father and Honey's white house that looks like a wedding cake inside and out, that doesn't seem to be made for kids but where there is now a baby, anyway.

She feels herself getting smaller in between those worlds that are getting bigger and starting to resemble the insides of her mother's books, places that she doesn't quite understand but that make her heart pound with excitement—and also with foreboding.

TEN

The next house sits on a mossy bank next to a creek. The move happens while she's away at Girl Scout camp. Her mother brings her home to this other place, where all her furniture and toys and clothes have been organized neatly into a sunny upstairs room facing the street.

As soon as he hears she's home, her brother Greg bounds up the stairs carrying a tortoise shell, but it turns out to be a live tortoise with its legs and head hidden away. He lives at the house, and they get to care for him for as long as they live here. They decide to call him Sam after agreeing that's what he looks like—a Sam. Their mother says no, that isn't his name. It's Tiddlywinks. But they won't hear of it; he can only ever be Sam. Deacon is in the new house too, and a new yellow, long-haired kitten named Sunshine that Sofia brought.

She now takes a different bus to school. She laughs to herself when she thinks about getting the buses all mixed up that first time when she was little. She knows the winding canyon streets, the shortcuts and the secret staircases so well now that she sometimes won't get on the bus at all, and instead walks home with Alicia and Yuko.

From this house, she and Greg walk to the corner bus stop, which is a yellow fire hydrant. She liked the old bus stop better, where she stood in the happy company of Alicia and her dachshund, Lucky. Now she has to wait with the meanest girl in their class, Yvette Cate. Yvette crosses her arms and squints her smirking blue eyes and calls her Martha Gay instead of Martha May. The other kids laugh nervously because no one wants Yvette turning on them next. Shadowing Yvette is a high-strung younger girl named Mary Kay. Sometimes Yvette asks *where you goin', Mary Kay, whatcha doin, Mary Kay* in the same taunting way she says *Martha Gay,* except Mary Kay stares right back and says nothing in a way that stops Yvette from asking any more questions and from ever daring to say *Mary Gay.*

One dull Saturday when everyone tires of sucking on giant Sweetarts on the swings at the park, Yvette and Mary Kay take her to a house on a little dead-end canyon street. Mary Kay's room is covered with the letters of her name in marker and crayon and paint and stencil. Colors, rainbow arcs, sun shapes, clouds, and buildings all made of Mary Kay. She wonders how it is that Mary Kay's parents let her do that. It seems wild and unbridled, like something girls do before running away from home and getting in trouble the way they do on television in the Afterschool Specials. Her own mother would punish her for daring to write on the walls of her sunny new bedroom. Walls are for posters and bulletin boards and hooks for her backpack and jacket. She just looks with wonder and also with envy at all the Mary Kays and the art supplies scattered on the dirty carpeted floor and giant waterbed. She wonders what would happen if she wrote her own name when no one was looking, someplace hidden and small that only she would know about, inside one of the giant Mary Kays.

Across the street from the new house are the blond brothers Peter and Paul and their mom. There's no dad there. Her mother says in a hushed voice that he went away long ago and that she shouldn't mention him. Peter is ten like she is, and Paul is six like Greg. So, everyone has someone to play with although mostly they all play together on Hoppity Hops in the boys' backyard or in Peter's room where she plays with Peter's pet rat, Barney. Barney bites sometimes, but she loves to stroke his black-hooded head and scratch his rough, wormy tail. Even though she's what everyone calls a tomboy, she prefers loving this wriggling creature to playing Legos with the boys.

One day they all tumble down the grassy roadside bank to the creek. The water trickles and gurgles over slick green moss, cement and rocks on its way down to the ocean. Their bare feet splash among the tiny tadpoles. Peter and Paul lead the way up the creek until they clamber back up the bank to a boxlike home, austere and modern with sleek wood panels and walls made of windows.

"This is God's house," says Peter. When she asks how he knows, he takes her to an open shed in the yard filled with flower and vegetable seeds, soil and gardening equipment. Peter tells her that no one's ever there, so he and Paul have been making a garden behind the shed. He shows her haphazard rows of tender shoots just sprouted and some that are further along. Peter says that whenever they use up seeds and soil, more appear in the shed. He and Paul have come in the morning, the afternoon and one time at night when their mother thought they were in bed. Never did they see any life or lights on in the house, but always there are more seeds. Then one day they came to find that a little wooden fence and gate had been built around the burgeoning plot, protecting it and acknowledging it and establishing space for more growth.

"God lives here, and he wants us to make him a garden," announces Peter, who puts them all to work. She plops down onto the warm grass, digging through the soil she pours from a bag and working with her hand and a spade. None of them know how to arrange the seeds or how big a hole to dig for them or how much water to give them, but they work anyway, energized by the sun's warmth, the creek sounds and the honor of having a sacred mission of mysterious origin.

She wonders whether, if God has given them this pleasurable thing, it's because it was unasked for and unexpected. Her friend Daniela, who lives in a small apartment behind Grama Lopez's house and is a Jehovah's Witness, tells her that prayers have to be said every night and the Bible read every day, in order to be delivered from Evil at the time of Armageddon, which will definitely happen within five years in a storm of fire and earthquakes. Daniela helps her memorize The Lord's Prayer, and she finds an old bible in Daddy Landon's office that she reads every day. Although it's hard to make it past the endless string of weird names, let alone understand what she's supposed to learn, she does it anyway. Then, after The Lord's Prayer, she tacks on a list of her own requests.

Sometimes God responds as He did the night of a mad brush fire. She sat up late in stomach-clenching fear as whirling, smoke-filled winds and the screech of sirens told her that danger was coming from over the hills. Her mother and Daddy Landon weren't at all alarmed, but she prayed anyway, and the winds stopped by morning.

More often, though, it seems He doesn't respond. Yvette Cate and math continue to torment her. Lux Adams, the sixth grader whose love she has prayed for since he kissed her under the Brooktree Bridge last summer, a shy, hands-in-pockets, all-too-brief peck on the lips, now goes around with the glamorous Maggie Robbins, who wears wrap dresses and espadrilles.

She often imagines that God is a glowering old man with a long white beard, pointing a bony finger at her because she hasn't been good and therefore doesn't deserve what she prays for. Even worse, she may not be qualified for deliverance from Evil and Armageddon and the fires and the earthquakes. She wishes God were more like Grama Lopez, who rarely says *no* to anything and when she does, is nice about it.

Yet sitting and planting in the garden of God's house, she has a different feeling about God than she does when she says The Lord's Prayer or reads the Bible at her desk. She didn't pray for this joyful moment. She didn't seek it as a way out of fear like she sought for the winds to stop the night of the fire or for Yvette to stop calling her *Martha Gay* or for the confidence to work math problems on the board. This happiness arrived simply and unannounced, wrapped in a thrilling mystery or maybe even a miracle that God, for some unknown reason, has decided she actually *is* good enough to experience.

She decides that she really doesn't understand God at all.

ELEVEN

She feels like a piece of fruit that's been yanked off a tree just as it begins to ripen. She would never dream of doing that to the figs on Grama and Papa's tree, twisting off those hard green knots in June instead of waiting until August when the tree becomes a riot of purple-skinned fruit needing only the lightest of touches before falling into her eager hands.

She misses the houses in Rustic Canyon they seemed to move into and out of each year. Her mother said they were finally going to stop renting and buy a lovely, bougainvillea-shaded house in Santa Monica, on a wide tree-lined street that led right down to the Palisades cliffs. She would go to Paul Revere Junior High or Westlake School for Girls, which is where Alicia is starting seventh grade right now, just as she is starting seventh grade miles away at Vista.

She loves the canyon, loves her school, loves that she beat Yvette Cate for class president when nobody ever beat Yvette Cate at anything. Lux Adams is in junior high now, but Kenny Fredericks likes her, and she likes him. They're partners in the square dance at graduation, which requires them to do lots of hand holding during rehearsals. She finally feels her ever present separateness begin to thaw and then melt into something akin to belonging.

And then something happens to the house in Santa Monica. It fell out of escrow, her mother says. Which sounds like it collapsed or slid down the cliff into the ocean.

In the spring, her mother takes her and Greg and Grama Lopez up to Santa Barbara to see the new house that Daddy Landon bought. It's in a place called Hope Ranch, which isn't really a ranch, but a long street lined with palm trees and a lake on one side. A road winds up a hill to a driveway and at the bottom of the driveway is a long white house with a red-tiled roof. Her mother is delighted with the red brick verandah that will be perfect for geraniums, and with the blue-tiled fountain that gurgles in the backyard. It's a serious house built by a serious and famous man whose houses grace architecture books and magazines.

She walks the serious floors, putting one foot carefully in front of the other atop the shiny large tiles, and looks at the serious high ceilings and both of the serious large fireplaces. She and Greg each choose their rooms on opposite ends. Hers is near her mother and Daddy Landon and next to an enclosed patio shaded by a large, leafy olive tree.

And then they visit the serious new school, a small cluster of buildings nestled against a grassy hill, where she and Greg take tests to see if they can attend. They meet a man called the Headmaster, not a Principal like at her old school. His name is Dr. Pepper, and she has to try really hard not to laugh, or to look at Greg, who immediately asks the man if he invented the soda.

It all seems okay enough, and her mother is so excited about moving to this place that she wants to be excited too, even though she doesn't see any kids racing their bikes down the street as they do down Brooktree Road. It's easy to forgive that this place doesn't feel like home, because she only has to be there for an afternoon, after which she gets back into the car and stares at the ocean on the ride to her actual home. She's dreaming of her return to school the next day and what she'll say to Yuko and Alicia who want to walk the playground at recess with her and not with Yvette Cate.

She finally understands what it is to feel happy, a feeling that she never really has except for when she's sick and her mother gives her a special cough syrup that makes her woozy and inexplicably glad about everything. But she knows that kind of happy isn't real because she always wakes up afterward feeling not particularly happy at all.

This happy is real, populated by a boy she likes who likes her back, by friends who love books and animals and stories and who love her too. She is becoming something, she feels, something that for once seems to harmonize with the things and people around her.

But then, suddenly, it's June, and elementary school is behind her forever. She graduates in a powder blue, Swiss polka-dot dress that Grama Lopez makes for her, looking into the brown eyes of Kenny Fredericks as they and the entire sixth grade class dance the Teton Mountain Stomp on the playground. Before them, seated rows of parents watch, fanning themselves with programs as a muggy sun breaks through the fog. Too soon, it's all over and there she is, standing arm-in-arm with Alicia and Yuko, reciting the final lines of the Robert Frost poem they all had to memorize.

Two roads diverged in a wood,
and I—I took the one less traveled by,
And that has made all the difference.

There's a party afterward at Yvette Cate's house, where the new graduates all stand around looking at each other over pizza and hot dogs, suddenly bashful and uncertain because elementary school, and the hierarchy and the context it provided for all their interactions, no longer exists for them. At the end, Yvette Cate hugs her and cries and says how much she'll miss her next year. She stands there in that hug, feeling happy but also sad that God has answered her prayers too late for them to do any good now.

And then comes July, and the move into the serious house in Santa Barbara. They spend the Fourth at Hope Ranch Beach, where her mother flutters about in excitement, perky in her red polo shirt and white shorts, meeting all the new neighbors who are so impressed with her fruit-topped meringue.

Bored by the adult conversation, the girl walks the beach parking lot alone, remembering last year's Fourth at Temescal Beach, the buckets of Kentucky Fried Chicken, running with Yuko and Alicia toward the shore and then squealing and running away when the waves crested and rolled toward them. Their parents took up a spontaneous game of volleyball, and then they all sat wrapped in blankets watching the firework show explode over the tops of the Palisades cliffs.

Fireworks aren't allowed in Hope Ranch, so there isn't any show. Waiting for the barbecue to end, she wanders among the parked cars. She comes upon one where there was music playing, her absolute favorite summer song: *Love…love will keep us together, think of me babe, whenever…*

She peeks into the car and sees three girls in the back seat, singing along with Captain & Tennille. She stares at them, mesmerized by their long, silky picture-on-the-shampoo-bottle hair, each a different shade of blonde, the slender legs in tiny shorts, the bright halter tops and flat, tanned bellies. When they see her, they laugh, and she knows that it's *at* her; at her flat brown hair and round awkward body that doesn't want to stay childish yet refuses to do anything else. She moves away quickly, feeling defeated and lonely. She misses her matching parts—gawky Alicia, whose hair stuck out at weird angles and Yuko who brought abalone and rice to school for lunch.

She realizes how different things will be here than they had been at home. And then she remembers that now this *is* home.

TWELVE

Once she senses that the car has stopped in the garage, she sits up in the back seat, throws up, and promptly lies down again, leaning away from the brown effluvium pooling next to her. She feels the capable hands of her mother helping her out of the car, through the house, into her purple and white striped pajamas and into bed. Then a pain pill is in her mouth along with water, and she dozes off.

When she awakens from her haze, feeling dazed and loopy, she knows without knowing that no one else is home. Both her mother and Greg overflow with a bouncing, kinetic energy that is there wherever they happen to be, even in silence. When they're gone, the house feels like a church where every little noise—Deacon's clacking toenails, the washing machine changing cycles, Sunshine scratching in the litter box—expands to fill all available space.

Lying under the daisy print comforter in a woozy cocoon, she feels vaguely annoyed that she should be wasting a precious summer vacation day on her damn ugly braces or rather, the wisdom tooth removal required by her damn ugly braces. Damn ugly braces compounded by damn ugly hair, damn chubbiness, damn pigeon-toed feet.

Damn, damn, damn. She sings to herself and laughs, the medication dulling the edges of her annoyance.

Big Bird sits propped against a cushion on the twin bed next to hers, a gift from Grama Lopez for her twelfth birthday. Floppy and ungainly on the outside like she is, sweet and at ease inside his totally weird bird body, which she definitely isn't.

She wonders whether she's too old for Big Bird, but then decides she's not. She still needs to come home from school to his bulging, guileless eyes and the permanently parted, smiling beak sprouting from his yellow feathers. He always looks like he's about to say something kind, a benign antidote to the new school where she's younger than the other kids in her class.

Too young for the slumber parties with the girls who are already thirteen, for the hushed slipping away from backyard tents to meet blond surfer boys bearing cigarettes and warm Coors. Because the other mothers all love her mother, she gets invited, but only as an outsider stationed to keep watch while her willowy classmates smoke and drink and French kiss with the boys. She escapes back to the quiet tent, into the warmth of her sleeping bag and pretends to be asleep when they return, breathless and giggling, smelling of yeast and ashes.

While they lay awake talking about boys, her head buzzes with strange other things she thinks she should be too young for but somehow isn't. The insides of the books her English teacher Ms. Henry keeps in the classroom, frayed paperbacks leaning against each other like old friends, sharing their secrets on rickety plywood shelves. Free for unlimited borrowing.

I would love to see Martha participate more in class, but it seems her nose is always in an unassigned book.

That's her first progress report from Ms. Henry, who must have written it while her nose was in *The Bell Jar.*

She's never heard of that poor husband and wife, Ethel and Julius Rosenberg, who were executed in the electric chair for being spies the year before she was born. She finds herself disturbed and obsessed just as Sylvia Plath was, wondering what it would be like to be fried dead by a machine. The more she reads, the more she thinks she understands Sylvia until she becomes convinced she'll probably go crazy and kill herself just like Sylvia did. She can't be bothered to think about the book she's supposed to be reading, about some boy getting involved in the American Revolution.

Then she finds Sylvia's journals in a library and reads them late at night, feeling as if she's reading her own future secret diary. She doesn't quite grasp the mechanics of life as a grown woman, but still she recognizes in herself Sylvia's dizzying feelings, the anxiety of awakening to all the ways she doesn't see things and people the way she thinks she should. How she isn't all happy and excited about her life the way she thinks she should be.

And she finds out that Sylvia had her wisdom teeth removed too. Her mother explains that they're called wisdom teeth because they don't come in until you're grown up, but they have to take hers out early to make room for her other teeth to move around.

Still, she doesn't like the thought of plucking things before their time. Not her teeth, not the figs or loquats at her grandmas' houses, not poor dead Sylvia. There are holes in her mouth now, bloody gaps filled with cotton. She moves her tongue around them carefully, tasting dry metal, and thinks again of the Rosenbergs.

The swimming red digits of the clock radio on her bedside table seem to read 12:18. When she blinks, the numbers stop swimming. She plays a game, seeing if she can keep from blinking until the minute digit on the clock changes, and then blink only once until it changes again. The minutes don't pass evenly, though. She's positive that some are longer than others.

Later she awakens, bewildered, not realizing she had fallen asleep again. The television is on; it's showing an episode of *I Love Lucy*. Lucy and Ethel are standing at a conveyor belt in a candy factory, wrapping candies but then having to shove most of them in their mouths because the belt moves too fast.

She wonders who made time and how it is that time passes as it does. Whether it will speed up, cramming her full of one experience after another so that she'll feel like Lucy and Ethel trying to keep up with all the candy. Maybe all of a sudden, she'll be a writer like Sylvia, pulsing with fear and wonder in the middle of a big city filled with people who are confusing, exciting and terrifying all at the same time. Or maybe time will crawl, and she'll forever feel invisible, standing watch over surfer boys kissing long-legged blond girls.

THIRTEEN

She and three of her eighth-grade classmates slouch low in their desks in the math room, rocking them back against the walls so that the front legs suspend at an insolent tilt above the floor. She writes on the smooth Formica top of hers, leaving cryptic comments and snarky suggestions in pencil for whomever happens to sit there next. School is out for the day, and they've all elected to spar and flirt and agitate in a setting more intimate and private than the after-school hub on the front lawn.

Bored, John gets up and draws the Spanish teacher's head on the chalkboard, and next to it draws a large penis.

"Dammit, John! Erase that! We're gonna get in trouble!" Francesca jumps up and tries to erase the drawing. A chase ensues. John corners Francesca and grabs her wrist, trying to get hold of the eraser. Francesca bites him. That's one couple.

Meanwhile, Robert scoots his desk closer to hers. They've been going together for a month, which means they sit together at recess and lunch on the eighth-grade benches. Last week he gave her a ring, a silver knot that he made in crafts class, which solidifies his status as her first, official middle-school boyfriend. And probably her last, since middle school ends in a month.

The romantic poles shift from season to season. At Christmas, Robert liked Francesca and John liked her, which she found out after her mother had to call John's mother. From almost the first day of school he waited every morning by the lockers, taunting her about everything from her pigtailed hair to the way she clutched her books to her chest, until she fled in tears to the bathroom to compose herself before class. The day after the phone call, John asked her to the Christmas dance.

Robert tries to look at her graffiti, but she shields it with her upright math book. She signs every entry *A. Nonymous* but makes sure no one sees her do it.

Bob + Diane = ♥

-BEST OF LUCK TO HIM. HE'LL NEED IT.
A. Nonymous

Mr. Healy is fat and sucks dick.

-GOOD THING DICK HAS NO CALORIES.
A. Nonymous

She pretends to be more focused than she is. She feels Robert's aqua eyes on her, striking beneath long camel lashes and a thick shock of black hair. She can hardly bring herself to make eye contact. She doesn't know why he likes her, or why, before him, John liked her. They should all forever love Francesca, with that Farrah Fawcett hair that cascades to her shoulders and that mysterious way of knowing how to torment and attract boys at the same time.

Francesca abandons her halfhearted attempts to police John.

"You made her hair all wrong. It should be in a bun." Francesca improves on the Spanish teacher as John leans in behind, closer than he needs to be. A hint of something secret and intimate flavors their laughter. They've definitely at least gotten to second base.

She hasn't kissed a boy since fifth grade. Lux Adams planted his lips on the corner of her mouth at an awkward angle once, under the bridge by the house on Brooktree Road. But that doesn't count because she was just a kid then.

She glances at Robert over her math book. He rocks his desk back and forth against the wall, shuffling a deck of cards. They whoosh under his nimble fingers before gliding silently together.

"Wanna play Fifty-Two Card Pick-up?" She knows the joke, but she lets Robert play it on her anyway, watching him bend the cards into an arc and then launch them over his desk.

"There's the fifty-two cards. Pick 'em up!" The cards scatter on the classroom floor. Robert bangs on his desk, laughing at his own joke, while she stares at the tens and kings and fours and aces. The Queen of Spades stares up at her. She sees on the humorless, stern line of the mouth an accusation, as if it's her fault the Queen wound up there, undignified and askew. She remembers Honey's long-ago card reading, something about the Queen of Spades and unhappiness, so she tears her eyes away from the card. She doesn't want to turn out like that Queen, but she suspects it may already be too late.

She remembers other things about that time, too. Her mother suddenly got a short haircut and stopped smiling after her father left for Honey. She can still see her mother at Disneyland, thin and lost inside an oversized pea coat, huddling next to Grama Lopez as they watched her spin, alone, around and around in a giant teacup.

That feels like it happened yesterday, but she had been four then. Only two years ago she moved here to Santa Barbara from Los Angeles, and that feels like it happened a million years ago. She can hardly recall anything about her sixth-grade graduation, which feels weird because those pictures of her with Yuko and Alicia in their long, fancy graduation dresses should be important enough to stay in her mind.

It occurs to her that time really is like the cards lying in their haphazard arrangement on the floor. You don't remember it in order, and it doesn't all stand out the same way. That must be what happens when you get older. Time isn't time at all. Just random pictures in your head.

She feels Robert looking at her again. Francesca has decided they should all play Truth or Dare, and dares Robert to kiss her. She sticks her tongue out at him, which is all she can think to do.

Robert grabs her and kisses her on the lips. His mouth is open and so is hers because of her surprise, and so their tongues touch. John starts hooting, and so she draws back, embarrassed.

And then it's over. Her first French kiss, from her first boyfriend, at a graffiti-riddled desk. As the Queen of Spades glares up from the grimy classroom carpet, she wonders whether this moment of thrilling newness will wind up being a snapshot she'll remember, or whether it will wind up face down, hidden and forever lost among all the others that should feel remarkable, but don't.

FOURTEEN

My mom has suddenly started going to therapy. To find herself, she told me, because she doesn't know who she is anymore. That's why she drives downtown to see Dr. Frank every week.

I don't get my mother or her friends. All of them go to Dr. Frank. Daddy Landon goes to therapy too, not because he doesn't know who *he* is, but because it'll help Mom feel better about getting to know who *she* is.

It's Saturday night. My parents' friends Shelby and Elizabeth Boone are here, and they just had dinner. I guess right now they're all sprawled on the living room carpet, drinking wine and listening to my *Saturday Night Fever* album. Their laughter and the Bee Gees drift into my room as I sit on my green beanbag chair watching *Love Boat* and *Fantasy Island.* I veer between feeling comfy and grumpy, between the coziness of being at home and the annoyance of not having anywhere better to be.

They're probably all getting high, too. I already walked in on Mom and Daddy Landon smoking pot in the living room one night when I went to the kitchen for a snack. They didn't seem at all bothered by my presence, which felt weird. I wish they'd acted embarrassed, because really, I just caught them with their parent masks off. But they just laughed and beckoned me over.

"You'll probably do it sooner or later, so you might as well try it now when you're with us." Daddy Landon hands me the joint, telling me to make sure to inhale. I do, but it makes me cough, so I hand it back to him and sit on the sofa with them for a few minutes until I get bored and wander back to my room to finish my homework. The pot doesn't do much except make it hard to remember what I've just read, and I find myself reading the same paragraph of *To Kill a Mockingbird* over and over without any of it sinking in. Which is frustrating because I'm really getting into the book. It feels like I'm losing the ability to be right there with Scout and Jem as they watch their father, Atticus Finch, defend the wrongly accused Tom Robinson. Instead, it's like I'm watching a movie that constantly starts and then stops so that I have to keep going back to rewatch it.

I don't get the thing of people not understanding themselves. There are Right and Wrong ways of thinking and doing things. If you're a parent, you take care of your kids. If you're a kid, you study and get good grades so you can get into college and get a job—and try not to get into too much trouble. If you're Atticus Finch, you defend an innocent man even though your whole town is against you. And if you're Scout and Jem, you make friends with the harmless weirdo, Boo Radley, because he's kind and lonely.

I stay up late. I've started writing stories and poems outside of my normal homework assignments. I don't think anything I write is very good. Actually, it's all probably pretty lame. But there's something about making up stories and finding the words for thoughts and feelings that makes me forget a little bit. Forget about things like Robert dumping me for Francesca, and also Francesca and my other middle school friends fast drifting away from me toward girls who wear makeup and whose parents let them throw parties.

Makeup isn't my thing, anyway. Mom's been trying to get me to wear a little Bonne Bell lip gloss. But when that happens, I might want to put away Big Bird and Paddington and the Barbie house I still secretly play with in my closet. When that happens, there'll be no going back. I'm not ready.

But I'm growing. I've put on an inch in the last year, and where Mom failed with lip gloss, she succeeded with a bra. So now I wear one, a stupid white lacy thing with a blue ribbon that looks like one of my grandmother's toilet decorations. It pulls and itches and gaps in some places and digs into my skin in others. It probably doesn't fit right, which isn't surprising because I refused to try on any others in the department store. I just wanted to run away from the whole womanhood thing. Like I said, I'm not ready.

Except that I can't run away because now I have breasts and a fucking period, which snuck up on me while I was in Portugal with Mom and Grama Lopez. The two of them rushed around Lisbon, trying to figure out how to say *Maxi Pad* in Portuguese, while I stayed in the hotel room, freaked out by what my body was doing. Mom and Grama told me that I'm a woman now, saying it like I'd won some big prize. But it doesn't feel that way.

Probably one day I'll want to wear makeup and kiss a boy who isn't Robert. But for now, I just want to close my bedroom door, fling off my gross lacy bra, sleep with Big Bird, listen to Billy Joel and Fleetwood Mac, read Dr. Seuss and Harper Lee, and think about boys and sex even though I sort of dread that all, too. I don't know. Maybe all of it can go together without me having to be one thing or another.

I imagine my bedroom door opening at some point, toward a future that seems blue and murky, like the fluid inside my brother Greg's Magic 8 Ball. *Reply hazy, try again* is the only answer I ever seem to get. I see myself floating down a hallway, with some doors opening and some closing, and others not opening at all. There are people, lots of them, but I don't see their faces. And some of them, I sense, are actually me, but I don't see those faces either. I can't tell if I have a married lady's face, or a mother's face, or the face of some career person in a suit with a briefcase. All I'm really sure of right now are my words and my music and my white bookcase half-filled with books, stuffed animals and the tiny glass horses I collected in elementary school.

I put my pen down on my desk, taking a break from a poem I'm trying to write called *The End of the Beginning*. Like everything else I write, I want it to be way better than it is. But like my bookcase, my poems and stories are only half full, because I'm still in my room. That hallway in the murky blue isn't ready for me yet. But when it is, hopefully it'll lead to places and things that are fuller and worth writing about.

Mom turns the music up because *More Than a Woman* is playing—her favorite song. I stand up and stretch, feeling my changing body, which is still a weird thing to me but also kind of exciting. I begin to move, first rolling my shoulders, then swinging my arms, then swaying my hips. I twirl, and then whirl, taking in everything around me: the daisy-print comforter on my bed, Big Bird on the pillow, the darkness outside my bedroom window, my record albums stacked under the turntable, my favorite The Beatles' *Sgt. Pepper's* on top. The spines of my books are perched upright and waiting like toy soldiers, Laura Ingalls Wilder and Sylvia Plath, Sidney Sheldon and Dr. Seuss.

And the empty spaces between all those things, waiting to be filled up.

FIFTEEN

love the place that's in between being awake and being asleep. The melting of the real world into my hidden world, where each is still separate but starts to drip into each other until, for at least a few moments, they become something totally distinct.

I sink into that place now, curled into the cave-like brown leather backseat of Daddy Landon's Mercedes. Daddy Landon has gone on another of his long fishing trips to Australia or New Zealand or Tasmania or somewhere. I never really know for sure. His friend Shelby is taking Mom and me to dinner. He's got the same green eyes as Daddy Landon, except he's younger, shorter and more muscular. And he always wears a suit.

All three of us are on the Scarsdale Diet, so all I eat at the restaurant is a hamburger with no bun and a salad with no dressing. My mother has finally stopped bothering me about my weight now that I finally care about it. Most of my chubbiness melted away when I went on my first diet last spring and noticed that boys liked me better when I'm thin.

I guess that's what gets me a senior boyfriend who takes me to his prom. I learn how to make out, and I learn that I love to make out. Then I somehow mess things up with that boy, so he leaves me for someone who goes to all his track meets and band practices. I suppose I didn't pay enough attention to him. But something changes in me after that. Now I look at all the boys and imagine them doing things to me.

Other times I just want to be a kid. Like right now, when the adults are driving and deciding everything, and I can just doze in the back seat. I feel like I'm floating, not asleep and not awake, feeling the comforting rhythm of the car rolling along in the dark.

"Y esta noche? Tu casa o mi casa?"

We all speak Spanish—me, Mom, Daddy Landon and Shelby. Grama and Papa Lopez immigrated to the United States from Spain, so Mom is fluent because it was her first language. I'm becoming fluent because I've studied Spanish since seventh grade and because I've been listening to my grandparents speak it for as long as I can remember. Daddy Landon learned to speak it, sort of, because he loves Mom. I don't know how or why Shelby learned it.

I open one eye. I thought I heard them talking about whose house to go to tonight, but in my half-asleep place, I'm not sure what I really heard or what it meant.

The conversation levels down to whispering, probably because Mom and Shelby remember that I'm here, even though they think I'm asleep. I quickly close my eyes as my mother turns her head to look at me.

When she turns away, I open my eyes again, watching. The car has stopped at an intersection. Mom and Shelby are looking at each other, their profiles silhouetted against the red glow of the traffic light. Shelby takes Mom's hand and presses his lips hard against it.

And then I see it. That feeling I have when I lay awake at night fantasizing about my ex-boyfriend, the waves of longing that stay hidden during the day. It's right there on their faces. An undisguised *wanting*.

I try to feel shocked; I know I should be. *This is wrong.* But I can't stop looking. I can't stop wanting them to do more, to kiss deeply and passionately. It sort of feels okay to want this though because it's like I'm looking at people I don't know. Not Mom and Daddy Landon's best friend but other people, like characters in a movie. And I sense they can't help it any more than I can help my own secret wanting. I feel a shameful, vicarious thrill that they live in a world where they get to act on their urges even though they have to do it in secret.

And then I start to feel sad. Not for Daddy Landon. I think he actually takes comfort in *not* knowing things. He doesn't really know or ask Greg and me what we do in school or who our friends are. That's Mom's job. And that annoys me because I can't stand not knowing things, especially things that are as obvious as the joy that Mom and Shelby throw out like flames from a huge bonfire whenever they're together.

I'm sad because something now feels forever lost. It won't come back, not even in that space between being awake and asleep. I can't ever not remember that look or not know what it means. I can't ever go back to that little kid space where not knowing separates me from Mom and Shelby and Daddy Landon and the awful, exciting mess they all live in.

I think about our family vacation this past summer, which feels so distant, but it's really only been three months. Daddy Landon took us to a ranch in Wyoming so he could fly-fish while Mom, Greg and I did ranch-y activities like horseback riding and playing billiards in the lodge. Mom spent most of the time reading in our cabin, Greg alternated between playing with and tormenting the autistic kid in the cabin next door, and I spent every moment I could riding Captain, the brown Quarter Horse assigned to me when we arrived.

By the second week, I'm allowed to help corral the ranch's herd of bison, who are regularly sprung from their enclosed pastures by a pissed off local native tribe. I'm terrified at first, scared of the reaching, extending, pulsing horsepower carrying me across the sagebrush plain toward that angry charging bull. I worry that on that razor's edge between pursuit and retreat I'll lose the reins or stirrups and wind up flattened by the whole crazy herd.

But after the fear comes joy, of the musky smell of sage mixing with my own sweat, of Captain cutting through the crisp, thin mountain air that rushes by me in a swirl of flying dust. I stand up in my saddle, digging my heels into the stirrups and leaning as far as I can into a happiness that suddenly falls upon me from somewhere—overriding everything else.

I'm afraid I'll never feel that again, that there's too much other stuff crowding it out, stuff that can't be obliterated, not even for a minute. I've crossed over onto the rocky shore of somewhere else, leaving behind a girl who somehow was both innocent and courageous enough to gallop into the midst of crazed beasts.

The light turns green. Mom takes her hand from Shelby's and places it back on the steering wheel.

I keep my eyes open.

SIXTEEN

Eyes open, eyes closed. So many ways to kiss and so many boys.

Chuck is a good kisser, so I want to close my eyes and lose myself. He gently bites my lower lip while using his tongue at the same time. He's come over to see me because I'm not feeling well today—some weird stomach thing with a fever. My fevers always run high, and so I'm a little shaky, which adds to the dreamy feeling. I stand against the driver's side door of Chuck's pickup, but I have to keep my eyes open so I can see whether Daddy Landon comes out of the house in his embarrassing bathrobe that has holes all over it. He smokes so much weed these days that sometimes I wonder if he just forgets to get dressed.

I'm a senior now. In the fall I'll hopefully go to one of the colleges I'm applying to. The counselor lady at my school said I need to be more of a joiner if I want to get in somewhere good.

I play junior varsity volleyball, so that's something athletic to list on my college applications. Even after a week of volleyball boot camp, I don't make the varsity team. When the sharpness of that disappointment dulls, I realize I won't have to train as hard being junior varsity, and that leaves more time for boys.

In order to check off the Groups and Clubs box, Mom gets me involved in Job's Daughters, the same Masonic youth group she herself had joined as a teen. In between ritualistic meetings where we all wear white satin robes and recite biblical stuff about womanly virtue and sacrifice, we hold car washes and bake sales and dances—things Mom thinks I should experience as a counterpoint to what she calls "the rarefied world of college prep."

Mom's counterpoint to the rarefied world of tennis clubs and fancy dinner parties is her yearly participation in a holiday food drive. She brings Thanksgiving and Christmas dinners to needy families who live downtown. The families don't seem that excited by the food they get from the Hope Ranch ladies. From what I can see, they all seem to be doing fine on their own without turkey and sweet potato casserole. I don't understand why they can't just be given money so they can buy what they actually need.

The Job's Daughters girls hug each other a lot and cry and squeal and flip their feathered hair, but when they come over to my house in Hope Ranch, they gawk in silence at the vaulted ceilings and yards of tiled hallways, just like they do on our group outing to Hearst Castle. I really want to explain to them that I only live there because of Daddy Landon. That if it were just me and Mom and Greg, we'd all probably live in exactly the same kind of tract house in Goleta that they live in, or even just an apartment downtown among the families that get the free dinners. Mom would still be a schoolteacher and knit and make casseroles for dinner, and I would go to a regular high school and then City College so I could get a job in a bank or an office. I'd tell them that I find myself in this serious house only because a rich guy found his North Star and took on her two young satellites as part of the deal.

But I say nothing and instead offer them cookies and punch as Mom taught me, because as Grama Lopez also taught me, most awkward things can be smoothed over by food.

There's a Masonic boys' group too, called the Demolay, and they elect me as their Demolay Sweetheart, which is an actual position where I wear a tiara and attend their car washes and bake sales and dances. Chuck is their Master Counselor this term, and all the Job's Daughters squeal and tell me how cute it is that the Master Counselor and the Sweetheart are together.

They might not think it's so cute if they knew that I'm "together" with most of the Demolay boys, which is probably why they made me their Sweetheart to begin with. I can't help fooling around with as many of them as I can. It makes me feel alive and fun and wanted and less anxious—temporarily. But then afterward I always wind up feeling more anxious because I know I'm going to get what my mother (with zero irony) calls a "reputation." That is, if I don't already have a reputation. I know boys talk to each other and then the girls eventually find out. But I can't stop. And I don't want to—not really.

Daddy Landon doesn't seem to have found out yet about Mom and Shelby. I watch very closely when they're all together. I look at Daddy Landon to see if he's watching them, trying to read his face for signs of sadness or anger or forced happiness. But there's none of that. He never seems to catch them looking at each other in that way I now understand. Their low, intimate laughter and intense gazes seem to emerge only when Daddy Landon goes to the liquor cabinet for yet another drink.

Mom and I tour East Coast college campuses in the fall. I see some Ivy League schools, Harvard, Yale, Princeton, but I'm most drawn to Wellesley. It's a girls' school—or "women's college" as the students there all call it—which I thought I'd hate. But there's something about the boy-lessness that's comforting. Maybe I can pull something worthwhile out of myself from the red brick buildings or the winding, tree-lined pathways. I imagine myself clad in head-to-toe black, head down into the wind as I stride with purpose toward a philosophy class. I kind of like that vision.

The heavy wooden front door opens with a creak. I slither out of Chuck's grasp and hop into the passenger side of his truck. The two of us peel out of the driveway, just as Daddy Landon emerges, bleary and blinking like a groundhog prodded too early out of hibernation.

SEVENTEEN

I wake up, slow and blinking, emerging from a food coma.

For months I've been eating everything in sight, craving nothing but gigantic late-night sandwiches piled with as much meat, cheese and mayonnaise as I can shove between two pieces of bread. And if that doesn't do it, I have another and then after that peanut butter or ice cream.

And then I got on the scale two months ago, the day after my high school graduation, and found I'd gained thirty-five pounds in six months. My mother pecks at me the whole time with comments about what I'm eating and how much, so I finally start the latest fad diet which consists mostly of fruit.

I manage to lose and keep off around fifteen pounds, so I decide to cheat tonight. I like to read while I eat, so I settle at the dining room table in my mother's newly rented house with a jar of peanut butter, a spoon and the local paper.

Lately, I've been scanning the classifieds, looking for jobs and cats. I wonder what will happen if I just come home one day with a kitten and announce that I won't be going away to Wellesley after all. That I'm going to be a secretary or a bank teller and take classes at community college and live in my bedroom and raise a cat. That I'll be meandering toward instead of rushing into the life that I don't quite know how to define yet but that my mother and Daddy Landon seem overly eager to define for me.

But I can't because what's done is done.

I'm set to leave in a week. I've exchanged letters with my new roommate and my mother bought me a rainbow comforter for the twin bed in my dorm room. I'm registered for philosophy, biology, psychology, and English literature classes.

I lose my virginity to a local boy named Patrick who dropped out of high school. Mom can't get me away from him soon enough. But in the meantime, when I'm not filing and typing at the ad agency where Mom got me a summer job, I spend all my free time with him, on the back of his motorcycle or in his bed in the tiny room he rents in a house downtown.

Daddy Landon finally leaves the serious house. And then comes back when Mom agrees to give up Shelby. And then Mom leaves when she decides that no, she can't give up Shelby, and moves to another house down the street with a swimming pool, the house I sit in now. I stay here sometimes when she goes out of town with Shelby, as she did this week.

Sated for the moment, I wander outside and slide into the pool. Dog paddling in circles, I daydream about staying precisely where I am forever, suspended in that place between a past that can't contain me anymore and a future that I think might be too big for me. A vast but demanding blank slate that I won't be able to fill in the way everyone tells me I can with all my "potential."

The sun sets, bathing the mountains behind Santa Barbara in a late summer pink-orange glow.

And after that, there is one less day left to remain suspended.

EIGHTEEN

It's Christmas Eve, again. The specialness of December 24th washes over and awakens me as I lie curled on my twin bed under the daisy print comforter. My waking mind is a swirl of glittering, tinsel memories. Crinkly wrapping, gold bells, bows, ribbons, candy canes and ornaments attached to Grama and Papa's Christmas tree in the window. The lights on the tree sparkle and tempt. Mesmerized by the lights, gifts, chatter, my family in their festive finery, cigar-shaped butter cookies coated in powdered sugar and individually wrapped in red and green cellophane, I become Christmas and I love the whole world. I set up the wooden nativity scene and reverently arrange the ceramic figures. This is my job every year and one which I take very seriously. Baby Jesus' benign blue eyes smile at me, mirroring my own goodwill toward all.

I'm in college now. Still, though, I can't refrain from indulging in the old reverie and the sweetness of what used to be.

I open my eyes. Between the heavy muslin drapes I glimpse the pale green, silver-tinged leaves of the olive tree outside my bedroom window. I climbed that tree earlier this morning to get over the brick patio wall, and carefully slid the glass door open to get into my room after a late night with Patrick. My parents still don't care for him and view him as little more than a going-nowhere pothead. They tolerate him as long as he doesn't interfere with my education. He was my first, though no longer my only lover—although he thinks there's no one else. Yet I'd be devastated to lose him, because I can't stand to lose anything. So I continue to sneak out and then sneak back in, drifting off to sleep afterwards with luscious memories of Patrick's hands and mouth on me.

Nope, I'm not a kid anymore.

Into my room walks my mother, brisk and efficient. She's on edge; she separated from Daddy Landon and moved out the summer before I started college. Now, she's back in the serious house with him, trying for the third time to make the marriage work. The purposeful thudding of her heels on the tile floor telegraphs that it's time for everyone in the house to be awake, regardless of how late anyone stayed up the night before. She yanks aside the long drapes and I squint at her, annoyed.

"We're leaving for Grama's at noon. What are you wearing?" She eyes the red cashmere crew neck sweater and plaid kilt I laid out neatly on the dresser; the miniskirt and halter top I wore when I hopped the wall last night are balled up under the other twin bed.

"Oh, that'll look nice—maybe with your pearls too? I think I'll wear black slacks with my gold quilted jacket." Satisfied that I'm adhering to protocols, she strides back out.

An hour later I'm suited up, girded for battle with the Ghost of Christmas Present, or CP, as I've started calling it. My new buddy. There's no gender there, just my sense of a hungry-eyed, shapeless form that feeds on discomfort and unease, kind of like my old grade school nemesis, Yvette Cate. This CP is definitely not jovial like the one Ebenezer Scrooge encountered.

I first meet CP the Christmas Eve that I'm fifteen. It taps me on the shoulder that Christmas after Auntie Di had her first baby. It's also the year I accidentally find out about Mom and Shelby.

And then the thing is gone, and all I see is the miniature nativity scene under Grama Lopez's tree, and I notice how the barn is peeling and faded. I had never noticed that it's actually made of cardboard and painted to look like wood. And suddenly, the gift wrap on the presents looks cheap and garish.

I don't meet CP again until the following Thanksgiving, when Mom and Daddy Landon get into a fight at dinner. Those glittering eyes were reflected in the shards that littered the floor when Mom threw a wine glass against the wall.

CP is now a fixture at every holiday gathering. Sometimes the thing seems less a ghost than a virus that's injected me with some of itself so that now I too hunger for the toxic waste of a fucked-up family. The ghost waits for me at Grama's house, where I'll become its accomplice. Until then, I get to marinate in memories.

I walk through the house, and the silence is imposing. Daddy Landon has just come out of his office, probably having girded himself with the armor of one last hit of weed. Greg lingers in his room, putting the finishing touches on a model truck. Mom places gifts in plastic shopping bags and takes a quiche out of the oven. No doubt dulled by the exhaustion of trying to prop up their foundering marriage, my parents don't say much. Like me, they're also gearing up for tonight. Only theirs is the determination *not* to see CP today. *All must go well, and it will,* says my mother's resolute busyness.

Sitting with Greg in the back seat of Daddy Landon's car, I feel like a pink peg in that board game *Life,* in which each player's plastic car fills with fellow peg-people as the game progresses. Blue for males, pink for females. You spin the wheel and whatever number comes up, that's how many squares you can pass as you move along the board. You get an education; you get married; you have kids; you buy a house. Today we're a white car filled with two pinks and two blues, lurching forward in stops and starts. Too bad there's no square that tells you what to do when your family is falling apart. Secrets and shame and limbo don't exist in the Milton Bradley version.

The highway rushes underneath me, hugging the gray Pacific. It's an *El Niño* year—there's weather coming. The surf is churlish, the beaches strewn with palm fronds and driftwood torn by rain and winds from other shores. CP knows we're coming. I look at the other cars we pass, at the tight jaws and wrinkled foreheads through closed glass windows. It seems that other ghosts are awaiting their guests too.

When we finally exit the freeway, we pass the corner burger stand that Grama Lopez used to take me to, brightening the glum afternoons when my father stood me up for his weekly visitation. Past the high school where Grama and I would meet Auntie Di after her cheer practice.

I adjust the strand of pearls, Grama and Papa's high school graduation gift to me, so that the clasp goes behind my neck where it belongs. I remember myself at ten, in a green dress printed with snowy white pine trees and matching tights, fidgeting in the back seat, eager to jump out of the car and bound up the walkway.

I adopt a pleasant, sedate expression to match my outfit as I help Daddy Landon unload the trunk. Laden with food and packages, we trudge up the porch steps. Grama comes to the door in her Christmas Eve uniform: white polyester pants and a red cardigan with a large Christmas tree brooch pinned to the shawl collar.

"I need my hugs and kisses! Don't you all look so nice!"

Her greeting is the same every Christmas Eve. I lose myself in her soft warmth, just for a moment, and Papa kisses my cheek. "*Chica Niña,*" he chuckles softly, his myopic eyes wet and tender.

Once inside, I inhale the Spanish Christmas Eve aroma, briny seafood *paella* mixed with the yeastiness of baking bread. Daddy Landon has brought plenty of wine, the expensive kinds he likes, which he spends all night drinking, along with anyone willing to join him. A plate of cheese, crackers and *lomo*, Spanish cured ham, sits on the counter. Borne up by the warm, inviting kitchen smells, I help myself.

CP beckons me from the living room. The Christmas tree that once seemed to reach the ceiling looks shrunken and crooked, the pine needles dry. The pile of gifts under the tree is meager. The statuettes of the nativity scene are chipped and dull. Mary's eyes look downcast instead of adoring. The animals are arranged in haphazard poses, ignorant of the miracle of this night. The little drummer boy faces the wrong direction, walking away from baby Jesus with his drum. The kneeling cow is for some reason up on the roof. Nothing makes sense.

My parents and grandparents brush by me on their way into the kitchen, followed by CP. I hear my stepfather's voice, tight and controlled.

"No, Ana, I keep telling you we DON'T need any wine from the cellar. Dammit, Amy, can you get that quiche out of the way?" I feel CP return to my side, ready to rumble.

A clamor out on the porch. Auntie Di, her husband Danny and their daughter Layla. The big sister I never had, the slim, long-legged cheerleader who was the first rock star I ever worshipped, is now a wife and mother. Three-year-old Layla squeals at everyone to look at her dance. Grama claps with delight, even though Auntie Di and her family live in the little house next door that Grama and Papa own, and Grama watches Layla most days while Di teaches at a dance studio. I watch my mother looking on; she's able to muster only a tepid smile. I wonder why it isn't enough for her to be the oldest child with the nicest house and the richest spouse and to know, as does everyone else in the family, that she's got it better than anyone. It must be some genetic urge. The oldest sibling's need to know better and to be better.

"I'd agree," says CP.

Auntie Di is hopping and chattering, passing out wrapped loaves of banana bread. Her husband, a talented but unemployed graphic artist, lumbers in with presents. I know what my mother says about them: Uncle Danny is shiftless, Di will never make any real money teaching spoiled little girls to pirouette and the two of them are living rent-free like a couple of squatters. Tonight, though, Mom plays the affluent and gracious married lady, charming and glib. CP plops down next to me on the worn sofa.

"Whaddya say we tell them all what she REALLY thinks?"

Grama's sister, Aunt Luisa, arrives next. She always talks about how things have to be kept from Mom, Mom's brother Uncle Johnny, or from Papa: "Don't let Amy know that Johnny hasn't paid back the money you loaned him. Don't tell Miguel that you covered Danny's car payment last month."

I feel myself exchanging a secret look with Mom as Aunt Luisa walks by because I know she's thinking the same thing I am: *Why doesn't she ever dress any better? My God, with that nice house in Santa Monica, you'd think she wouldn't have to look so tacky. What is it with the too-short black pants and ugly brown boots?*

CP snickers.

I'm ashamed. It's Christmas Eve. I'm both too young and too old for this, obscene in a way, like a toddler pageant queen in heels and makeup. But I can't get excited about steaming cheese bread and cellophane-wrapped cookies and be oblivious to everything else. There's no in-between place, it seems.

CP winks at me. "Great night for a game of Truth or Dare. How about it?"

More relatives arrive. Mom's brother, my Uncle Johnny. My stepsister Linda, who's Daddy Landon's daughter from his first marriage, and Linda's husband Bill. Sofia, the family housekeeper and nanny who lived with us for six years until she got her nursing degree and finally—mercifully—left us.

Linda and Uncle Johnny exchange casual glances, but the sly smiles that follow confirm for my now older, wiser eyes what's going on. As I watch their cautious choreography and note the charged undertones to the brushing of forearms as Daddy Landon hands them each a glass of wine, Sofia sits down beside me and hugs me around the waist, greeting me in her reedy, Colombian-accented voice.

CP whispers to me. "It's okay. She deserves it. Come on. Give it to her. Right here, right now, in front of everyone."

But I don't. Instead, I shift a little to minimize contact and try to stifle the sound of her years-ago yelling and hair-pulling whenever Mom was out at night after my father left. The rage, the dolls and toys thrown at my head. Chasing me, grabbing me hard when I awake suddenly in my darkened room, my hammering heart compelling me to go sit by the front door and wait for Mom. Screeching.

"What you doin' outta bed? You diabla, you goin' to hell. Your mother never comin' back. Never! *Nunca!*" And later, when I start school and my new friends come over, Sofia for no discernible reason swooping down upon me, bony pterodactyl hands flinging a package of cookies off the kitchen counter and onto the floor, Oreos scattered everywhere that Sofia then makes me get down on my knees and pick up in front of the other little girls. Mortification envelops me as they look on, too intimidated to say anything. Still, I feel their pity and embarrassment, and the shame that makes me want to disintegrate into a million little pieces and fly away. *Fuck her.*

Grama calls everyone to dinner. The dishes are lined up on the gray formica kitchen counter. Saffron-stained rice mixed with crab legs, shrimp, chorizo and chicken drummettes. Bread pie filled with chunks of chicken, sausage and onion. Cheese bread and Grama's endive salad.

"Here, honey, take a plate." I hear Grama's voice and look down at the counter and see the food, the same as it is every year but really, nothing's the same anymore. I think for a minute that I don't really need CP, that the fragrant steam rising from the *paella* can coexist with infidelity, that Grama's wrapped cookies on the cheery Santa Claus-shaped plate can live alongside shame, and that maybe one day I may be able to stomach sitting next to Sofia. And that the bad of one thing doesn't always have to cancel out the good of something else.

I fill my plate and sit down at the round mahogany table, which has been made longer for the occasion with an insert. There's a piece of colored glass on top of the part where the table leaves attach to each other, green and blue swirls that together become my favorite color, turquoise. The table had originally been in the house I lived in with Mom and Daddy Landon after my father left. Mom used to have her girlfriends over to play Pan on this table, the game set's red and blue chips scattered among plates of canapés.

I stare at the little glass piece now just as I did back then, when I thought it was a secret passageway that led to a deep, endless ocean.

NINETEEN

I really don't want to be having this conversation, perched all tense on my dorm room bed with Jimmy sitting across from me on my desk chair, his apprehensive eyes on me. I want to be messing around with him or eating a gooey grilled cheese sandwich at the student center or messing around and then eating a sandwich. Or I might as well just be studying.

"Why do you even need me there? I have two exams next week. I'm not in a party mood." I know I sound like a bitch. But I don't want to tell him the whole truth. He knows I hate how he gets when he drinks. What he doesn't know is that I feel shut out, a mousy dullard compared to the pliant university girls who know how to navigate the world of keg parties with their feathered Loni Anderson hair and snappy small talk. I don't know how to do that. It's not my world.

"You can study in the bedroom. We'll tell everyone you have exams." He's trying to appease me, but I can tell he's getting impatient. I squeeze my clasped hands in between my knees and hunch my shoulders in an attempt to close in on myself.

Everything comes so easily to Jimmy—his grades, the scholarship money, jobs, his sunny disposition, the ability to juggle everything. The only thing I have are my books—the novels and poetry and plays I read for my English major and the glossy photos of paintings and sculpture in my art history books. And the grilled cheese sandwiches at the student center. And Jimmy's devotion to me.

I take a perverse comfort in being the only thing that doesn't come easy to him.

"No, I'll study at the library. You have the party. I'll be fine." Better to split the scene and leave him to import his drinking buddies. I sigh. Why can't he be content with the movie and concert dates that punctuate our study time?

"I'm not going to get drunk. I promise."

He's careful around me. I know that. He stopped getting really crazy when we got serious, when I told him that his late-night drunk dialing while his buddies hooted in the background was a turnoff. That more than three beers in him scared me when he was driving. He tells me all the time that *I'm* what keeps him secure and happy now. That he doesn't need the alcohol the way he did before he met me when he felt so lonely and lost after leaving home for Boston University.

But it seems he still *does* need it sometimes. And when he does, he staggers around and gets loud and is just—different. That's when *I* feel lonely and lost, and because I can't stand it, I'll be at the library.

Then we're driving back into the city, to his apartment off Kenmore Square on a little abbreviated street bordered by the subway and a pizza joint next to cheap Chinese food and a laundromat. Modern, concrete city buildings. No ivy-covered halls like the one that wraps itself around me at Wellesley as I sleep, eat, study, and sit around with my handful of quirky friends.

I'm sorry to leave the haven of my school, my dorm, my room. I feel like myself there, where nobody cares that I wear the same pair of sweats for three days and don't wash my hair or that I eat raw cookie dough in the living room while pulling an all-nighter.

I love to withdraw into my little burrow with its twin bed and dark wood desk, my turntable and speakers perched on a wooden crate. I'm a Resident Advisor on my floor, meaning that in exchange for listening to my dormmates talk about their problems, I have a private room. I'm an essential part of the fabric of dorm life without the messiness of being anyone's family member. My overarching purpose is to get a serious education. And most pleasing of all, I recognize myself in the crowd that surrounds me—all in various measures smart and neurotic and aligned in the pursuit of learning. We're all weirdos, but definitely not dimwits.

And some are my friends. Girls like me (although at freshman orientation we're all told to refer to ourselves as *women*), interesting oddities from Massachusetts, Ohio, New Jersey, Iowa. Book-smart, off-beat, outspoken misfits. The topics of William Blake, constipation, Salvador Dali, punk rock, and blow jobs can all appear in the same conversation. And there are no boys around to impress or self-censor for, which makes for even more compelling discussions.

When I'm not laughing in the kitchenette while eating whatever baked goods someone's made, I'm taking great pleasure in academic life. There are answers to everything in my books, or in what the professors say that I can review when I go back to my neat, organized notes. Or at least there are ways to go about finding the answers. There is structure.

I look at Jimmy now as he drives—at his coarse brown hair swept back from his forehead, at his straight, dignified nose. I met him at the annual Hawaiian Lei party hosted by my dorm at the beginning of my sophomore year, a mixer where Wellesley students in sun dresses and their hopeful male counterparts from the city, clad in tropical shirts and anticipation, gather to drink and to assess the social landscape.

Having volunteered for snack duty for an hour, I'm obligated but not happy to be there. Strangely tentative girl-women, the same ones that I sat up with the night before, howling our opinions like a pack of fierce she-wolves, now circle eager boys in an annoyingly subdued dance. My fellow students, the MIT frat boys, the Harvard guys, and a smattering of townies, the local boys who show up to drink and hope to get lucky. They all look the same—unrecognizable shadows flickering under a rotating mirror ball.

The dance becomes louder and more brazen as the kegs empty. A short but confident boy who looks like Al Pacino approaches as I stand behind the protective barrier of chips and pretzels. I try to ignore him, but his beer-driven persistence makes me finally agree to join the dance. He leads me out onto the floor, and I close my eyes and spin and sway to The Police, not caring that he's drunk and I'm not, because he's nothing to me.

Then, against my better judgment, I give him my number, hoping he'll lose it on the bus ride back to the city. He doesn't, and calls me the week after. Sober, he's intelligent and fun, kind and warm and earnest. He doesn't overthink—he just *is*.

Today, his simplicity annoys me. It allows him to navigate in ways I can't. So, because later tonight he'll be leaving my territory, I'll have to leave his first.

He leans over from the driver's seat to kiss my cheek and takes my hand.

"I love you."

I smile and squeeze his hand, saying nothing. I know I'm not easy. I don't tell him very much about myself. I don't open up. I keep the upper hand by not revealing myself. I'm sure I intimidate him with my seriousness. I often wonder why he's so in love with me.

Jimmy and his roommate immediately begin busying themselves with party preparation. I'm on the outside looking in at their happy, uncomplicated anticipation. I *want* to get excited, but I can't. I tell myself that my academics are just so very demanding that it's hard to cut loose. But that isn't it. I slip out after giving Jimmy a quick kiss.

My boyfriend likes the attention and respect he gets from partying with his friends, most of whom live in the dorms. Jimmy's family can't afford on-campus room and board, so he lives off campus with a roommate and works. He can't afford to be a kid anymore—except on nights like this. It astounds me how he finds the energy to work thirty hours a week, pull straight A's, throw parties and commute to and from Wellesley to court me.

Twenty minutes later finds me bent over my art history text, trying to concentrate on Classical Greek architecture but instead thinking about Jimmy's jovial wave to me as I left the apartment. And about the moment of fear I felt right after that, at being alone and cut off from the excitement I think I'm supposed to be experiencing. And then, an unexpected exhilaration as I drove over the Harvard Bridge in the crackling autumn night with the lights of the city winking at me.

I raise my head and look around the beige, fluorescent-lighted rectangle of a room I'm sitting in on a Saturday night at MIT. The sad-looking crowd of mostly foreign students, veiled by a haze of cigarette smoke borne of circuit theory and whatever else they labor at. It's still early in the semester; the students probably haven't yet acclimated themselves to American social rituals, or they're not interested. Like me, they take refuge here.

Two hundred pages later, it's midnight. The party has to be over by now. I collect my books and hurry out of the library, relieved to leave behind the inhospitable wooden chair, the dirty ashtrays, the dingy walls.

I take my time driving back under the comforting cover of night. Buoyed by anonymity and solitude, I cruise along the river, aimlessly touring deserted parking lots as if I'm a kid on a skateboard. I can stay out all night if I want. No one can stop me but me—or rather, my concern for Jimmy, who'll be worried if I stay away too long and who no doubt has already begun glancing at his Seiko.

I park the green Vega and stride toward the welcoming lighted windows of the apartment building. But then I hear it. Music pounding up the stairs from Jimmy's basement unit. Bruce Springsteen. I love Springsteen, but tonight he sounds to me like just another townie trying to get laid.

My hope that everyone would either be gone by now or not have shown up at all is dashed. I open the door to a keg party in full swing, the small apartment crammed with Jimmy's friends and friends of friends. The acrid smell of warm beer rises from a puddle under the keg and invades my nostrils. Half-full bottles of cheap hard liquor leer at me from the kitchen counter. People are laughing loudly. I smell weed. Girls in shoulder-padded mini dresses and slouchy ankle boots lean into boys who hold plastic beer cups and laugh at stories that they all seem to understand. I don't know any of them, and I don't think they'd care to know me.

Where's Jimmy? I look around, wanting to be rescued. The phone is ringing shrilly through the sounds and the smells and the sights.

And then I see him, stumbling his way through the mass of bodies toward the phone.

"Jimbo's Whorehouse. How can I help you?"

An uproar of appreciative laughter. Jimmy laughs back and drapes his arm over the shoulder of a big-haired brunette in a gold lamé tube top.

I push through the dense, buzzing activity into Jimmy's room to pick up my overnight duffel. As I slip back out, I see girls dancing by themselves, swaying and shimmying with an easy, oblivious sensuality.

Back in the car, I try to gather myself. And then I see him running toward me. Because I desperately want to be able to defeat the frustration and the loneliness, I roll down the window, hoping he'll have the magic words to steady me—but knowing I can't go back in there.

"Don't leave. Please. It's okay. I'm okay. Really. I need you. I've only had a few drinks."

I hear the desperation in the speech that veers between slurred and staccato. I see it in his bleary eyes. However many beers and screwdrivers he's had aren't enough to keep the mask in place. I'm tired of being sad and mad and trying to figure out why. I roll up the car window and drive away, back toward my school and my room and my books.

I don't even make it to the turnpike. I can't leave; I don't know how. So, I sit for two hours in a dismal all-night coffee shop down the street from the apartment, again trying to concentrate on the schoolwork that in this moment I wish could mean more.

Spent, I return to the apartment, grateful for the darkness and silence that finally and mercifully greet me. I shrug off everything—my clothes, my anger, my sadness, my loneliness. I crawl into bed and wrap myself around Jimmy. The tension drains from my body, not from love or connection or exhaustion, but from a desire to sink into that suspended place where there is neither Jimmy nor me, neither a here nor a there.

TWENTY

A*ugust*

I know that I shouldn't—that I'm playing with fire. But he's just so…sexy.

The black Corvette rumbles through the muggy midnight darkness, its driver holding the wheel with one hand as the car careens through the sleeping suburb. I hold myself rigid in the passenger seat like an old schoolteacher ready to rap my own knuckles with a ruler. Inside, I'm thrilled and greedy, eyeing the passing homes and gardens that seem to rise from the river like towering, iced confections.

May

I sigh, laying my pencil down. My art history final, the last of my junior year, is done—for better or worse. I turn in my blue book and shuffle out of the lecture hall, away from the remaining oily, bedraggled heads still bent low over their exams. No one on campus seems to have showered for days.

Drained as I am, I can feel myself lighten with each step that takes me back to my dorm, toward summer and toward Jimmy. The campus is awash in a riot of color, the pinks and yellows and greens of springtime in Massachusetts. All of it bears me up and carries me along with the peonies, mulberry trees, calling chickadees, my fellow students trotting back to their dorms after finals like horses to a barn after a seemingly endless trail ride.

Jimmy has finished his year and is home in Maryland waiting for me. He already found a summer job at a popular Mexican restaurant on the Rockville Pike, which is great news yet makes me nervous. I'll need to work too, and I don't know if I'll find something as good. It's his hometown, not mine. But I want, I *need,* to show that I'm as good as he is, as smart, as responsible, as industrious. For God's sake, he even stopped drinking for me. So now he's so perfect that I really need to step it up.

Twenty-four hours later, I barely make my flight out of Logan. I have to pack up and clear out my dorm room, which takes longer than expected because I procrastinate. Then my ride to the airport never shows, so I have to call a cab at the last minute. Jimmy would have handled it all so much better. He would have started his packing earlier, found a more reliable ride and still aced every final.

I'm proud of him. He's in the first class of Boston University's new law program that will earn him both a bachelor's and a law degree in six years instead of seven. I plan to apply to law school in Boston in the fall so that we'll both get our degrees at the same time. There'll be long days in the library and nights spent eating macaroni and cheese and watching Jimmy's little black and white television in his dank basement apartment. But before that, I'll probably be engaged like my freshman roommate who's marrying her boyfriend next summer after graduation. *Martha and Jimmy Farrell. Mrs. James Farrell.*

I burrow into my seat, under the blanket, and as the plane lifts off, I think about Jimmy's thick brown hair and his big, dark coffee eyes. One more hour before I see him and then spend the whole summer with him and his family, nestled in their sweet little home on a sweet little street in Olney, a suburb whose name sounds quaint but also warm and inviting like a bosomy old grandmother.

August

He decides to take me back to his house. Warring tendrils of guilt and excitement spar for dominance in my head, but the more aggressive of them wins out and so I go along with it.

We recline on lounge chairs in the solarium, sipping iced tea that his mother in her pink velour tracksuit and white Reeboks is more than happy to serve, almost stumbling in her excitement that I'm there. I'm embarrassed to be seen in a miniskirt and kitten heels, which seems silly since I know exactly what I'm doing there. I'm not a friend and I'm not a Girl Scout. I'm a sexual interest that may have the staying power to become romantic. She assesses me with eyes that see something there that she likes for her son. I'll take it.

"I'm glad you're here," he says after his mother goes upstairs to bed. "Thank you for coming out with me." He says this in a sweet, courtly way that touches me.

"You're who I'm looking for." He looks into my eyes and takes my hand, but I feel as if he's telling this to another person and that I'm somewhere else.

It's not the first time he has said this. He said it when he met me. And now he's kissing me and taking me to the kitchen for more iced tea and then kissing me some more.

This is not the boy *I* was looking for. The boy I was looking for is on the other side of the river right now, asleep in the foldout bed we share in the basement of his parents' house or playing Frogger with his little sister in the den. He's the boy of the future I mapped out with a compass made of common sense.

But this boy stirs up something else, something messy and prob-lematic that threatens to push me into a mire where common sense can't save me because common sense suddenly doesn't motivate me. I watch him slink around the large house like a spoiled young tom cat, the only child of a surgeon and a society wife. He's three years older than Jimmy and me, but his intriguing combination of impulsiveness, charisma and passion makes him seem younger. And, for some reason, he decides to focus his likely temporary attention on me.

Jimmy seems wizened by comparison, an old man knocking around in a twenty-year-old body. The prospect of law school, of side-by-side studying, of frugality and predictable routine, all of it suddenly starts to look gray and dreary. I'm someone else in this moment. If not ex-actly the blazing life of the party, then maybe the calm counterforce in the gravitational field of somebody who is.

He decides to make popcorn, but it starts to burn while we're making out. He throws open the French doors that lead to the pool. I watch the smoke waft out the door, dissipating along with my good judgment.

July

It's easy to get a job at one of the herd of restaurants lining Rockville Pike. Within a week of arriving in Maryland, I'm hired by a Mexican restaurant a few blocks away from the one where Jimmy works. The tips and the hours are good. When our shifts coincide, Jimmy waits for me in the parking lot in the old Chevy Vega we bought together. I lob myself with gratitude into the security and certainty of him as I slide into the passenger seat.

On our days off, we go to movies, concerts and the local public swimming pool, just the two of us. With the pressures of school on hold for the summer, we can do as we please. We don't need anyone else. My fellow employees are uninteresting. I dismiss as low-brow their token attendance at the local state party schools and the constant rounds of keggers and bar-hopping that seem to punctuate their summers off. I'm not like them, I tell Jimmy. What do I have to say to pert cocktail waitresses looking for husbands under the guise of half-hearted attempts at education? Or to their male counterparts, second-string jocks artlessly slinging guacamole alongside me? When they ask me to their parties, I beg off, claiming to be hard at work studying for the LSAT. Which I am—sort of.

Then I start to notice that Jimmy complains. A lot. His tips aren't as good as he'd hoped. His father's diabetes is getting worse. He's not sure he'll get the financial aid he'll need for the coming school year. The worries and fears I can leave behind on Sunday nights when I hop the bus from Boston back to Wellesley are constant and inescapable now. I find myself missing the lightness of my witty friends who laugh as much as if not more than they study. My family is across the country. I'm getting to know Jimmy's family by living with them, his parents and his two little sisters. I'm sleeping in their house and eating their food. A stifling mask of endless cordiality is required by that arrangement. It makes me crave my space—and my people.

I'm anxious, too. Jimmy is already enrolled in law school because his university program is combining a law degree with an undergraduate degree. Unlike me, he doesn't have to worry about the LSAT or law school applications, whether his grades will get him in, or how any of it will be paid for. He'll get his financial aid—and if he doesn't, they'll give him a scholarship to cover the shortfall because that's how good his GPA is.

I don't tell him any of this. And I can't bug my parents, because my father is in India with his guru and my mother is in Paris trying one last time to save her marriage to Daddy Landon. So, I listen to and comfort Jimmy as best I can as I try to deny the ugly doubt taking root like a weed inside me.

August

I'm a veteran at El Toro now, which means I've lasted beyond six weeks. I know the policies, the routines, the subtle ways to increase guest tabs to maximize tips. The managers view me as one of the stronger servers there because I can handle a lot of tables and have an excellent memory.

Eventually they ask me to train new hires. I don't care much for being shadowed by trainees. By now, the restaurant feels like my only escape from a crowded house, so the prospect of people hovering over me at work is unappealing. But it doesn't hurt to curry favor with the management so that they'll give me the coveted weekend dinner shifts where multiple margaritas kick up tabs and tips.

On a quiet weekday morning before the lunch shift, they send me a boy, tall with curly hair the color of peanut butter cookies. Long eyelashes, slow-blinking amber eyes. Lanky but soft at the same time, the start of a beer gut peeking over his belt line. He looks like the usual type who walks into a job here. Cute and lazy, but smart enough to figure out how to get by doing the least work possible without getting fired. And a likely flirt—I've already seen him chatting up the cocktail waitresses in the bar. Not my type, and I certainly wouldn't be his. Even if I were looking. Which I'm not.

"I know the deal already," he tells me, interrupting the introductory speech I'm supposed to give all the trainees. "I worked at Adobe for a year." El Toro's competition. I don't bother asking why they fired him. Instead, I head over to my first table of the day, two plump matrons wearing loud print blouses.

Weekday lunch shifts are low and slow. No one orders much. And generally, no alcohol.

"They'll order two taco salads," I mumble, annoyed. The cheapest item that has the most calories because of the fried shell and the creamy avocado dressing. But no one ever seems to realize that.

"No way. They'll go lower. A la carte. Trust me. Two chicken tacos with ice water each." It isn't that funny, yet I feel welcome, long-dormant laughter bubbling up, the kind that's inappropriate and uncontrollable but soothing to my parched mind. I'm sick of the managers with zero management skills and the customers who condescend to me because I wear a uniform and a name tag. I'm sick of the smell of refried beans that clings to me in the car when I leave. I'm sick of myself and the rutted track I'm finding myself on.

"No," I intone, mock-seriously. "The word 'salad' will make it seem like they're being healthy. I'm sticking to my prediction."

"Okay, fine. Whichever of us is wrong has to buy the other a drink."

"You're on." What the hell? Meaningless banter.

The women end up ordering the salads, and so he loses.

"Well, shit. I guess I just can't resist a good bet. I'm even addicted to the lame scratchers at McDonald's. But now I get to take a beautiful girl out for a drink." He raises an eyebrow and gives me a sweet smile.

Okay, so maybe there'll be follow-through. And then this boy named Allie starts telling his boy stories, first about one of the cocktail waitresses with a sleazy reputation, the one who's been grabbing his ass all morning, and then, randomly, about his father's multiple businesses that he, Allie, will be taking over at some point.

"I'll never have to work in a place like this again. See that 'Vette outside? The one in the parking space reserved for customers? That's mine, and it ain't gonna sit where I can't see it. And in a couple of years, it'll turn into a Ferrari. Poof." He makes a fist and then splays his fingers.

I start to walk away, toward my next customers, as that information rolls around my brain. But then he takes me by the shoulders and turns me around so that I'm looking straight into his amber tiger eyes.

"I could really take care of you." He says this differently. The delivery is soft and serious.

I don't know how the rest of my shift passes, but it does. My head lost as the rest of me goes about the robotic business of taking orders and refilling chip bowls.

I realize I'm hungry. I've been wanting to escape from routine and seriousness, but I realize that I also want to escape *to* something, to a place that's lighthearted and fun and interesting. I also find I *do* want to be cared for, in a way where I don't have to feel so responsible for figuring everything out. The life that stretches before me, work and school and then more work and more school and the paying for more school, feels frightening and unmanageable. And now, just because of a dumb boy with a sleek car, I wonder if I even *want* all of that.

I avoid Allie for the rest of the day, and then I'm off work for a few days so that Jimmy and I can drive down to the beach resort town, Ocean City. I'm going back to Boston in a couple of weeks to start my senior year, so the two of us have planned a getaway.

The night before we leave for the shore, Jimmy and I argue, and so the drive takes place in silence. Jimmy's worried about the cost of the trip because really, the two of us should be saving money for school. But I'm tired of the constant quibbling over every expenditure. All I want to do is get away—from the restaurant, from the constant blare of the television at Jimmy's parents' house, from his sisters and their endless, shrieking fights.

Dejected, I slump in the passenger seat, feeling old and tired. I wish I'd spent the summer at home in California, even though I'm not sure there currently *is* a home there anymore. I realize I don't have anywhere to go but here. It isn't really a matter of choice.

Once at the beach, we settle into our motel room, and I start to feel better. Jimmy apologizes and tells me that everything's going to be fine. The two of us splash around in the warm Atlantic and stroll hand-in-hand down the boardwalk. He buys me a hermit crab in a little terrarium. We ride the Ferris wheel and kiss at the top when it stops.

On our last night together, we stand at the end of the pier watching a thunderstorm roll in. The wind gusts from off the ocean, salty and bracing. Jimmy pulls me close, the protective gesture warming and endearing. Yes. We'll both finish our education and then things will start to even out once we get our careers going. He's a good, solid guy, and he makes me want to be a good, solid girl.

We get back after our weekend to find a letter for Jimmy from the university claiming he owes them an additional two thousand dollars' tuition. The peace of our vacation promptly evaporates in a maelstrom of panicked phone calls, punctuated by periodic shouts at his sisters to shut up and turn off the television. I go to bed, looking forward to escaping to work the next day.

As I stand at the hostess desk fastening my apron before the start of my lunch shift, I feel a playful tug from behind and look back to see that Allie has survived training.

"Where ya been? I thought I'd lost you!" He finishes tying my apron, an intimate gesture that makes me catch my breath.

"Nope. Still here, unfortunately."

"Good! Wait'll you hear who got caught making out in the bathroom…" I laugh for real, which hasn't happened since I last saw him. I love gossip, and I like that this guy worms his way into the center of things.

"I sweet-talked what's-her-name into giving me a station next to yours. That way, you won't leave my sight this time." He winks and saunters off.

It seems that he—cute, and definitely in demand—is actually interested in *me*. He certainly can't be serious. He probably spreads the charm thick on everyone. But then another server comes up to me at the register and says that Allie has a crush on me and asks whether I'll go out with him.

"I don't know." Yes, I do.

For the rest of our shift, we exchange smiles, or sometimes laughter, after he takes me aside to make fun of a customer. At the end of the day, he comes up to the bar when I'm cashing out and sits down beside me.

"Today was fun! Fuck, I can't believe I'm saying that about this place. I want your number. I owe you a drink!"

I wish I could hesitate, but I don't. I actually give him the phone number to Jimmy's parents' house, hoping I'll be next to the phone when it rings or if I'm not, that I can concoct a believable story.

Fortunately, I'm right there when the call comes later that night while Jimmy and I are watching TV.

"Hey, cutie. I'm working a double shift, and I had to hear your voice to get me through it." I chat with him, keeping my end of the conversation as neutral as possible so as not to arouse suspicion. When I hang up, I tell Jimmy it was a guy from work wanting to get some people together for drinks.

He gives me a look. "I thought you couldn't stand those people."

"Yeah, well, they keep bugging me, so I might as well just go. In a couple of weeks, I won't have to see any of them again."

He calls again, fifteen minutes later.

"I can't stop thinking about you. Come out with me. Tonight."

"Yeah, you know, I'm already home and it's late. I think Friday will work." I do my best to sound congenial, yet detached.

"Cool. We're on. Oops, Gotta run. Manager Blob, I mean Bob, is up my ass again."

I take a silent, jagged breath. I've just made a date, in front of my boyfriend, at his parents' house, with a guy who doesn't know I have a boyfriend. I wish it were May again or even my freshman year or high school even, and that I could just get a do-over.

Jimmy's talking to me now, saying he can't drive me back to Boston. It'll be too expensive and time-consuming, besides being hard on the car, and airline tickets are pretty cheap right now anyway. He looks worried as he says this, expecting me to get upset, which I would have—yesterday. I wonder if I should argue with him for appearance's sake, but I don't have the energy for pretend or even real anger so I just look at him and let him make of that what he will.

On Friday, I walk into work carrying a bag containing the outfit I'll change into at the end of my shift. It's been a while since I've put much thought into what to wear. Allie bounds up to me like a puppy, abandoning a gaggle of cocktail waitresses. His vitality immediately jolts me into a good mood.

"We're still on for tonight, right?" He tugs at the strings of my apron as he always does.

"We are indeed," I reply matter-of-factly, disguising that I'm loving this.

"Good. I got us stations next to each other again, though. Just in case," he whispers before walking off. I stare after him, suddenly flustered. He makes everything seem so…easy.

As my shift wears on, I notice that something has happened so that my coworkers now view Allie and me as an item, which seems to dissolve the barriers that had existed all summer between my fellow servers and me. Suddenly they're joking with me and asking me questions and I'm finding that I like it. A lot. I realize how isolated I've been this whole summer, socializing with nobody other than Jimmy's family and his friends from high school.

These people are fun and actually not that different from me. They feel the same frustrations as I do at the restaurant, the frequent bad tips or no tips, the butting heads with incompetent managers. At the same time, I feel special, singled out by Allie every few minutes for a joke, a snarky comment or a friendly squeeze.

At one point, he even clues me in on his secret methods for cheating the restaurant out of money and not doing the side work required of all the servers at the end of their shifts. It puzzles me that he does this; it's obvious he doesn't *need* the money. When I ask him why, he says the job doesn't even pay minimum wage due to tips that in reality we all might or might not get, and we have to pool all of it anyway for the busboys and runners, and the managers are morons. Stealing the money and skipping the work, he reasons, are an easy and well-deserved *fuck you.*

This, which might have offended my sensibilities a week ago, now titillates me. That night, I start to do it, too. I like that Allie doesn't put up with shit. Why should I?

After work, I climb into his gleaming black car, sparing a moment of remorse for Jimmy. This becomes alarm as Allie lights up a joint and then takes a hit. *Oh, God. Jimmy wouldn't do this, let alone expect to drive afterward. Damn. This is a mistake.* When Allie offers me the joint. I shake my head no—vehemently.

"What's the matter?" He looks at me, confused.

It isn't that I'm a prude. I smoked a little weed in high school, and more than a little during the first half of my freshman year in college, until a D in biology snapped me out of my hazy lethargy. I just have no more use for it. I've outgrown it, and—I thought, anyway—the people who haven't.

"I, I don't know. I just don't see the point of it." What I don't say is that I don't know if I can deal with someone who's high when I'm not.

Allie crushes the joint in the ashtray and sighs.

"Look, I'm not smart the way you are. I don't go to college. I didn't even make it past tenth grade. I don't care, though. I just want to have a good time. With you. Please, don't be mad."

He looks at me. He truly doesn't understand my sudden irritation, and neither do I, really. I smile.

"Just drive."

Later at his house, I wander into the kitchen with him for more iced tea and then we stroll hand-in-hand into the solarium. Sitting with him on a loveseat, I finally tell him about Jimmy. I'm vague about the problems I say we're having, because I can't really articulate them and because I'm afraid of them. Allie seems unfazed, which I assume is because he thinks he can eventually win me over.

And then I talk to him. Not about Jimmy or the LSAT or law school or my future or even about the silliness at the restaurant, but about the Aston Martin my father had when I was a kid and how riding in Allie's Corvette reminds me of that. About how I miss California and don't know if I really want to commit to another three years in Boston. About Deacon, my old beagle in Santa Barbara, who still whimpers when I come home, even though he can't see or hear anymore.

And then the talking turns to kissing, and then to more than kissing, and then I'm upstairs in Allie's bed, and he's kissing my neck as I look over his shoulder at the baseball posters on the walls and the water polo trophies on the shelf. I stay with him until almost 3:00 am. He drops me off at my car in the deserted restaurant parking lot, and I rehearse a story about having to sober up at somebody's house.

Jimmy stops questioning my absence when I tell him I'm working double shifts to maximize my earnings before I go back to Boston and then hanging out with the crew afterward. I tell myself that I love Jimmy but that I need to sow my oats, to have one last taste of danger and excitement before settling down. *Please never find out*, I say in my head to Jimmy's warm sleeping body when I slip into bed late and curl against him. *I don't know why I'm doing this. I promise I'll stop soon.* Responsible, patient Jimmy. He'll be a good husband.

My departure date draws closer. In the mornings before I leave for work, Jimmy helps me pack, putting my shoes in plastic bags and rolling up my clothes so that I can fit everything into my suitcases. We talk about the larger apartment Jimmy and his roommate have rented for the coming year and how we'll be able to walk to all our favorite eateries.

At night after work, I jump into the Corvette. It doesn't matter where we go, cruising the Rockville Pike or the sedate residential neighborhoods of Potomac or the alphabet streets of D.C. We wind up in Allie's bed most nights, where I close my eyes for a few delicious minutes and dream about a life with an uncomplicated boy who awakens lightness and ease in me.

"I love you," he says.

"I love you, too."

I sense that he means it—or at least that he thinks he does. It may just be that I'm different and my difference excites him into saying that word because he doesn't know a better one. I don't know if I love him, but I say I do because I know I love at least the *experience* of him, the impulsiveness, the not being afraid to do as he pleases and grab for what he wants. And I love that he wants *me.*

The night before my return to Boston, Allie and I join our coworkers at a bar for the annual *Adios El Toro* party, where the summer hires gather for a goodbye bash. Twenty-five of us sit around drinking and rehashing the highs and lows and the dumb jokes about the restaurant that accumulated over the summer. We exchange phone numbers and addresses and promise to keep in touch; Allie sits with his arm draped around me in a sweet display of possession, kissing me and in between kissing me, buying everyone rounds of drinks.

As everyone gets progressively more drunk, someone gathers the group together for a picture. Slightly dizzy, I look around, photographing with my mind the spectacle of everyone throwing their arms around each other and making funny faces and rabbit ears. I'm a part of this moment, actually in it and having fun and not standing outside of it for once. I feel happy and funny and entertaining, wishing I'd gotten to know these people sooner. They're all so…nice. It occurs to me that this is how my life should always feel—relaxing and fun. After all, I'm only twenty.

Quite suddenly, it seems, the buzz wears off; the happiness and camaraderie evaporate, leaving exhaustion in their wake. This needs to be over.

Allie cries as he hugs me goodbye in the empty parking lot. I say I'll call and come visit, or he can come visit me at school, though I know none of that will ever happen. As I drive away for the last time, the tears I want to cry refuse to come.

The next night finds me back at Wellesley, sitting in my dorm room among my unpacked boxes and suitcases, starting to fill out the law school applications that are waiting for me. Staring out my window across the lamp-lit campus, I set my pen down and reach for the joint Allie gave me the night before. I take a long hit, feeling the tingle, a protective, warm blanket that both dulls and soothes.

TWENTY-ONE

I miss my cozy dorm room at Wellesley. I miss the Christmas lights and tinsel I threw around my tiny window one highly caffeinated night during finals, and my oddball collection of friends and dorm-mates. I'm exhausted and eager to be done with exams; yet at the same time when the moment comes to leave for the airport to fly home for my last Christmas break of college, I feel an unexpected sense of loss as I look around the small room for the last time. There's only one semester left until graduation.

What I don't miss is Jimmy. I think the time apart will be good for us, but I haven't called or even thought about him other than when he's called me. I figure that time will take care of all that so that I won't have to—but there's no need to think about it now.

My flight is turbulent and shaky, as if the plane is as loathe to leave Boston as I am to leave my cozy little haven. I get stuck in Dallas due to fog and spend hours stuck in a chaotic maelstrom of angry and anxious people.

I land in Santa Barbara some fourteen hours after starting my journey and stand for a time at the curb, waiting for my mother. I haven't been home in a year, having spent the previous summer with Jimmy and his family. I'm no longer the startled animal caught in headlights that I was when I first left this airport over three years ago, terrified to move forward but unwilling to stay in place.

My newly single mother arrives looking trim, tan and energetic despite the late hour. When she learns that my luggage hasn't made it with me from Dallas, she navigates the bureaucratic maze necessary to retrieve it with the matter-of-fact expertise I've always both admired and lacked. I'm glad she wasn't there to witness my meltdown at the Dallas airport when my carry-on bag broke and spilled its contents in the middle of the concourse as I rushed to catch a flight that I didn't know had already left. I sat down at a random gate and cried from frustration and from the cumulative exhaustion of too many all-nighters during finals week, until a kind flight attendant took pity and guided me through the proper channels toward my eventual flight home.

My mother drives me to her rented home in Montecito, talking the whole time about the house, her new boyfriend Alex, and the plans she has for my long winter break. I watch the freeway exit we'd normally take approach and then recede, the one we'd have taken to reach the serious house.

Mom's new home is a square, two-story affair nestled into a hillside. Far below, the lights of downtown Santa Barbara twinkle gem-like against a black ocean backdrop. Mom's made her home warm and welcoming. Twin pots of her beloved geraniums, vibrant blooms of red, pink and white, greet me on either side of the front door. Her Lladro ballerina occupies a new place of honor on a ledge above the fireplace.

Mom shows me to my room. She hasn't had time to finish decorating, so the walls are a stark, empty white. I feel sad seeing the daisy print comforters from my old bedroom on the two twin beds. I remember the trip to the department store to buy them back in seventh grade. Standing before the silly-looking things now, I feel a brief flash of affection for the girl who once loved them so.

With my toiletries and pajamas still en route from Dallas, I have to borrow everything from Mom. In a way, it feels pleasing and intimate; in another, it's disorienting to be a transitory visitor at home—which isn't even really home because I've never been here before and have no idea if I'll ever be here again. Once again, I actually miss school, where I have my own space, belongings and a familiar and comforting routine.

I sleep for much of the next day, awakening in the early afternoon to an empty house and a note from Mom saying she's gone to finish up Christmas shopping. I get up and wander the unfamiliar space. I plug in the Christmas tree lights, and as they blink, I caress the familiar ornaments that I know so well—the egg-carton bulb I made in preschool, with its random splashes of color and haphazard glitter, the ice skates with paper clip blades that Grama Lopez crocheted, the Styrofoam and pipe-cleaner snowman made by Grandma May. Picking up a package of silver tinsel, I complete the decorating by adding icicles, strand by strand.

Daddy Landon is still in the serious house. I suppose I should call him. I can picture him beating around the house in his ancient blue terrycloth bathrobe, red-eyed from too much pot and heartbreak. Greg still lives there, but he's seventeen now and not around much. I decide to put off the call for another day; it's too much to deal with. I'm getting a headache, anyway.

And then Greg bursts in. I barely recognize the tall, muscular creature whose every nerve ending seems to vibrate with a strange, hyperactive energy. I wonder if he's coked up. He's been my shrimpy little brother for so long, taking his lumps and bumps and beatings from me, and now he's towering over me—an antsy behemoth with pierced ears and tattoos and a new broad, sinewy physique. Fifteen minutes is all he can spare. There's a party he's going to somewhere and some other stuff that's hard for me to comprehend because he's talking so fast. So, I decide to stop him the only way I know how, the way I did whenever he had gotten upset as a kid: I start reciting a stupid rhyme from our favorite issue of *Mad Magazine* that we used to read over and over again. And that snaps him out of whatever trance he's in. His voice joins mine and then the crazy goes out of his eyes for a minute as he hugs me before whirling out the door.

I get only one night alone with my mother, because her boyfriend is coming up the next day. I wonder what the rush is, but I know I have to take what I can get. Mom is all the time like the ball of mercury I once held in my palm in seventh grade science class: impossible to contain, impossible to pin down, one body seeming to shapeshift into many and then back into one again. So, I just link my arm happily in hers as we walk to a movie theater to see *Beverly Hills Cop,* which I've already seen twice but I don't tell her that.

Early the next morning, I wake to the burr of a sports car. Through the slats of the window blinds, I see a man exiting a white Jaguar XJS and hear the *crunch-crunch* of the gravel as he walks the path to the front door. I hear my mother's soft, throaty laugh, the one I know very well but haven't heard since the days of Shelby Boone.

I make myself presentable, walk downstairs and find myself looking into the green sea glass eyes of a more vibrant version of my stepfather. The confident bearing of a well-to-do man combined with a touch of Greg's kinetic energy, even though he doesn't seem that much younger than Daddy Landon.

Alex takes the two of us to lunch downtown at a trendy new cafe populated by trendy people who keep stopping by our table and who all seem to be my newly single mother's new best friends—women with spiky bleached hair and hoop earrings rather than the Talbots-clad matrons from the old days. In between the socializing, Mom and Alex do little more than laugh, exchange private, knowing glances, and feed each other bites of Cobb salad and grilled salmon. I'm relieved when they decide to play tennis after that, because that means I can have Mom's car for the afternoon.

I really can't put it off any longer, so I drive to the serious house, north on Highway 101 past State Street and the huge Moreton Bay Fig tree by the train station, the tree everyone says is a thousand years old. I feel unburdened for the few minutes it takes to make the drive, free for the moment from the widening gap between the old and the new.

The road to the serious house has been re-paved since I last drove it, but all the homes look the same. In my mind's eye is twelve-year-old Greg doing wheelies on his tricked-out BMX bike, Deacon waddling along behind him, doing his best to keep up. What I do see as I pull into the driveway are dry brown geranium plants on the verandah, the unlucky ones Mom left behind for some reason, dead in their terra-cotta pots. Which is weird because Mom always says you can't kill a geranium—they're like flowering weeds.

And then I walk into a mausoleum. Cavernous as always but now almost entirely devoid of furniture because Mom has taken it all. No clattering, cooking sounds emanating from the kitchen, no Muzak that Mom constantly had playing on the radio even though I always begged for something, anything else. Not even Greg can dispel the gloom. He's at home, in his room, but once again is shortly on his way out—this time to pick up motorcycle parts at a friend's house. So much like our mother, another who I wish would stop moving, just for a minute. My heart reaches for him, but he's gone again. I can hardly blame him; I don't want to be here either.

I stand alone for a few minutes, scratching behind the ears of Deacon, the aged beagle who hasn't been around me me for a year but who whimpers and wags his tail when he recognizes my scent. I remember the first night he came to live with us in Australia, a puppy with huge white paws and silky brown ears that I stroked as he lay snoring at my side.

Daddy Landon emerges from the master bedroom, looking just as I expect in his tattered robe, clutching a wad of tissue. He's recovering from the flu, the one he always gets just before Christmas. He hugs me for a long time and then has me sit on the burnt orange sofa, the only remaining piece of furniture in the room. I look into the green eyes that are the same shade as those of Mom's new boyfriend, only older, and sadder.

I don't want to sit. I want to flee, which makes me feel horrible. But I do sit for twenty minutes as he sniffles and sneezes and goes on about how people change and how everything must come to an end, eventually. And then when he actually says *ashes to ashes, dust to dust* in that mournful voice as if he's eulogizing himself, a friend of his that I don't know mercifully shows up and after a polite couple of minutes of pleasantries with that guy, I make my escape.

But not before slipping off to see my old room. Like every other room there, it's nearly empty. There's just a small mattress covered by Greg's old Sesame Street comforter from which Cookie Monster, Bert and Ernie leer up at me with their manic wide, open-mouthed smiles. I remember wrapping Greg up in it and dragging him as fast as I could up and down the slippery tile halls of the house on nights when our parents were out just as Auntie Di had once done for me. After allowing myself to stand for a minute in what used to be, I leave via the patio, climbing the olive tree and hopping over the whitewashed brick wall the way I did at night in the used-to-be as Mom and Daddy Landon slumbered, oblivious, in the next room.

I don't see Daddy Landon again before the end of my college break. After he recovers from his flu, he goes on a fishing trip while I celebrate Christmas Eve in L.A. with Mom's family at Grama and Papa's house and then spend Christmas Day with Mom and Alex in Marina Del Rey, where Alex lives on his boat.

They decide to sail to Catalina while I spend a few days with Grama and Papa Lopez, which is fine, as I think I've spent enough time looking on, feeling awkward and out of place, as Mom and Alex openly revel in their infatuation. They plan to return on New Year's Day, the day before my twenty-first birthday, when there will be a party with Mom's family. Thankfully, I don't have to worry about squeezing in a visit with my father—he and Honey have decamped with the kids to an ashram in India for the holidays.

I'm grateful for the few days' respite in the bosom of my old life, the least complicated part of it anyway, cocooning with my grandparents. I sit on the sofa wearing Papa's soft old flannel nightshirt and watching television until he goes to bed and then Grama and I stay up to watch *The Tonight Show.* Days when I'm not out with Grama, lunching at Sizzler or the local Chinese place that we call Brown Sauce Palace because that's what appears to drench every dish, I sit in Uncle Johnny's old room, rifling through the ancient dusty drawers just as I used to, running my hands over old fabric remnants and remembering the outfits Grama used to make me. I find a piece of tartan and remember the kilt with buckles and a pin that she made to match the one Auntie Di had; I hear the revving of the Singer sewing machine that now sits dusty and dormant on a dresser.

On New Year's Eve, the three of us sit at the kitchen table playing dominoes and eating roasted chestnuts. Dick Clark conducts his Times Square festivities on the tiny television on the buffet, but all that distant excitement seems canned and artificial. For once, I don't wish I were somewhere else. I don't look out the window and wonder where the real action is and why I'm not a part of it. Instead, I look *at* the window and see in it my own reflection and those of the two older people bowed in concentration over their tiles, framed by the light of a warm and fragrant kitchen.

My birthday party happens at a nearby Mexican restaurant. Auntie Di and her two little daughters, Uncle Johnny, Grama, Mom and Alex, and me. Greg has flown to Seattle to meet up with a girl he's in love with that he, honest-to-God, met on a train, and Papa stays at home, content to celebrate with me there when everyone returns for Grama's cheesecake. I watch Auntie Di's intense focus on her girls; her bobbed mom-hair in place of the cheerleader waves, her six-year-old Layla who still wants to pirouette and jump for everyone's entertainment, and the new baby Mara who lays big-eyed and quiet in her lap. I watch Mom and Di's brother, my Uncle Johnny, grimace at Alex in silent, not-so-subtle disapproval of Mom's abandonment of her marriage to Daddy Landon.

And now, the morning after that, I'm in Mom's car again, driving away from Grama and Papa, who stand at the curb waving as I pull away. Grama cries when I get in the car, and Papa turns away after hugging me so I won't see his lip quiver, but I do see it. I don't want to leave them; their loving faces tug at me, and I wish myself back in their little house. But Mom expects me up in Santa Barbara for a party she's hosting to officially introduce Alex to her new friends.

I turn onto the freeway and slip a Bruce Springsteen tape into the cassette player, *Born in the U.S.A.*, which I've been listening to nonstop since I've been home. As I pick up speed, I begin feeling that familiar sense of freedom wash over me—the comfort I feel from wheels turning underneath me, taking me away from one place toward another, yet letting me be nowhere because I just keep moving.

TWENTY-TWO

Feeling spaced out from the long flight, I stand on the long moving walkway that transports me toward the baggage claim at LAX. They supposedly renovated the airport two years ago for the Olympics, but they must have never gotten around to this part. I recognize it from when I made this same journey years ago, when Mom, Daddy Landon, Greg and I arrived home from Australia. I look at the tiny mosaic tiles on the walls that gradually move through the entire color spectrum as the moving sidewalk rolls along: green, yellow, orange, red, blue, purple.

Grama Lopez and my stepmother, Honey, are supposed to pick me up. I imagine them looking just as I remember: Grama's short strawberry blond hair sleek and straight around her face instead of teased over her head like when I was little. And she'll be proudly wearing her red-framed glasses that are "just like Sally Jessy Raphael's." Honey will sport the same short platinum hair, except cropped short on the sides and big on top. She'll sparkle in some brightly colored jumpsuit with shoulder pads, rhinestone lapels and, of course, a matching belt.

It occurs to me that this may be the closest I'll ever come to having my parents stand together anywhere they're not obligated to do so—through their appointed representatives, my stepmother and my maternal grandmother. Before I even reach them, as I anticipate the hugs and bustling over luggage that will mask any awkwardness between two women whose only connection is my brother and me, I feel as uneasy as I did at my high school graduation. Everyone stood together yet apart, clumped in safe, separate bubbles among the other guests, shuffling and making nervous conversation on the verandah of the serious house in Santa Barbara. I'm still not sure how to act in these situations.

Two nights before that, I'm lying in bed with Geoffrey in his house north of London. I feel the desperate intensity with which he seeks me for the last time, but I'm already slipping away. Hovering above the lovemaking in an impatient holding pattern, wanting to speed away like I had from Patrick, from Jimmy and from Allie.

Two weeks before that, I'm in India, a trip that starts with my father and my half-brother Mikey, a mission to meet God, as my father puts it. I eventually do meet him, and his name is Shanti Ram. He says *yes, do law*, so now I finally feel I have a purpose. And my father is doubly delighted, because I'm going to be an attorney like him and because I've also found *his* God.

I stick around the ashram by myself for a few more weeks, walking the rocky hills among little boys driving goats and oxen down to the Chitravathi River. I sit for daily meditation and the singing of devotional songs, because I figure I should after coming all the way here, but it all falls flat without my father there to interpret the experience and point out all the ways Swami is at work in my life.

Finally, antsy and feeling the need to get on with it now that I've been given a purpose, I take a taxi down one long, endless shimmering road to Bangalore, where I board a plane back to London. I spend a couple of weeks wrapping things up with Geoffrey, who I suspect I'm not quite finished with. And he certainly isn't finished with me. But it's time to go.

Goodbye, India and goodbye, Geoffrey—at least for now.

Goodbye, Sotheby's and all the young lords and ladies I've had alongside me, touring Blenheim Palace and Spencer House. It's the first thing I've left unfinished and hanging, if I don't count all the boys, most of whom are left twisting in the wind after I helplessly lose interest, even though I'm sure each time I never will.

I wind up in London because first, it's either go abroad or go home and apply to law school, and at that time I'm not yet convinced of the wisdom of the latter. Plus, I have the vague sense of missing out when my friends go to Europe during junior year while I decide to stay and serve in the student government.

Second, the Sotheby's program has much to do with art history, which absorbs me in college along with my old friend, literature. I always read to escape from the unpleasant or the merely boring. Thus, majoring in English is a no-brainer, although Mom regularly wonders aloud (which is how she wonders everything that casts doubt on my stated intentions) how I'll ever make money with that. She suggests I should go for economics instead.

But then, while my friends are off looking at the real thing in Europe, I take a survey course and find I love the visual images, paintings mostly, that tell the story of the times in which they're made. The funny Byzantine religious paintings with their gold backgrounds, Baby Jesuses that look like miniature old men, and everyone sporting halos that look like dinner plates. And later, the sensuous, full-bodied figures of Leonardo and Michelangelo, who even though they are all biblical, look like they're about to lie down and make wild love in the green Tuscan moss.

And then the Surrealist works, Picasso's *Guernica* and de Chirico's *Mystery and Melancholy of a Street,* art that seems to me haunted by their makers' sensitivity to truths they can't name. And for me the most arresting, Dali's *The Persistence of Memory,* the melting clocks and the ant-covered timepiece against earth becoming sand becoming water becoming air.

I decide that since I have the time to delay and to play, I'm going to do it with art, envisioning a year of museums and galleries and private collections under the tutelage of the learned experts at Sotheby's, which might even lead me toward job opportunities, vague as they first seem.

In reality, I spend much of my time flirting with boys on woozy nights at Stringfellows or Annabel's when I tag along with people who can get me in, between visits to country homes where I stand taking notes on furnishings and portraits. The young counts and baronesses who are in the program with me largely view the experience as a comma in their privileged lives, a pause before the next thing, joining the family business or marrying a fellow privileged person or having a baby with the wealthy husband they already have. I envy them the certainty of what lies ahead and their cavalier approach to clubs and flats and travel. They never have to think about anything. And just as much as I envy them their certainty, I envy the certainty of the others who are more like me, living within budgets and with the necessary determination to parlay this experience into something if not lucrative then at least sustaining—a career-starter position, an assistant conservator at a small gallery or a public relations something-or-other at a larger museum.

I never find out how anyone's story ended, because one day I just stop attending the classes and excursions. I move in with Geoffrey, who I meet at Stringfellows and who pursues me until I give in, even though I'm not really into him. But he likes me, pays for things, takes me places and is very attentive. He's a welcome and grounding diversion from the conversations, if I can call them that since I can't really contribute, about skiing at Klosters and summering on Ibiza. And I realize, after all's said and done, that I prefer to hold the images of melting clocks and sinister street shadows in my mind's eye or contemplate them in silence in the quiet of museums. I don't want to sell them, publicize them, publicize the places where they live or hang around with the people who do.

And now here I am, standing still on a rolling walkway that transports me into a tableau that feels just as odd and removed from me as a Baroque court painting, yet it's me. I'm moving toward my father's wife and my mother's mother and a future that's been decreed by the God of my father. I think about *Las Meninas,* Velázquez's depiction of a child princess being tended to by her retinue of handmaidens and dwarves. They constellate around her, but she is oddly detached—either because their undivided attention is a matter of course, or because their constant navigation for her of the minutiae of her daily life has separated her from herself.

I stand glued to the rumbling walkway under my feet and look at the mosaic tiles passing by, feeling for a moment as if I am just part of a strange, moving art installation.

TWENTY-THREE

pull into Grama Lopez's driveway and under the carport. I've left work early because my throat is killing me, and I have that slightly chilly feeling at the tips of my fingers and nose that usually means my temperature is rising. I'd guess it's about ninety-nine-point-something now, but it'll likely hit 103 before this is over. My body runs extremely hot and fast to shake off illness. When I was young, Mom and Grama gave me enemas, doused me in Jean Naté, wrapped me in cold towels—anything to cool me down until they realized that the fevers just broke on their own as mine will tomorrow or the next day.

I work for Honey's brother-in-law, her sister's husband and a partner in a medical malpractice defense law firm. I'm a legal secretary there, at least until I start law school in the fall. The firm defends doctors who maybe or probably didn't do right by their patients, which means a lot of letter-writing and brief-filing until the other side caves and accepts whatever they can get from the malpractice insurance company, who's the true client and the deep pocket. I spend a lot of time transcribing dictated readings of medical records and synopses of depositions. Laparoscopies that don't detect what should be obvious. Laparotomies that infect and kill the patient. It all has to be someone's fault—someone who can and should pay.

The late spring air is thick and close with low-flying, gray clouds when I leave work. I assume it's just the early June gloom that creeps in from the ocean and settles into the city basin for days and sometimes weeks. But then it starts to drizzle, and then rain, and by the time I get to the house, the windshield wipers on my worn brown Honda Civic are on their fastest setting, hypnotizing my fuzzy mind with their metronomic beating against the wet glass.

I don't have an umbrella in the car—no one does in Los Angeles because people here always manage to be taken by surprise by actual weather, even when it's predicted. I just hunch over, and with my purse over my head, run across the yard past Grama's clothesline.

As I run, I hear a tremendous crack followed immediately by a tinny screech and then a boom that feels like it's originating from inside my skull. I wonder for a moment if I'm having an aneurysm, if this is what it feels like in the seconds between the brain exploding and death. But then it registers that no, that's not what's happening. It's lightning, a white-hot flash that strikes the top of the umbrella covering the patio set, twenty feet from where I stand.

I stumble into the house, past Grama who stands at the stove making soup after I call to say I'm coming home sick. I shake off my wet purse and shoes and climb, fully clothed, into bed in Auntie Di's old room.

With rain clacking on the roof, I pull the thin bedspread tight around my neck and press my lips together to keep my teeth from chattering. And then I slip into a timeless twilight, where at some point I'm dimly aware of Grama covering me with a heavier blanket and of snippets of Oprah coming from the television in the kitchen.

Papa sits on the edge of my bed, his weathered face beaming with joy. Tears fill my eyes. I somehow know he's okay, which I've wondered about since the summer afternoon two years ago when Grama came home to find him face down on the living room floor, cold and stiff. I felt, on my last Christmas break from college, that it'd be the last time I saw him, my mind forever imprinted with the sight of him waving to me from the curb as I drove away from the house.

But here he is now, saying nothing. Just smiling in a way I'd never seen him do when he was alive. His had been the reticent smile of someone with a hard life, who worked a series of backbreaking jobs so his family could have more, yet still, he was ever on the outskirts of their accomplishments, a stranger in a strange land.

Then it's Daddy Landon in his sad blue bathrobe, alone in the big house in Santa Barbara. I'm sitting next to him like I did that last time

I was there before he sold the serious house. Greg calls to me from his room; he needs help. I go, but he's somehow little again, not a teenager, and he needs help reading the instructions for a model truck he's building. I try but can't read them because the words are blurred.

But no, I'm not there; I'm on the patio of Daddy Landon's apartment, the one he takes after Mom divorces him. Still, I hardly say a word. I look down at my hands and pick at the remnants of an old manicure. Grama does most of the talking. I don't know what to say or where to look. His left side has been paralyzed since the stroke and his mouth droops down at the corner so that I have a hard time understanding what he says.

"Amy broke his heart, that's what. It never would have happened if she'd stayed with him." I can't believe Grama is saying that right in front of poor Daddy Landon. But then I realize she isn't. I'm not in Daddy Landon's apartment. I'm in Auntie Di's bed and Grama is on the phone to Aunt Luisa.

And then I'm standing in front of the Residenz Fountain in Salzburg, where they filmed *The Sound of Music,* and Geoffrey is getting down on one knee in front of smiling tourists and suddenly there is a ring on my left hand, a large ruby encircled by diamonds. It seems that he's asked me to marry him, and it seems that I've said *yes.*

I see Papa and Daddy Landon together in an empty room, and then Geoffrey, but I'm not sure whether he's in London or Los Angeles…

My hands are clammy and clenched into fists under the blanket when I awaken. The ruby ring on my left ring finger has gotten turned around and is now digging into my palm. The house pulsates with a dark quiet. I have no idea what time it is. The rain seems to have stopped, although I hear dripping from the rain gutters on the roof.

I feel sick and weak, and my heart is pounding, but I don't know whether it's from the illness or from the endless loop of fevered dreams.

The lightning strike—was that a dream too? No, that really happened. That it did makes my heart pound faster because now I'm thinking it was a warning, a harbinger of punishments to come. Thunder and lightning are rare in L.A. Just one strike, and it happened steps away from me. I must be doing something or several somethings wrong. Have I just had a major signal from on high that I'm going off the rails?

Daddy Landon…I've all but ignored him since the stroke. It's been all about my father and Honey and sliding into the slot created for me at their house on weekends. I'm like bread in a toaster there now, hunkered down and warming up, ever ready to pop up and please. Church on Sundays, crashing on the top bunk in my littlest brother Jordy's room after a late night of videos and candy. Honey makes steaming pans of cheesy lasagna and mesmerizes me, her breathy whispers touting the sacred joy of marriage and family. My father reports to me about his cases and I report back to him about my week at the law firm. Photos of Shanti Ram adorn the walls. Having been to the ashram in India, I'm in the club now so I get to nod with sage understanding when he riffs on Swami's teachings, which is what he mostly does when he isn't working.

There isn't enough real estate in my head for that and for the remains of Daddy Landon. I *did* just sit there and pick at my nails the one time I went to see him. Grama visits him every other weekend, alternating with his daughter Linda. There's no slot for me there. The one that was created when he married Mom feels sealed off by their divorce, and I haven't been able to detect a different opening. I guess I'm just not *trying* hard enough.

Greg has landed himself in jail after getting involved in some breaking and entering rap. I'm not sure of the details and I don't really want to know, but Mom's angry clucking over it has gotten on my nerves. She's spent the past year sailing the world with Alex. When anyone does hear from her, it's via a crackling phone line from Belize or wherever she has momentarily alit like some maddening, hyperactive bird.

I shouldn't have gone so far away to school. Had I stayed, Greg wouldn't have gotten in trouble. He only had the fuzzy presence of Daddy Landon getting high all day and drunk all night and Mom completely absent as she gads around first with Shelby and now with Alex. And now Greg isn't talking to me because I wouldn't visit him in jail. Why should I? No one forced him to commit a crime.

I probably shouldn't have gone to London, either. Another year away from my floundering brother, just so I could screw around looking at art and shacking up with a random English guy.

Geoffrey…*why* did I say *yes*? I should've just ended things kindly but cleanly when I moved back here from London. Instead, I let him come visit me in the fall because I was bored and hadn't met anyone else. Then, after a few dates with guys who don't show any interest, I visit him. He takes me across the Channel for a road trip and then there we are in Salzburg because Geoffrey knows how much I love *The Sound of Music,* and there are people there looking on and smiling when he gets down and takes out the ring.

Who refuses a public marriage proposal in front of a famous fountain in Salzburg? I don't, I can't, and so I accept, spending the rest of the trip in internal panic, wondering how and when I'll manage to get myself out of it. And now a month later here I am, listening to his excitement every time he calls and talks about moving to Los Angeles and starting a business while I'm in law school.

Geoffrey is a good person who loves me and is willing to uproot himself just so he can be wherever I am. The problem is that all I am is flattered. I don't think I'm who I'm going to be yet, and who I'm going to be is someone who will become bored with Geoffrey. Or, more accurately, I'll get bored with whatever version of myself I'll fall into if I settle down with him, because it will feel like a dead end. I'm *already* bored, but I've never known how to end things unless there's a Man B in waiting. And I do know that it's just a matter of time until there is one.

My temperature starts to spike again, and I gladly give myself over to it, grateful for the temporary release from the ever-elusive adult way of thinking.

TWENTY-FOUR

My stepfather is dying.

Daddy Landon's chest rises and falls but I don't hear his breath, just the industrial hiss of the machine that does the breathing for him. Tubes containing different colored liquids drape from somewhere under the sheets, tentacles keeping him momentarily afloat. I can't look too closely, or I'll faint. I already feel as if all my blood is sinking down toward my feet.

I've never been around the dead or dying, except for my grandfathers' embalmed bodies: Papa's when I was twenty-one and Zhido's last year. Chilled, made-up mannequins reclining on satin beds in fancy wooden boxes. They're dolls that I stare at with a morbid curiosity. They're not the men I had loved.

This is different. I hold Daddy Landon's chilly hand because I think that's the kind thing to do. I feel my body and mind recoil from the contact, my own cells rebelling in visceral self-preservation against the shutting down that is happening in front of me. Life running from death.

Mom stands with her arm around me. She's left her boyfriend Alex on his boat in the Bahamas or Bermuda or somewhere so that she can speed here with her usual efficiency to usher her ex-husband out of this life.

"It won't be long." She sits on a chair next to the bed.

"Lanny, can you hear me? I'm here, and so is Martha. We love you." I've heard about people fluttering their eyelids or giving some other signal that they understand. But Daddy Landon doesn't respond.

The two of us stand there in silence, not in that moment as mother and daughter, but as sisters, complicit in the abandonment of a decent man. She fled to slake her thirst for freedom. I fled in search of the biological father who left but whose blood runs through me and who now beckons me from this ending and toward a beginning or at least a do-over. I don't want to think that I'm like her, but I am. We both have to keep moving and seeking, and if it turns out that it's just leaving—well, that's just the unfortunate semantics of it.

Mom sees me blanching from the sights and sounds and smells, so she tells me to go outside to greet the visitors who she's let know that this is the end.

Greg won't come while I'm here. For two years, we've been as ships passing in the night in silent agreement to disagree. His studied avoidance of me hurts, but I still don't see why I should have visited him in jail or why that still has to be an issue.

Wrung out and somewhat disoriented after my first year in law school, I'm happy to take the manageable job of distant death docent on this June day that can't seem to decide whether to be gloomy or sunny, waving friends and well-wishers inside to be assaulted by what I can't handle. The task requires more conversation than I'm comfortable with, but still, I prefer the animated voices of the living to the inanimate machinery of the dying.

Tinkling silver bracelets announce the approach of Rose, a massage therapist that my mother counts among her many and eclectic collection of post-divorce friends. I find myself enveloped in a purple, crushed velvet hug.

"Oh, sweetie." Her hug lasts a long time. I hide my face behind the drape of her red-ringleted hair. Its strawberry smell reminds me of the cologne my friends and I all wore in eighth grade. The memory rattles my rickety thirteen-year-old self for a minute so that tears blur my eyes, and a small sound escapes me.

Rose lingers with me outside the hospital for a long while, talking of darkness and light and energy and other things whose unseen existence comforts me. Law school's attempts to make a skeptic out of my inner mystic have so far been unsuccessful.

Shadows fall across the lawn in the middle of the hospital quadrangle. It's the golden hour, and the sun has decided to make a late appearance. The statue of the hospital's namesake, St. Francis, seems to radiate a molten glow. His palms look orange, and the cement animal figures at his feet take on the same hue so as to look like aliens.

"There's a dark cloud here. I'm not really sure what's going on. Hmm." Rose's delivery is matter of fact. She says it after looking around, as if hailstones are suddenly going to start dropping from the sky. She doesn't say anything else. She just smiles, gives me another hug and walks into the hospital.

Restless, I wander over to a bench next to St. Francis and his animals. I want to know what Rose means. I'm afraid she's talking about me, that the darkness is my shameful, secret relief that soon I won't have to worry about Daddy Landon anymore. I've been a neglectful daughter, and he knows it and the whole family knows it and maybe that's what's killing him in addition to Mom cheating on him. We're bad news, the both of us. But Mom is better at disguising it and never comes off as a black cloud.

Just before dark, I feel a tugging pain in the side of my neck, the same one I felt that afternoon two years ago, right before I found out about Daddy Landon's first stroke. I know he's gone before they tell me, before I see my mother and Rose exit the big glass doors, crying arm in arm.

TWENTY-FIVE

peel out of the Loyola Law School parking lot, singing loudly. My classmate, Drew, makes me a cassette when I tell him I love Crosby, Stills and Nash.

I've got an answer…I'm going to fly away…What have I got to lose?

The Honda careens around the curving exit lane as I wind my way down in circles until the lot spits me out onto the street. I'm driving straight from here to my father's office to tell him what his firstborn, the only girl, has managed to do.

A chip off the old block.

Life is pretty okay. No, it's *good*. For once, I can subtract the cautious from the optimism. I've just been named Best Advocate in the school moot court competition after spending dogged weeks in the law library, nights poring over cases that help me formulate novel arguments in the death penalty scenario that's the basis for this year's case study.

Fueled by a strict routine, I stay the course, all but living at school during the competition prep period, which consists of writing a mock appellate brief and then preparing to argue both sides of it before a panel of volunteer judges. Toast and juice in the morning at home with Grama Lopez, the drive to school for morning classes, yogurt and fruit for lunch, more classes and a little research time in the afternoon. Then a veggie burrito for dinner before spending the rest of the night at the library until it closes at midnight, my research punctuated only by a trip down to the basement snack room for a bag of microwave popcorn. I lose weight during this time, which is fully intentional in an attempt to buoy my confidence. I generally don't lose weight without trying unless someone breaks my heart.

Paring down does buoy my confidence, but so does the sheer enjoyment of delving into the material. I've proven myself just an average student at law school, doing well only in courses that I find interesting. The writing, the advocacy and also entertainment law because somehow, it's easier for me to remember and apply case law that comes with a little colorful celebrity gossip, like Bette Midler getting pissed at Ford Motor Company for using one of her songs. The rest of it is mostly confusing. I need more time than what's given during a final exam to sort through potential solutions to the byzantine questions presented.

The moot court competition gives me several weeks to ponder and deliberate and read and contemplate. Which always comes easy to me, especially when there's enough time to get things truly figured out. I love nothing so much as to take tea with my own mind, even though that can be dangerous. But something additionally pleasing yet unexpected comes from the school exercise. I find a group of fellow misfits who, like me, have neither the grades nor the inclination for Law Review but who are sharp and funny and happy to debate the whole make-believe case study with me. And all of them are glad to see my name posted at the top of the list, above theirs but also to the exclusion of those pompous Law Review people, the kings and queens of footnotes and proper citation format who thought this would be a no-brainer and found to their dismay that it wasn't.

I get to be a rock star for a little while. Big Woman on Campus, which has netted me a few minutes of big fishiness in a little pond and also the attention of the Big Man on Campus.

Dave is a strapping, rough-hewn sort. Hiking, rock-climbing, snow-camping Dave. But also, in the top ten percent of our class and Law Review editor, getting here via Stanford with a stop at UCLA for an MBA. Unlike most of my moot court cohorts who, like me, got here mostly unremarkably: former actors, postal workers, undergrad English majors, people casting around for the next thing to do.

As the top advocate, I along with the three top scorers below me, will represent Loyola in the national moot court competition.

"Oh my God, we're going to Nationals!" is what I shout to Barry and Dawn and Tina as we all crowd around the Moot Court Office when the results are posted on the door. And then I laugh, out of joy but also because I never would have believed I'd utter such a thing since I always associated the word *Nationals* with sports and cheerleading and other things that are strictly for athletic people and joiners—and I've really never been either.

But here I am now, a joiner. I'll have to get to know and work with a new set of people for the next competition as well as help administer next year's on-campus competition.

As I drive, belting *Suite: Judy Blue Eyes* out the open car window and into the smoggy L.A. sky, I feel myself drifting off as I always seem to after hitting a peak, wanting to fly away and savor it alone. Savor the newfound acclaim that (for a second anyway) will prove I belong here. Savor the prospect of another romance, which will reflect back to me (also for a second anyway) a little queendom and a little power and a little glory.

I take one last look in the mirror, admiring my new suit—a jacket and skirt in a go-out-and-get 'em shade of red. I grab the leather document folder, a law school graduation gift from my father's sister, and then head out the door and down Sunset Boulevard toward my destiny.

I'm a grown-up now. For real and forever. Not in the legal sense. I've been an adult on paper for almost nine years. But now, today, I've reached the true beginning of the next chapter.

Goodbye, education. I'm done with classrooms and professors and exams and summer jobs.

Goodbye, summer break and Easter break and Christmas break. I'll have to find a new way to mentally divvy up the year. And goodbye, especially, to the "Summer to End All Summers," which was the summer I've just had.

Exhausted and sure I failed, I stumble out of the airport Hilton at the end of day three of the California Bar Exam and into the heat of a late July afternoon. Disoriented, I eventually regain my bearings and head to my father's hilltop house, where I sometimes sort of live when not downslope with Grama Lopez. I plop onto the plump green leather sofa, hide under a blanket and carb-console myself with pasta and chocolate cake until I'm sick. I probably just failed the bar, and before that, just as I'm starting to crack the bar prep books, my fellow law student boyfriend Dave dumps me good and hard for a more compliant classmate. Someone willing to go camping and rock-climbing and do other uncomfortable and inconvenient things that I do for a while because of the novelty of it all and because the sex is good. Eventually, as my enthusiasm for roughing it wanes, so does his interest in me. Things have not been going well.

A few days after the bar exam, I spend an afternoon alone moping around a shopping mall, depressed and obsessed with the guy who doesn't want me anymore. I haven't told my father exactly when I intend to start as an official associate at his firm, because I don't know. I *do* know that I need time. For something.

The something comes roaring up in a cinnabar red BMW M3 as I step off the escalator into the mall parking lot. Behind the wheel is good old Drew from law school, a portly, balding but amusing troublemaker who skipped his classes and made snarky comments to and about most people on campus yet still somehow managed to graduate while also keeping his fat ass from being handed to him. I'd heard the gossip (which seemed to be the chief pursuit of anybody not involved with Law Review) that he wanted more than friendship with me.

"Hey," he says, powering down the window. "What's up?"

"You. Getting me out of here."

My enthusiastic would-be suitor is happy to oblige. I slide into the buttery leather passenger seat of that red car and I'm off, leaving my cares and my beat-up Honda behind me in the parking lot, never to return, at least not until I have a meal, see two movies and am driven up the coast fast and with abandon because Drew feels the spontaneous, optimistic urge to introduce me to his mother in Thousand Oaks.

Hours later, we make out in the deserted mall parking lot, pressed up against that sexy red car, my head spinning as I taste his bad-boy cigarette mouth. Not because I'm falling in love or anything even close to that, but because here's my chance to have one last good time.

The following eight weeks are a hopped-up carnival of nonstop good times. Drew inserts himself into my absence of a routine, yet nonetheless manages to win the hearts and minds of my father, stepmother and teenage half-brothers, Christopher, Mikey and Jordy. My father stops bugging me about my start date at the firm. Honey talks eventual marriage and the boys start out every day asking where Drew is.

Joy…and pain…like sunshine…and rain… Rob Base and DJ E-Z Rock provide the summer soundtrack as we careen through the hills, singing along again and again, sometimes alone with Drew but more often with one or more of the boys hanging out the back window. Disneyland, Six Flags, all-night diners, wherever, whenever, with whomever.

When Drew isn't around, I paddle in the pool with my brothers, making up nonsensical water aerobics routines with Jordy or laughing at Mikey's jokes about what a boring putz my ex-boyfriend had been. My father's Doberman, King, lopes circles around the pool, barking at us to hurry up and get out. Mostly, I just tread water in the deep end, gazing up over the tops of the tall cypress trees bordering the property, at the endless summer sky smiling down on me. I listen to the soothing whirr of the pool equipment, the happy sounds of boys being boys echoing from their bedrooms, and I turn my face to the sun.

I think I'll start work after Labor Day, but then to my delight the dog days of summer offer to extend themselves when Drew decides to carry me off to Fiji for a couple of weeks on a whim after I say I was there once as a kid. I throw a few things in a carry-on and wearing my brother Christopher's outgrown board shorts and tee shirt that I've been living in for weeks, I find myself on a midnight Air New Zealand flight with Drew to Nadi. We gorge on a huge fruit and cheese platter that the flight attendant spirits out of first class with apologies when they run out of meals. We spend the rest of the time gazing out the window as the plane flies through the night, chasing dawn.

And then comes a respite I don't realize I'm craving. I join Drew in his cigarette habit because it seems the thing to do, knowing that once we're home, I never will again. We stretch out on random beaches far off the tourist track, parking the rental car on the side of a rain-rutted road where dark, bashful children in threadbare shorts and jerseys giggle and sell us bags of syrupy mangos. Evenings we sit on the resort verandah eating spicy sweet *gado-gado* and watching storms build and then dissipate far over the Pacific.

One afternoon near the end of the trip, I lie on the sand with my arms stretched out above my head, legs submerged, hypnotized by the endless gentle rhythm of wavelets spending themselves on the sand. Here and there, glistening just below the tide line, lie the queer blue starfish that I've never seen anywhere else. I remember how I had so desperately wanted a pair as pets that I snuck two of them back to the hotel where, the next day, I found them black and stinking inside my pink suitcase.

Drew sits hunched over next to me, his soft doughboy body slathered with SPF million sunscreen yet still somehow turning an angry red, dragging on a cigarette and blowing smoke rings.

"Hey," I say, breaking a long silence in which we've both been gazing at the ribbons of cumulus clouds parading overhead. "What if we just dropped out? I mean, you know, went off the grid?" I've heard the term somewhere, but I'm not exactly sure what it entails other than opting out of the rat race.

"Fuck, I got nothing going on." That's true; he's yet to line up a job. "Let's just stick around for a while. We could hit Tonga after this, then the Cook Islands. We can stretch this whole thing out for as long as we want."

I sit up and take his cigarette, feeling the still-strange tingling sensation of the smoke inside my mouth. I like being with him here, away from all that's familiar, and love that he's so beholden to no one that he can go away and stay away for as long as he damn well pleases.

But then something starts to break my heart a little. Maybe it's the thought of those beautiful blue starfish suffocating to death. Or the clouds building up over the horizon that will put on their nightly show in an elsewhere or collection of elsewheres that I'll never see because I suspect that my life's trajectory contains other but not necessarily better plans for me. Or the very accommodating boy sitting there who loves me but who I know I'm going to hurt. I dig my toes deeper into the warm, wet sand and gently touch the living starfish half-buried near my feet.

"Never mind," I say. And even though we have another week left on the island, this afternoon feels like the end of my Summer to End All Summers.

And now I'm walking through the wood-paneled double doors, into my father's firm, so that real life can finally begin.

TWENTY-SEVEN

An astrologer named Mallory is talking about a Death Vortex. I listen to his radio show on Thursdays in my office in Hollywood, gazing over my desktop at the silted downtown skyline that glows orange in the morning haze.

Mallory seems like an alarmist on the one hand, with his predictions of thousands of souls primed to leave the planet. The End Times are near, he claims. Current planetary configurations portend the fulfillment of biblical prophecies as never before. I personally think that while people may be heartless and stupid, they seem to have been that way since the beginning of time, and yet the world still turns.

On the other hand, Mallory might be right. The country is at war. I sit with Drew in his apartment a few weeks prior, both of us nervous and glum as we watch the news and see the opening volley of green tracer fire arcing against a black Iraqi sky. I think of what's going on underneath those emerald ribbons, people huddling and terrified, buildings and streets destroyed, daily life and all its pleasures large and small getting razed along with military targets.

And while an ocean and three continents separate me from where it probably *is* the End Times for all intents and purposes, here I sit making the world safe for title insurance companies. I meet with my father's law partner who tells me what arguments to make to persuade a judge to clear the title to a home, usually in favor of a bank that's loaned money to someone who took title by questionable means. I spend time in the windowless law library flipping through dusty case books, finding precedent for those arguments. I write it all up neat and tidy in a brief, and then stride clickety-clack into the courtroom in my smart suit and high heels to nail it all down.

This is me, the professional, the place everything has led up to, the end of the path that Shanti Ram pushed me onto four years ago. But I think he let go before I was ready to lose my training wheels because, rather than taking off on my own, I'm tottering. I can feel hard and unforgiving ground rising up to meet me.

It's been barely six months, but I already know I don't and never will love this. I hate it, in fact. I wish being an attorney was like any given episode of *L.A Law*, where work and personal lives intersect in always-thrilling ways, and where the personal always takes precedence, unfolding in wine bars and hillside homes in Silverlake. Law school was sort of like that. Even though everyone was broke and stressed out, there was enough color and drama to keep things interesting. Who was dating whom, what embarrassing or lame comment someone had made in class. Who had made Law Review or won the Moot Court competition.

I wonder how people do this sitting-in-an-office thing for decades. A life laid out like a long, straight train track through a flat landscape. I'm on that track now, and the thought of staying on it fills me with panic.

My father has done this. He had a nightclub once. I have a vague memory of it, a glamorous couple holding their wedding reception there, the bride in a white lace minidress. *Rounders. Wannabes. Has-beens and never-weres.* That's how my father now describes the club's clientele all these years after he gave up the club in the divorce. He dismisses the entire first thirty-five years of his life, in fact, all the years before he found Shanti Ram, including the ones he spent married to my mother.

He occupies the office down the hall, having given up all *child's play*, which is what he calls everything that took place before he simultaneously found God and started his second family. *God. Work. Family. This is the focus of a householder.* The oft-repeated words of Swami.

I hang around his corner office as much as I can, now that we work together, or more accurately, now that we work in the same firm since I mostly work for his partner. Making up for lost time, I'm hoping, as we sit and talk about whatever crosses our very similar minds in happy sympathy.

Well, not exactly happy. I don't know if I'd call either of us that. But we're definitely sympathetic, because we see ourselves in each other. Nature trumping nurture. I often wonder, for example, how it is that although I didn't see much of him as a child, I somehow have his same weird love for and tendency to hoard Bic pens, medium point, in every color except purple.

I love talking to him. I pad softly down the carpeted halls of the firm from my office to his, hoping for the rare moment when he isn't on the phone or with a client or in court. Sometimes when he's on the phone, he motions for me to come in anyway, and I sit waiting, eager to pounce on whatever food for discussion he offers up.

We both love celebrity gossip. And Chinese food. After I go to India, I decide to become a vegetarian like him. We walk across the street to Panda Express and talk about Julia Roberts and Kiefer Sutherland over Styrofoam boxes piled high with noodles and tofu eggplant.

It feels too soon to talk about what I really want to talk about, which is why everything with him is about God and Love and Duty even though there seems to be no pleasure for him in any of it. There are pictures of Honey and him in the office and in their house during the club days and after, when he managed rock bands in the seventies. The long wavy black hair I remember, the diamond stud earring, the Aston Martin, the confident smile of someone who believes himself to be winning.

I want to know why he's so tamped down now, why he sits morosely at his desk in the moments when he's not distracted by clients, calls, court, or me. Why, when I sort of lived at his house during law school, he walked in the door dark and moody at night and on weekends, shutting himself in the master bedroom while my half-brothers clamored inside and outside the house, shrieking through the hallways and then biking down to Westwood to smoke and shoplift. I want to know if that's my future as well, if today and all the tomorrows on that straight track are hurtling me into that same prison. If I really *am* a chip off the old block.

Other things, I realize, are never to be discussed at all. The afternoon I spend with Honey late last summer. We loll in the pool together, floating on yellow rubber rafts and peering up at the sky in between the pointy cypress trees. After, we sit at the kitchen table together, towels wrapped over bikinis, drinking Crystal Light and doing our nails.

"You're going to want your own place soon. A career girl needs her own apartment," Honey says as she expertly strokes Ballet Pink over my nails. "I know you love your grandmother, but you can't stay with her forever."

I reply that's the plan, that even though rents are high in L.A., I should be able to find something since my father has promised to help repay my student loans. It'll be a tax write-off for the firm and free up some income from my modest starting salary. *A win-win situation* was how I describe the arrangement to Honey, echoing what my father told me as he smiled, showing the dimples that are another thing I've inherited from him.

Honey pauses mid-brushstroke, and in that moment the girlish afternoon evaporates, leaving me feeling cold and exposed.

"Oh no, sweetie. No. Noooooooo. That isn't going to happen. I don't know what you're thinking." Honey's breathy, Marilyn Monroe voice is at jarring odds with what it just delivered.

I feel my eyes do that thing they do, darting around the room like mad pinballs, just as my father's do whenever he tries to wrap his mind around something. I'm trying to analyze the words that were just said, trying to figure out what went wrong but also wishing they could all just be stuffed back in as if they'd never been spoken. I sit there in awkward silence.

Honey gets up and strides into the master bedroom, slamming the door behind her. I look down at my nails and close my hands into fists, my thumbs smearing the polish into jagged streaks and blobs.

Nobody ever brings up the matter again.

So I've been paying for the education that I'd have done differently or not at all if I'd realized I'd be on the hook for thirty years. The white envelopes arrive every month at the apartment I really can't afford on my salary but which my littlest brother Jordy persuaded me to move into so he could use the mailing address as proof of the residency required to attend Beverly Hills High.

I live in a pretty pink and white confection of a building with curlicue railings on the staircase and languid awnings that shade the walkways. I miss Grama Lopez and our cozy nights in front of the television with popcorn and crochet patterns, but I knew that was too easy and comfortable. I was turning into an old lady there. It was time to move out.

My dutiful day at the office ends, Mallory the astrologer having kept me company as I churned out a Motion for Summary Judgment and then a research memo. When I get home, my newly adopted cat, Abby the tabby, greets me along with this month's student loan payment vouchers. I place the bills on the cardboard box that acts as a temporary coffee table until I can afford an actual one. And there they will sit until I receive the next paycheck, most of which will be devoted to the vouchers, much as the last one was mostly devoted to rent.

I try not to think about my credit card situation. I know better than to use plastic for monthly living expenses, but that's what I'm doing. I look around my half-empty apartment, at the dark gray industrial carpet on the floor, at the white particle board bed frame from Ikea that Drew assembled for me, and the pink leather sofa I splurged on.

I assume I'm no different from everyone else my age, strivers who start out the way I have and who immediately and regularly find themselves with too much month left at the end of the money. Still, I wonder how it is that people go on like that and stick with the striving and get married and have kids and just bury themselves deeper and deeper.

TWENTY-EIGHT

A *nd now my bitter hands cradle broken glass*
    Of what was everything...

Pearl Jam. I hear Eddie Vedder's voice rasping from my brother Michael's bedroom as I stand at the refrigerator picking at leftover pasta salad.

A large Costco sheet cake lies on the white-tiled kitchen counter awaiting Jordy's fifteenth birthday party tomorrow. Jordy let me call the corner piece with the blue flower in return for a ride down the hill to meet his friends in Westwood after the party. Fair enough.

This is a moment that ought to sit well, when the rhythms of family should grant me comfort. My father works at his computer in the master bedroom. Honey has gone to the market. Michael and Jordy gather behind closed doors along with Pearl Jam, undoubtedly scheming at something I don't necessarily want to know about. The oldest, Christopher, amasser of accolades, is in his room bent over homework before leaving for soccer practice.

Honey fills the house on the hill with food and décor. My three teenage brothers fill it with varying decibels of messes, music and bickering. It's a buzzing port that my father docks into late at night and on weekends, craving peace and quiet after long workdays but receiving some measure less than that. He's an uneasy visitor in his own home, a silent catamaran seeking shelter among the braying cigarette boats disrespectfully cavorting in his wake.

I visit uneasily as well. There is no camaraderie in our shared awkwardness in this house. My brothers, my father's guru Shanti Ram, the practice of law and the goings-on at the law firm float between us as both padding and distraction. Also, between us but solidly on my side of the water as far as responsibility goes, is the matter of my school loans. I understand that he can't help, even though it was Honey who said it and not him, but I'm struggling with the payments along with my growing alarm that I chose the wrong profession. This is all or partially my own doing, so that also floats between us, but more in the middle. The space between us is expanding with what's been disregarded or just left unsaid, the kinds of things necessarily produced by the business of maintaining a fragile relationship. But no current seems capable of carrying any of it away.

I wander into Michael's room where he and Jordy sit cross-legged on the floor sharing a joint. In the twin bed huddles a beautiful blond boy who reminds me of a young James Spader.

"That's Aaron. He's in withdrawal. Don't tell Dad. Mom thinks he's just hung over." Jordy delivers a staccato summary, managing yet another tricky tableau with his usual quick-thinking efficiency. Michael hands me the joint. I take a shallow hit, buying time, aware that while perhaps getting high isn't the best response, there doesn't seem to be a better one I can think of at the moment.

Home from the market, Honey enters the room. She takes the joint from me.

"Hi, Aaron." Honey glances at the boy as she exhales, handing the joint back to Michael before exiting to unpack the groceries.

Aaron stirs, mumbling.

I sit on the floor between my brothers. I wonder if I should try to find out what's going on before the weed starts to pull my focus.

"Is he going to be all right?" I study the figure under the comforter, wondering if some authority should be called and whether he has parents.

The year before, Michael locked himself in his bathroom with a Swiss army knife one night, saying he wanted to die. Mishandled by a thoughtless girl, he lost his already tenuous grasp on the possibility of an acceptable future. Seventeen years had taken their toll on my father and Honey's medically troublesome, non-achieving, non-adorable middle child. It must have become unbearable to feel like a dull, technical difficulty-fraught intermission between the two dazzling headline acts that are Christopher and Jordan.

"I'm okay. The worst is over." Aaron mutters from deep under the comforter, his voice jaded like a sick-of-it-all old man. His weary certainty tells me this probably isn't his first time at this particular rodeo.

I sat outside the bathroom door the night that Michael contemplated doing himself in, wondering what people were supposed to do in such situations. Every few minutes I returned to the master bedroom where my father sat in his recliner, thumbing through *Newsweek,* while Honey lay on the bed with Jordy, trying to distract herself with television.

I didn't actually say anything, but my father apparently interpreted my silence as accusatory.

"What do you want me to do about it? Jesus Christ, we've sent him to therapy, special schools, I've exposed him to Swami's teachings. There's nothing left to do. If he wants to off himself, so be it." He returned to the magazine.

"And he can't stand *me*. He wouldn't breastfeed, and it's only gone downhill since. The heart surgery, the brain surgery, the learning disabilities. This is all too much." Honey sat up, her head in her hands.

Jordy ignored the entire incident, having long ago written off his brother as beyond salvage and useful mostly as an on-call henchman.

Aaron sits up now, pallid, his white-blond shock of hair matching his skin. Jordy sits next to him and pries his lids apart, peering into his eyes.

"He's dehydrated and needs salt." Following this declaration, Jordy orders Michael into the kitchen to have Honey prepare soup.

The plan for Jordy is eventual medical school, which suits the loyal caregiver in him one hundred percent but the equally vibrant and mischievous libertine in him zero percent. I'm fairly sure the libertine will win out but eventually will be kept in check by his natural focus and drive. Jordy likes to be at the center of everything, but he also likes to be in control. I can't imagine Jordy ever being at the mercy of anyone or anything.

Michael eventually opened the bathroom door to me late that night before crawling into the empty bathtub and lying down, flicking the blade of the knife in and out of its slot in restless contemplation. I could say nothing to ease the cumulative effect on Michael of being Michael. I was just his errant half-sister. I didn't know the half of his personal hell, but he deserved more from me than nervous retreat, which was generally my first instinct.

I just kneeled by him, stroking his hair in an awkward gesture of comfort, the movement of my hand countering the rhythmic scrape of metal against metal.

"You need somebody to do that for you," was the only thing he said.

"Let's do it for each other then," I replied, kissing him on the head and eventually helping him into bed after he'd had enough of the unforgiving bathtub.

Aaron now leans back against a pillow, exhaling a long-held breath.

"You're not bad." He tilts his head to the side and squints at me, his calculating assessment making me want to inject him full of a lethal dose of whatever he's withdrawing from.

"No, I don't mean it like that. I mean…you're here." His voice is small. He has shape-shifted for a moment into who he must have been before his premature acceleration out of childhood.

I get up from the floor and sit next to Aaron. I don't know what to say to this kid I've never met before who is sweating and shivering in a strange bed, any more than I knew what to tell my own brother as he lay in his own bathtub flirting with the idea of no longer being here. So, I kiss him on the head as I did Michael, a substandard benediction from a one-off substitute sister. And then I drift out the front door, finding myself driving down the hill to my apartment and finding also that my cheeks are wet. My own tears always manage to surprise me— as if they're someone else's but somehow wind up on my face.

I feel an invisible but strengthening force field that is getting harder for me to slip through each time I gun my car up that hill. When I enter that house, I wander from room to room, perching alongside a brother or my father or Honey, orbiting aimlessly like a restless, visiting ghost.

And then I find myself suddenly flung out of that orbit, becoming an untethered relic of an inconvenient past.

TWENTY-NINE

I no longer have a job, let alone a career to speak of. Nothing, in fact, to wake up for.

"Let's take a drive and check it out." Seth is on edge, eager to move.

Normally I'd jump on that. I love taking long rides with him. It's one of our favorite things to do together, and cheap, which is good because we're crammed together in a studio apartment. He's the only one working.

But tonight, I'm scared. I've had an irrational fear of fire for as long as I can remember. The thought of driving on purpose toward a raging brushfire fills me with dread.

In the few months we've been together, I've learned that Seth gets annoyed by fear, particularly mine. So, I suck it up and get in the car, heart pounding, hoping the winding canyon roads won't lead us straight into an inferno.

At the same time, it's kind of thrilling. Seeing the smoke this afternoon billowing like a mushroom cloud above the Santa Monica Mountains excites me. Driving down Olympic Boulevard toward the apartment today, having cleared my few things out of the office and walked out for the last time, I see that plume and feel good. *Burn, baby, burn,* I think to myself. *Bring it on.* The Santa Anas have been raging all afternoon. Those devil winds that blow all hot and bothered out of the desert only to leave a lingering chill in their wake. I can tell, looking at that smoke through the eyes of someone who's lived here a long time, that the winds are going to make that fire bad, that the winds are making *me* bad, my battered heart gladdened as it is by the thought of scorched everything.

I've been scorched too—by the flames of my own impulsiveness. I leave a job that I hate, move out of an apartment I can't afford and default on student loans I can't repay. I don't know what all that will lead to just yet, so here I am sitting next to Seth in his Nissan Sentra, driving toward whatever rages under that big black cloud.

Pacific Coast Highway is closed beyond Gladstone's. We park the car and sit on the beach. An angry red glow bathes the night sky behind the hills to the north. Rows and rows of kids sit alongside us. But we find out that they're not kids—they're volunteer firefighters from Oregon. They sit with sandwiches and bags of chips, waiting to be called out. They're cheerful and greet us with big smiles, as if we're all at a tailgate party. *What's wrong with you,* I want to ask them. *You should all be petrified.*

Too soon, Seth starts fidgeting. He wants to be on the move again. I'm learning that about him, too, that he can't stay still for long. We get back into the Nissan. He's determined to get up close to the fire, so because we can't head up the highway, we drive up Sunset and hang a left on another canyon road. Now the glow has become an array of distinct bright orange lines of flame that dot the hills above Malibu.

After several miles driving uphill, Seth guides the car up to the end of the road, a big, dirt-covered expanse where new homes are being built—side-by-side McMansions. We can't go any further, which is good because the flames are now clearly visible on the hillside opposite. A pickup-truck full of kids, boys and girls in flannels and Doc Martens, pulls up next to us. They take beers from a case of Heineken on the flatbed, and I see a bright red glow inside the cab before smelling the skunky aroma that follows a few seconds later.

Seth wants to get out of the car. I don't, but I get out anyway. I'm so nervous that I'm shaking as I emerge into the smoke. The winds are mad, rushing in all directions, sparks like angry fireflies scurrying across the canyon. One of them alights on a Manzanita bush in front of me, at the edge of the lot where the hill drops off into the gorge below.

Mesmerized, I watch the ember burrow into a leaf. I wonder if these shrubs are like eucalyptus, if there's oil in there that will make the whole thing suddenly explode. My fear morphs into fascination as

I watch that hungry ember become a small flame, taking over one leaf, and then another and then another.

Just this morning I was in my office, packing up the little I'd take from there—a ceramic fish my brother Mikey made for me in his art class, copies of a few of the briefs I've written just in case I ever need to show anyone that I can. A week before that, I left my old apartment, and helped Seth and a couple of guys we found standing outside a hardware store load my stuff into a U-Haul to take to a storage unit.

And a month before that, I was standing in my father's office telling him that this was it, that I was done. After three years, it was time to move on, even though I didn't and still don't know what I'm moving on to and he didn't ask. He made no eye contact when I told him. He just looked down at some papers in front of him and mumbled that it was good I'd made a decision. But what I'm doing doesn't seem like a decision, because I'm not really choosing to leave. It's choosing me.

"Holy fuck!"

I look up to see one of the kids from the pickup truck standing next to me, both of us watching the flaming leaves become something more as the whole bush begins to take fire. He stomps it out with his shredded combat boots, finishes his beer in one swallow and then jumps into the truck before it peels away back down the hill, blasting Nirvana against the wind and the distant scream of sirens.

THIRTY

I know that I shouldn't, that I'm playing with fire. Again. But he's just so…sexy. Again. That's how it always starts, I think, remembering Allie and others who came after.

All these Israeli men are sexy. They surround me at Banner Entertainment, from the CEO on down. Salacious dark eyes that drill into whomever they're beholding. Hair everywhere, curly and cascading or cropped close. Shaggy beards. And no sense of personal space. They invade, standing all close and appraising, waiting for an opportunity, for the momentary letting down of the guard so they can… whatever.

Whatever hasn't happened. Yet. But it's getting close.

I sign up with a temporary agency six months after leaving the law firm and moving in with Seth, who, after a time, starts to make impatient noises about me getting a job. And he's right; I don't know how long I can go on without a car after the Honda finally dies—and without a dime—crammed into a studio apartment with Seth and the cat. Days spent eating Jujyfruits and splitting my time between Seth's small television and the library down the street are becoming repetitive and disheartening. It's definitely time to do *something*.

The agency sends me to Jonah Banner. It's the fourth or fifth job they send me on, and I'm the fifteenth or twentieth temp personal assistant he's tried. My previous jobs end because people come back from vacation or sick leave. Jonah's assistants are sent away because they can't understand his heavily accented dictation, or they bring him espresso in cappuccino cups, or they get flustered while rolling the dozens of calls that come in and go out every day.

Because I'm adept at figuring out and then accommodating difficult or demanding people, I prove to be a good fit for Jonah. It's not hard to keep him happy. I'm smart, at least in the ways that the job requires, and I don't have to be told things twice. I manage Jonah's driver and the office kitchen help. I also manage Jonah's wife, Laraine, who always seems to call when he isn't there and when he is purposefully vague as to his whereabouts. I just call the driver and have him tell Jonah that Laraine is looking for him along with whatever cover story I've concocted, so that everyone is on the same page.

Jonah knows I'm an attorney, so he never grabs my ass or looks at my tits. We understand each other.

I'm confident that I won't be Jonah's assistant forever—that he'll begin using my brain for better things. So, when Jonah hires the flamboyant and receptive Simon Lu to run the new Children's Entertainment Division, I become fast friends with him. Simon's gay but thinks that nobody knows and appears willing to help me move up the ladder.

A constant parade of company executives, television show talent and various favor-seekers stream in and out of Jonah's office. I'm the gatekeeper. They have to get by me to see or talk to him. My first Christmas at the company sees piles of gift baskets on my desk as thanks for the access I've granted or as a tacit plea for that which I haven't.

In short order, I organize the office and get the filing up to date so that I have time to sit and read or crochet. Plus, Jonah is often out of town, and when he is, he doesn't care if I'm at my desk or not.

Color and interest texture the days. Sometimes I'm at the office as early as 6:00 am if Jonah feels motivated, and sometimes I'm there as late as 7:00 or 8:00 pm, typing up deal memos and ordering in dinner for meetings that run late. I don't have much time to think about Seth or my father.

I've been with Seth for over a year now. After Jonah hires me as a permanent employee, we can afford to move out of Seth's studio apartment and into a large one-bedroom just off Santa Monica Boulevard. Our life together is starting to take root, even though he's moody and sometimes gets angry in a way that makes me nervous, but not nervous enough to leave him because I ruined my credit after bailing on my student loans and would have a hard time making it on my own. And he does love me and has learned to love my cat. He's not a bad guy.

There's been no word from my father since I left the firm last year. There had been much to say then that I didn't—that I was unhappy, that the apartment in the proper zip code rented for the benefit of Jordy's attendance at Beverly Hills High was too expensive. That it was weird and hurtful when Jordy told me and not his parents that he was gay—the unwelcome shock when they found out was something they decided I had laid upon their previously tidy doorstep with some sort of malicious intent. Even though my littlest brother's sexual identity seemed pretty obvious.

Something or someone eventually has to give. I not only hope but actually believe that my father and I will one day speak, even though right now it doesn't feel that way. For now, I guess it's easier to rack up career credits than try to crack the code for slotting back in.

Between Christmas and New Year's, the office is dead. Jonah works from home and then takes Laraine and their kids to Aspen. I take a couple of days off and then go into the office because Jonah gets bored on vacation and wants me to send out some memos and roll some calls.

On New Year's Eve day, I come in early for a couple of hours to tie up loose ends and tidy the office in preparation for the post-holiday onslaught.

As I'm getting ready to leave, I look up and see him standing in the doorway.

"Hi," we both say at the same time.

"Maaaarty." He says my name slowly after I introduce myself, as if he's trying it out on his tongue.

It feels good to hear him say it. My bright and shiny new name. *Martha* became *Marty* right after leaving the law firm. My stepmother Honey had always compared me to the biblical Martha, the dutiful one making dinner or whatever while her sister Mary sat at the feet of Christ. Honey had said that as if it were some sort of compliment.

I'm not Martha anymore. I've been cast from the father's house, and the sons seem to be getting along okay without me there to chauffeur and babysit. So now I'm Marty, the wanton Pink Lady of *Grease*.

Or at least someone more interesting than the put-upon shrew of the Bible who got stuck cleaning up after her sister and the Savior.

Jonah has hired Adam Drezner as a Director of Something, and he thought they had a meeting today, but Jonah must have forgotten to tell him he was going to be out of town. I reschedule him for the following week, and then we both just stand there looking at each other.

His eyes don't bore into me that way I'm used to from other men at the company, nor do they shift down toward my cleavage or my crotch and then linger there. And his eyes aren't dark; they're bluish green, caressing, assessing. His hair is sandy and cropped; he's just finished an obligatory tour of duty in the Israeli army.

This I learn as we walk back to the deserted parking garage. There's no reason for either of us to remain, but we do, talking about random things like how we both think camels are so ugly they're cute and how Adam keeps a photo of one on his desk for no reason. When he says he lives just a few blocks from me, I feel obliged to tell him I don't live alone, because I know he's going to ask if I have a boyfriend and the omission feels like a lie. Though right now I don't give much thought to Seth and for the first time even sort of wish that he didn't exist. I like Adam and I can tell he likes me. I haven't felt that raw mutuality for a long time and realize I don't and never really did feel that with Seth.

After the New Year, it seems that Adam is ever present, at every meeting where I take notes and serve drinks, in Jonah's office sitting in on conference calls. I remember he always orders pasta *puttanesca* from La Scala Presto and the spicy tuna bento box from the sushi place, so I don't have to ask him. He knows I love the waving cat statues that are in all the Asian restaurants, and one day he brings me one.

"Is Adam in love with you?" Jonah asks one day after he sees Adam lingering at my desk. I laugh because I don't know what else to do, hoping I sound appropriately dismissive. But I wonder too, and I keep thinking about him and that helps me tolerate Seth and the lack of anything interesting to do when I'm not at work with all the people who seem to do interesting things.

Adam lingers around all the unattached girls at the office. I watch them toss their flat-ironed hair over their faces and cast their eyes down. It bothers me—a little. Although I'm not free, I kind of hoped he'd carry the torch for me.

One night I attend a company screening with Seth. Adam introduces me to someone he calls his girlfriend, a willowy Israeli girl named Maya. They speak Hebrew in hushed tones. She laughs and caresses his arm, her long chestnut hair covering one eye. I feel awkward standing there with Seth, like we're two stiff cardboard figures hovering on the outskirts.

At work, Adam and I continue to flirt. I start to stay at the office long after Jonah leaves because I know Adam stays late. He's kind and gentle, and even though I now know he's a player like the rest of them, I don't care.

After a month, the two of us find ourselves once again in the empty parking lot. We've run out of banter and the air between us is getting thicker the closer we get to our cars, which are always parked next to each other. I think for a moment of Drew four years ago, and Allie six years before that. And then suddenly, it's happening again.

I'm pressed up against a car under flickering garage lights, but it's Adam's and I don't care that it's a decrepit Toyota Corolla and not a sleek Beamer or a muscle car. And then I forget about Drew and Allie and Seth and my father and my debt, as my hard edges soften and then liquefy into a pleasing essence that feels like *me*.

I don't go any further with Adam than kissing and a little furtive groping although it would be easy enough to go back to his place or even just the back seat of his car and then tell Seth that Jonah kept me busy until late. Which is true often enough that it would be believable.

Instead, I pull back, get in my own car and drive home to the guy I feel bound to and bound by. I'd like to flatter myself with the fiction that it's a matter of wanting to take the high road. But if it were that, I wouldn't have let things get this far.

I just need the sure bet right now, the security of someone who knows my closeted skeletons and will help keep them propped up. I don't know that Adam—or anyone—would take me as is, with rickety finances and an inconvenient boyfriend. Upending my life right now is too risky; I can't even qualify for an apartment.

I'd love to be the opposite sort—someone who like Sheryl Crow could "have some fun until the sun comes up over Santa Monica Boulevard," without everything having to feel so high-stakes all the time. But I realize that no matter what anyone calls me or what I call myself, I'm still Martha. The older I get, the harder it is to be a true Marty and the easier it is to hang back in the shadows where there is neither fun nor sun.

THIRTY-ONE

My heart cries out for something fierce—I don't know what, exactly. But for now, this will have to do.

I have a career, finally, like an actual adult. My temp job that turns into a permanent secretarial job morphs into a promotion to a quasi-executive position. It includes both a sunny office and an assistant of my own in a building in Burbank with a window that looks out onto *M*A*S*H* Mountain, where they filmed the opening credits for the television show. I'm a part of the Hollywood industry now, the sector that churns out TV shows for kids.

Banner Entertainment produces shows that run along the silly yet inexplicably hugely profitable end of the kids' entertainment spectrum. I am its Director of Communications, a vague but interesting position created for me by a senior executive who likes and respects me. I sit in on departmental meetings and help create five-year business plans and toy lines and television story arcs. I go to New York for the Licensing Show in summer and Vegas for the Consumer Electronics Show in winter. I read memos and trade magazines that arrive in my inbox and write outgoing memos in turn.

The sun sets over the hills beyond my window, casting shards of light onto the shrubby hillsides. My office stereo stays tuned to the smooth jazz station. Rick Braun, Dave Koz, Sade. Drum and bass with some piano or sax thrown in. Adult background music for work or the dinner parties which I don't host now but may someday.

Simon Lu heads the company's creative division. It's his imprint on the story arcs, toy names and packaging design. Like me, he has a law degree but also an MBA. He managed to parlay his education into a fun and high-paying career, and he seems to have faith that I can, too. He compliments my handbags and shoes and takes me to champagne bars in New York when we travel there on business.

"Enjoying a truly fine champagne is like drinking gold dust," Simon remarks as we linger over a bottle that costs the same as Seth's and my monthly rent. Buzzed and starry-eyed after that, I meander the Manhattan sidewalks back to my hotel on West 57th and stand at the window of my lush room that overlooks Central Park.

At the end of my workday, I slide into my white Mazda Miata for the long drive home. Red brake lights flash on and off in front of me as the army of commuters slogs across the 101 and then plods up the 405 toward the city. I feel myself preparing to cross a double yellow line on the other side of which there is no champagne gold dust.

Seth is always home when I get there, though I often wish he weren't. He's an optical sales rep, which involves driving around his territory, small cities and towns off feeder freeways and splayed across a portion of the sprawling Los Angeles city limits. Mostly, though, he stays home smoking weed and playing video soccer. He's figured out that he can visit one or two accounts per day and then call in to his bosses from the pay phone across the street from our apartment to make it sound like he really is driving around.

Seth is less than thrilled with my career trajectory. He wants me to make money, but what's required for me to do that keeps me away— and distracted.

When I'm home, my head is filled with what I need to accomplish next and the unfamiliar joy I'm starting to feel as I finally begin to mesh with my improved circumstances.

"The trash can is overflowing. Didn't you even notice that?"

I stand in front of the mirror each morning, blowing out my hair with a round brush. I play with the makeup I bought after getting a makeover at Bodyshop. I still need to practice with the lip liner, brow pencil and eyeshadow palette.

"You never make the bed anymore. This place looks like shit."

When I sense the emotional temperature in the apartment rising (and I'm never quite sure when that will happen or for how long) I stay in the bedroom and read or journal or think about how I haven't spoken to my father, stepmother or half-brothers for two years. I'm doing okay without them, spending my days in a pretty office learning and troubleshooting and smoothing over personnel issues, all under the expert guidance of the wonderful Simon Lu. I'll show *them…*

An unfortunately audible sigh escapes me as I place a tuna sandwich and chips on the coffee table in front of Seth on a Saturday. He leans forward on the sofa, furiously clicking the buttons on the game controller and staring at the screen.

"What? You have a problem making my lunch?" He picks up an edge of the plate and then drops it, hard, against the coffee table. My body tenses, and I hold my breath—but nothing breaks, and he mercifully stays seated on the sofa, absorbed by his video game.

What I won't show anyone is the fading purplish-yellow bruise from a couple of weeks ago. It's embarrassing, and I'm horrified.

I thought it was just another mood, that if I got out of his line of sight, he'd calm down. But he followed me into the bedroom. He wouldn't let it go—whatever it was I'd said—and pushed me down on the bed, shaking me hard. He wanted to punch me in the face; I saw his fist draw back, but then his eyes changed. There was the briefest flash of uncertainty, perhaps a split-second realization that he was about to do something that could never be undone. But he wasn't uncertain enough. His fist landed on my thigh instead, hard.

He apologized, as he always does after yelling at me, but sounded more desperate that time now that he'd finally crossed a line.

"I have problems, I know. I need you." I always settle for his remorse. I'm a textbook patsy. I'm disgusted by that and by the fact that he now sees me as someone he can assault more than just verbally .

I guess I *am* someone he can do that to. I'm not going to tell anyone. I'd rather die than have anyone know. I have nowhere to go. I'm estranged from my father, and my mother is ensconced in Santa Barbara with her third husband and a real estate career. Both my credit and my confidence are forever shot. I'm not even sure I know how to do the alone thing. My mind spins and spins, but all it can come up with is: *I can't.*

I've been at Banner Entertainment long enough to earn a week's paid vacation time. Seth books a trip to Laughlin, a small casino town on the Colorado River. We were supposed to go to Vegas, but after the fight, he cancels that and then is unable to re-book a hotel room after we make up.

I sit in the passenger seat of Seth's black Volkswagen, staring out the window at the rocky red mountains that jut out of the desert floor along Highway 40. Hell's Kitchen is what they call this area. Drew told me that when he took my brothers and me on a road trip. It's been five years since that Summer to End All Summers, after which I sent Drew away and then faded away from the home and the family I'd tried so hard to mesh with.

It's August, when the winds gather up moist ocean air and nudge it into the desert; thunderheads billow up from the Gulf of California and sail upriver. My spirits lift when the clouds begin to crowd out the blue sky as we make our way down the winding road to the hotel.

We check into a room overlooking the river and unpack in silence. Seth and I are awkward together. I don't want him to touch me anymore, not in that way, and he doesn't try. When he puts his arm around me as if I'm a genderless comrade, it feels as if something inside of me might be forever dead.

I sense the storm coming, so we head downstairs to the patio bar outside the casino. We stand under the pink awning as the squall makes its way up the river, and the seconds diminish between each lightning flash and the thunder that follows. The lush smell of desert scrub meeting rain makes my heart pound as if I've found a long-lost lover. I dash out from under the protective awning and stand on the slippery red tile of the open patio. Wind bends the rain sideways, lightning forks and flashes all around me, and thunder crashes like cymbals in a mad symphony.

I'm at one with that symphony, along with the musky redolence of the wet desert and the raging clouds that scud overhead. I give myself over to it all, allowing nature to express the madness that I can't.

THIRTY-TWO

The digital clock on my desk reads 12:18. I feel a strange sense of déjà vu and feel like I need to remember this as I hang up the phone. Also, that strangely, it's December eighteenth.

I keep typing after the call, the rhythm of my fingers soothing me as they fly over the keyboard, keeping up with my boss' flat, emotionless voice, which also comforts me. I have to finish the dictation tape, which I hope never happens because then this limbo will end, to be replaced by something worse.

"Mikey's gone." Two words from my father, tight and contained.

A pain in my brother's hip went misdiagnosed for months. And then, when they finally figured it out, the only solution was amputation and chemo, which would only buy him time. Mikey wouldn't do it. My father combed the world for healers who advised shark cartilage injections and coffee enemas, but Mikey wouldn't have that either. He carried on as he always did with junk food, action movies, video games, beer, and weed. And then he decided he was done with all that and told his father he was ready to go. And then he did go, in the middle of the night, his brother Christopher at his side. Two frightened lambs huddling together in the dark, one too young to die and the other too young to have to live to tell.

I keep typing, willing away the pain that should not be mine to feel after my feckless absence from Mikey's life.

"He doesn't want to see you." More tight containment from my father after Aunt Rosie told me that Mikey was sick. I hadn't seen or talked to him since I left the firm. The shaky ground under my feet somehow collapsed into a black hole that disappeared me for weeks that turned into months and then years.

"George would like to hire you full time as his assistant."

My stupid competence at all things organizational makes me the darling of every office I've temped in since getting canned from the one job that actually meant something to me. This place is no different, so I sit here as I've sat elsewhere, typing for George as I did for David and before him Helena, all of them marveling at my ability to get work done fast without asking a million questions. If not exactly climbing upward, I'm at least moving laterally, trying to find my footing again. Slipping and sliding while Mikey lay dying. Typing and filing and photocopying, getting things done and filling up time so I don't dwell on what can never be made neat and organized.

I get up from my desk at some point, five minutes later, an hour, I don't know, because time doesn't seem to be a thing right now. I find myself sitting in my car across the street from my father's house. I get there just as two suited men guide a stretcher down the walkway toward a waiting van. I imagine Mikey's frail body, translucent skin stretched over bone, the bulbous tumor protruding from his hip. That was what would be left of him, what I'd see if I walked over and lifted the sheet. In death, he can't stop me from seeing him, but still, it wouldn't be right. I sit motionless, averting my gaze until the van is out of sight.

"Hey, hey, sweetie!" My father hugs me as I walk into the house. He is jovial, almost giddy, which is weird because this is the first time we've seen each other in over three years—and also because his son has just died.

"Mikey's in Swami's loving arms now," he says. I basically said the same thing at the office before I left, telling my concerned coworkers that Mikey is with God, that his passing was beautiful and peaceful, all the hopeful crap that people say after the end of someone else's messy, brutal dance with terminal illness. I don't believe myself and I don't believe my father, but I linger, taking comfort from his moist cheek against mine.

I hang back after that, uncertain. I haven't been here for so long. King the Doberman holds no grudges. He lodges his snout into the crook of my arm and whines in happy recognition when I crouch to greet him.

Clumps of visitors circulate. My father is drawn away by a group of healers who had worked on Mikey as best as he'd let them by coding him with mysterious numerical sequences written on slips of paper or chanting from afar. I need to get it over with, so I break through one of the clumps to find Honey, who allows me to kiss her cheek as I mumble my sympathies but turns her face upward and away as I do. My tie to my stepmother warrants more than a garden-variety, Hallmark condolence, but no space exists right now for anything approaching real.

One of their friends, who hasn't seen me in years, turns and asks how old I am now, which sounds like an indictment of my absence from the family. Like I should be mature enough to figure all the awkward out, or at least to know how to fit myself in around all of it. But no, he's just making conversation.

"Thirty-three in two weeks. Same age as Christ at his crucifixion." A random, occasion-inappropriate thing to say. People laugh, but it probably wasn't the best response, even though people shouldn't go around asking the age of anyone who's clearly over twenty-one. A few more minutes elapse and then I find the door, awkward loose ends trailing behind me like toilet paper on a shoe.

Four days later, I stand at a podium in front of the altar at Good Shepherd Catholic Church. My father had followed me out of the house the day Mikey died, asking me to speak at the funeral.

"Mikey loved you. He would want you up there."

I don't buy it. If Mikey was so pissed off in life at my having left, he certainly wouldn't want me as a spokesperson in death. Mikey wasn't wishy-washy. But I don't say that. In this thing, at least, I can do what's asked of me.

Christ hangs on a cross behind me. In front of me, Honey sits in the front pew surrounded by her four sisters, an army clad in fur and sunglasses. Her armor against the freak of nature that was the death of her child, her enduring personal crucifixion. In the second pew sits my father, surrounded by the healers and shamans who have become his friends but who couldn't fix Mikey. He stares at the back of his wife's head, the chasm between them vast and unforgiving. I know in that moment that they won't make it.

I have no notes. I don't know what to say about this boy that my father's guru, Shanti Ram, once predicted would grow up to be a famed scientist. Suicidal in a bathtub, lover of Metallica and weed and tragic waifs who broke his heart. A teller of inconvenient truths who once jarringly (and rightly) told me to stop trying so hard all the time. But who also admitted me into his aloneness without expecting me to do anything about it.

I find my voice, but the words I'm too ready to say about God's will drop down from my head and into my mouth like fake coins, tinny and trite. Instead, I talk about heroism—Mikey's uncomplaining acceptance of everything that fate visited upon him in his short, difficult life, my father's persistence in scouring the world for help, Honey's strength. But it occurs to me as I speak these things that no one is really a hero in this kind of death. Deer suddenly seeing headlights are caught in a vise of instinctive response. They freeze, or run, or refuse to believe a car is even coming at them. The drive is to remain upright for as long as possible, whether you're the one dying or the one watching. There is no army of willing, trained warriors in any of this who know what the hell they're getting into.

The grief, the hot, roiling pain that ought to well up from my heart and pour out of me remains inaccessible.

With nowhere to go, it takes over my body instead. At the end of Mikey's service, I slip out of the church, opting out of the reception at the house. Back at my apartment, I slide my hot limbs and throbbing head into bed and enter a fevered dreamscape where I wander endless highways littered with roadkill.

THIRTY-THREE

My feet feel heavy beneath me, dragging across a carpet that's a combination of gray and beige, or maybe just a combination of dirty and dirtier. My father lies curled on a small sofa, his back to me.

I move between my father in the small waiting area and Grandma May's hospital bed inside the Intensive Care Unit. He has fallen into a twilight zone that he can't seem to emerge from, while my grandmother has fallen into a coma that she will never emerge from.

Family members arrange themselves in a loose and fluid deathbed tableau. After my father's sister, Aunt Rosie, arrives from Michigan, it's decided to release Grandma May from the machines and medicines that can no longer do anything for her.

"Where's your dad?" they all ask. One by one they go and peer at him too, gingerly, as if he's an exotic zoo animal, returning only after they satisfy themselves that he isn't going to be getting up. The practical business of Grandma May's dying will have to be managed without him. He's been through a lot.

I hope I'm better at this now than I was nine years ago at the end of Daddy Landon. I've taken the day off from my television development job, and if necessary, I'll take off tomorrow as well. I allow Aunt Rosie to wipe away the fluids from my grandmother's nose and mouth, but I am there, and I will stay there for however long it takes for her body, realizing that its mechanical helpers have departed, to see itself out.

Grandma May hasn't said a word to me, or anyone, for two years. Her sharp, acerbic mind is gone, yet a large part of it lives, rattling around in my own brain. The part that wants to go and shake my father into presence alongside his family, even though I know I can't because it hasn't even been a year since Mikey died. But in me also is the heart that loves him still above all others, just like Grandma May loved him above all others because he was her firstborn son. And she loved me because I came from him. Neither of us ever had to do anything to please her. Sharing her blood was enough

My grandmother has both gifted and burdened me with my predominant genetic load. My physicality has gelled into hers—the fine brown hair that persists in doing nothing absent professional assistance, the lanky, loose-limbed body that is flexible but prone to flab. All of that is one hundred percent the woman who came into this life as Annie Maritch and through marriage became Annie May, joining herself to a man who arrived here as George Maloof but who renamed himself after the department store that to him embodied all that was the American Dream.

We're also alike in the lack of any real inclination toward motherhood, despite the wobbling into a troubled marriage that in her case produced three children, two of which she adored once they arrived because they were boys. My future still holds some wiggle room, but I sense myself heading in the same general direction no matter how much I tell myself I won't. I definitely share her preference for pets, particularly cats, over people and for friendly books over friendly humans, and her penchant for caustic storytelling.

I remember being a kid and wandering Grandma May's garden of roses, the American Beauties and Forty-Niners. Touching the succulents in terra-cotta pots lining the cracked porch, their turgid leaves patient and yielding under my small, curious fingers. The clothesline in the backyard, wooden pegs holding gauzy old-fashioned slips that danced like restless ghosts. Loquats and figs, magnets for the buzzing and chirping life that descended on languorous summer days. Sherlock the Siamese cat, brown tail swishing madly as he crouched before a sunning lizard. Watching him as Grandma May read me *Butterball* over and over again, as focused on the cadences as Sherlock was on his prey.

As much as she loved us all, Grandma May would never have had children had my old-country Lebanese grandfather not essentially raped her into it. No one has told me this exactly, but I sense it in the way that kindred souls tied by blood are able to crack each other's vague codes, burrowing like ticks into each other's hiddenness.

"Oh, I wasn't really interested. But he made me. Didn't you, George?"

"After your father came along, I was finished with all that and moved into the other room. But he wouldn't take no for an answer and then came Rosie and Rafael. Isn't that right, George?"

If Grandma May hadn't had the accidental misfortune of walking into my grandfather's speakeasy to help him with his accounting, maybe she would have been able to hole up behind closed doors with books and magazines and cats and music instead. Or maybe teach school or become a comic actress or writer, and I wouldn't be standing here trying to create a last-ditch happier story for her.

When his mother is gone in a minute or in an hour, my father will finally awaken and say that he was communing with her in the spirit world, helping usher her into the beyond. Despite my own baseless but persistent faith in a vibrant post-death universe, I'm not satisfied. I want to penetrate his real story the way I could Grandma May's. I want to put my arms around him and cry together over her in her final moments and over Michael's final moments that are now forever lost to me. To be two flesh-and-blood people mourning other flesh-and-blood people in the world of the living and the feeling.

I've already been a willing co-conspirator with cowardice, allowing it to beckon me away from my loved ones and their messiness, naming itself a thousand other things. Now it's time at least to call myself strong and to show it, to do the hard, heartbreaking things that are a part of the business of living and dying. I didn't do it for Daddy Landon or for Michael.

I sit at the edge of Grandma May's bed, holding her hand, resolutely refusing to look away from the face of a dying woman who loved me solely for me.

One last, gentle breath, and she's gone.

THIRTY-FOUR

I've been taking secret drives to the beach through Rustic Canyon, past the houses I lived in as a kid, and along the roads that slope from Sunset down to the ocean. It's September. Unemployed for three months, I've started to realize a certain troubling pleasure in being adrift. It's a relief to avoid the overly traveled ruts made by the cars I see every morning on Santa Monica Boulevard as I sit on the balcony drinking coffee in my ratty old sweatpants. People all just sitting in traffic, waiting in line to get to jobs they don't want to do, and then just reversing direction eight or ten or twelve hours later.

My last job is a year spent in a beautiful circular Beverly Hills office with high ceilings. The position comes with an important-seeming title, *Director of Development.* The company consists of one guy and his assistant. My job is to work on concepts for kids' television shows. It's my second job in that business, so I know that the ideal programming is essentially a half-hour toy commercial. That way, the programmers can make a ton of money off deals with companies that make action figures and play sets.

I spend a lot of time in that job driving back and forth between Beverly Hills and a big toy company many freeways away, where somber Japanese men in dark suits listen to my presentations, disconcerting me with their refusal to make eye contact—which I later find out is a cultural thing. And there's also something off-putting about the manipulation of children and their imaginations so that humorless and unimaginative men can profit off the mass production of identical pieces of plastic crap.

The only enjoyable thing about my time there is coming up with an idea for a girl's show about teen angels with superpowers, and then putting together a promotional video. To develop the required toy line, I pass a few days sitting with two ladies who make dolls and doll clothes, playing with fabric and glitter and sequins. We come up with four dolls with diaphanous gowns that turn into bad-ass crime fighting power suits. The toy presentation is a hit with the toy company. The dark-suited guys smile and nod at the thought of competing with Mattel's Barbie.

Then some higher-ups in Japan decide that a girls' show and toy line can't possibly compete with Barbie the way they need it to. So that's that, and I return to chasing dragons and robots and other creatures and contraptions that boys like. Which sort of takes the wind out of my sails. Not long after, it's quietly decided that there's nothing further I can do for the one guy and his toy-manufacturing contacts. I sign a release, get three months' severance and slink home to my apartment and my sweatpants.

When I do land the odd interview every now and then through old contacts, I find myself sitting in front of various mid-level executives who all look the same, hearing myself parrot all the vague cliches for success I've heard everyone say. *Zig when everyone else is zagging. Think outside the box.* The thing is, I don't believe a word I'm saying, and I can tell that my potential colleagues don't believe me either. They shake my hand, thank me for coming and say they'll be in touch—when we all know that they won't. And then once again I slink home to my apartment and into the sweatpants.

Seth wishes I were more like the dutiful commuters in their econoboxes and the interviewers behind their desks. Like him. He just opened his own optical business and works hard at it. Of course, he wants me to be out there making money, pulling my weight, doing something so that one day the two of us can stop renting and start owning. And I really, really *want* to want that too, but I don't. I'd rather he just does it all for the both of us so that I can just, just—I don't know. The problem is, there's no period to that thought, no *plan* that I can hold up like a trophy as evidence of a method to my madness.

Today I find myself at Temescal Beach, again. I lurk there most frequently because one day a pod of dolphins suddenly appears, and they all begin leaping into the air for no apparent purpose other than to amuse themselves. Still, I believe they're putting on a special show for me, sympathetic fellow creatures, giving me the message that it's okay to be here instead of chasing dragons alongside everyone else. I imagine myself in that moment to be a dolphin-in-exile, beached and disoriented among completely baffling fellow mammals.

I sit on a towel, eating a protein bar and gazing at the water, hoping for another dolphin show or at least for the emergence of a friendly fin. At the vast expanse of ocean between here and Hawaii, and Tahiti beyond that, and Fiji beyond that. I imagine the cold, uninviting water off this coast little by little mellowing into something deliciously placid and warm and crystalline far beyond here. A nearby lifeguard station stands lonely and boarded up on its peeling wooden stilts, as they've all been since Labor Day. The sand is deserted but for a few foreign tourists. The beach has the feel of a fairground after the carnival has left town and everyone's gone back to their lives.

I pick up the copy of *Newsweek* I brought. I subscribe to it because I think it's important to keep up with what's going on in the world despite the isolation that's come with unemployment. I read it cover to cover, even the boring *Science & Technology* section. I don't want to be unprepared at, say, a dinner party, even though I've rarely been to a dinner party. At least not the kind of dinner party my mother and stepfather used to put on where people discussed current events and drank dusted-off bottles of rare vintage wines. On the few occasions when Seth and I entertain in our apartment or go to someone else's, the food is ordered in or it's potluck. And no one discusses current events.

This week's *Science & Technology* section features a big spread on what they call the New Rich, the Internet millionaires. I look at a photo of a guy in his late twenties who looks like he just rolled out of bed. Torn Levis, scuffed Converse sneakers, curly, unkempt hair. He splays across a lounge chair. Behind him, an infinity pool appears to extend off a cliff against a setting sun that bronzes the facades of office buildings in a valley below. One of them is his, and that building, the infinity pool and the glistening dark-haired wife in the adjoining chair are the product of a thought or series of thoughts that came along at the right time and in the right order so that he went from being a scruffy college dropout to a scruffy millionaire. The mechanics of his idea, of getting investors and figuring out a business plan, don't interest me. But, I spend a long time staring at the photo.

As the afternoon starts to die, I trudge away from the beach and up the street where I parked to avoid the pay lot. Once back on Sunset, I hang a right on Brooktree instead of continuing east toward the apartment. Past the house where I lived during sixth grade and then past the house where I lived during fifth grade. I preferred the latter because of the redwood trees in the backyard that bordered the creek and because the house came with Tiddlywinks, the resident tortoise who Greg and I renamed Sam.

Over the bridge crossing the creek, and then right, past Auntie Luisa's old house, and then back down toward the beach. I see the cement stairway where actors and models and the physically fit and those aspiring to be any or all of those things congregate for cardio, tramping up and down or just wishing to be seen tramping up and down. When I lived in the canyon, the stairs were there, but the only people who used them were those who actually wanted to go someplace. They had never been an actual destination.

I don't know why I'm led to go home this way, or why, instead of continuing on toward home, I pull into the parking lot of Canyon Elementary, my old school. I find myself getting out of the car and walking into the office where Mrs. Rothman used to sit.

I assume the stout Mrs. Rothman is retired or dead. In her place is a small woman with a smooth black bun and darkly lined lips.

"Who are you coming to get?" the woman asks as she picks up the phone. I guess they have phones in classrooms now so that they no longer have to send Mrs. Rothmans around to go get kids.

"Oh, um, no." She thinks I'm a parent, which feels weird, but shouldn't, because I'm actually three years older than my mother was when I started the third grade here.

I hear myself say that I don't belong to any kid, but I'm wondering if they could use any volunteers at the school. The woman disappears for a moment and then another one emerges from an adjoining office. She's the principal, who tells me that if I want to work with kids as opposed to helping out in the office or the library, I need to apply for an instructional aide position. And that it pays $9.75 per hour, so I'd be making a little money.

I take the paperwork she hands me. Before leaving, I stop for a moment at the chain-link fence that surrounds the playground. I stare at the library building, the one that used to be a stand-alone schoolhouse and was the entirety of this place a hundred years ago. The tetherball courts, handball walls, vanilla-yellow lunch tables outside the cafeteria where I sat with Yuko and Alicia, eating grilled cheese sandwiches and brownies from the cafeteria on Fridays or rectangular tiles of pepperoni pizza on Wednesdays.

I linger for a while, feeling the restless breath of the ocean calling me from just around the bend, just as it did back then.

THIRTY-FIVE

Little Jackie doesn't look well. Her gray eyes are half-shut beneath her long brown bangs and her voice is slurry, drunken almost, as she tells me she feels weird.

"Bottom drawer, sweetie. Capri Sun and a cookie, okay?"

She'll lose consciousness if her blood sugar dips too low, which I accidentally learned from one of the other fourth graders who told me that Jackie is diabetic. With the school cafeteria ladies unmoved by this dilemma and Jackie's mom spotty about sending her girl to school with food, I labeled the bottom drawer of my desk *Jackie Snacks.* Her classmates know it's hers, and to their credit, they don't raid it.

Selena sits at her desk, listless. The bullying episodes have lessened but not stopped. I catch the eye of Renee, who seems hard-wired for caretaking, and then look over at Selena. Renee takes the hint, along with her colored pens, and goes to sit next to the forlorn Selena.

I need to have another word with the perpetrators. Unbeknownst to all but me, courtesy of their mothers, José wets his bed and Paul has to be given growth hormone shots due to his small size. I would never openly reveal this, but it wouldn't hurt for the boys to know that I know. We all prefer to hold certain things close to our chests, private things that might open us up to judgment or ridicule.

I circulate the room, among the towheads, black curls, cornrows, braids, and buzz cuts, bent over and absorbed by their geography projects. Boys and girls alike are obsessed with wrestling, or rather WWF, which from what I've seen features less wrestling than random body slamming and endless trash-shrieking. Because I couldn't get them off the subject long enough to generate interest in the actual land masses

Earth has to offer, I've allowed them to create their own world maps with continents and kingdoms named after The Rock and Undertaker and Stone Cold. The only criteria are that the maps show actual knowledge of compass direction and mapping terms.

This classroom is my first long-term substitute teaching job. I volunteered as a teacher's aide at my elementary school last year, and from that felt moved to take it a step further. I can't teach full-time unless I invest time and money in getting a full state credential. But for the moment, this works. The school district calls me in the morning, and then I have somewhere to go. Seth is happy I'm making money again, so things are calmer at home.

I walk into this room as the latest in a long line of day-to-day subs after the regular teacher departs on an extended medical leave that seems to be more of a mental health thing. I find little more than a dying potted plant on the teacher's desk, the whole environment wilted before a room of restive fourth and fifth graders who, because of the neighborhoods they live in, are classified as "at risk."

Eyeing each other with suspicion, the kids and I form an initially uneasy truce based on a mutual lack of expectation. I'm here to make money doing something not horrible, and they're here as a matter of law. If they sit there without making trouble, I don't care what they do as long as they look like they're doing something productive whenever an administrator walks in.

The truce gradually becomes a refuge as we all stick to the bargain and get comfortable. I replace the dying plant with a hardy succulent and clean out the cupboards. I go to the dollar store and buy everyone their own pencil box, pens and pencils.

And then at some point it's tacitly decided that they're a little willing to learn and that I'm more than a little willing to teach.

I hate math and have little idea either how to do it or how to teach it, so I just make sure they have their times tables memorized, assuming that eventually they'll have a teacher who will be more into it. I do try to bestow on them my love of reading and writing and history, which meets with only marginal success, so I wind up letting them learn about whatever interests them. Which leads to maps of imaginary wrestling kingdoms, as well as essays and book reports about wrestling.

I do manage to teach them how to ask questions, how to find information, how to know what to believe and what to doubt. Are the stories in the magazines about The Rock and The Undertaker and Stone Cold true or false, and if the stories are false, why would the magazines make them up?

And then I teach them some things I wish someone had told me. About money—what it does and doesn't do. About not letting parents, or the world, drain the joy from them. About remembering this time in ten or twenty years and not forgetting what they love now.

I make them play at behaving, telling them they have to walk in straight lines from the playground to the classroom, and from the classroom to auditorium assemblies. They can't say the f-word around littler kids or grownups. They have to try their best on the standardized tests. Inside the class they can swear, sit on the floor, eat snacks, and know that the stupid tests mean nothing but money for the school, which the school needs to keep art and music. The world outside is just a game they have to play, with a set of very specific and oftentimes weird rules. When they figure out how to play that game, then they can make up their own. I reinforce this with Friday class parties once they show me they can play by the weird set of rules for the rest of the week.

As my time in the classroom nears its end, I have my charges write their autobiographies, based on timelines of their young lives to date, with each chapter focusing on an event on the timeline. I order special bound books for them to copy their final drafts into, with blank covers for them to illustrate.

Erika writes about the time she shoplifted lip gloss from Rite Aid— and how the look on her mother's face when she found out made her feel worse than the stealing did.

Brady's third chapter is about his parents' worst fight ever before his father left for good, after a strange pregnant lady came to the door demanding to see him.

Jaleel's first chapter is about the night he found out that his sister was really his mom.

My mother, who had been a teacher until Greg was born, visits me in the classroom one day.

"You have a very nice daughter." José shakes her hand formally.

I put Mom, a former teacher herself, to work with one of the reading groups, the more advanced kids who are reading *The Phantom Tollbooth*. She enjoys this. It was one of the books Greg and I loved as kids. We catch each other's eye while I work with another group, and I feel a very rare fullness.

Mom leaves at lunch time.

"This is *you*," she says, gesturing at the kids and the classroom before embracing me in a long, tight hug. She sways with me slowly, the two of us awkward together, like a middle school couple at a dance, until I break away.

I don't know whether this experience is just a pause between one thing and another, or whether it rises to the level of a calling. But it's something, and I'll remember it.

The regular classroom teacher eventually returns, still frayed but in need of her full paycheck, and the kids grudgingly go back to playing by the rules of state-sanctioned learning. Before that, though, I make each of them pinky-promise me they'll re-read their own stories once a year on their birthday, just to remind themselves of who they are.

THIRTY-SIX

" I feel like we're all on a conveyor belt. It just keeps going, and everyone just drops off at the end—whenever that end is. Some people try to hold on to the sides to keep from falling off, but eventually, we all go." I ponder Mom's words as they echo through the tiled chamber of the spa mud room where we sit in companionable enjoyment of goop and humidity. She closes her eyes and leans her head against the wall, grateful for a few moments stolen from the care of her mother.

Grama Lopez isn't doing well. Neither of us mentions the possibility that she won't be around for my wedding next year.

I'm about to start a new job in a law firm as I contemplate applying for a teacher credentialing program. Document production is a fancy term for word processing, which is a fancy term for typing. But the pay is decent. I made it clear to the firm that because I have no desire for the stress of actually practicing law, I won't be lobbying them for an attorney position. It will be steady money, unlike the spotty substitute teaching I've been doing. That was the deal Seth made with me—marriage in exchange for my getting a full-time job.

This is how the conveyor belt moves. We think it's creaking along when, in reality, it's a speeding bullet train. Yesterday I feasted on purple figs, entranced by the sweet, sticky juice that ran between my fingers as I rocked Grama and Papa's porch swing. Today Papa is gone, and Grama dangles at the edge of the drop-off.

I used to think the conveyor belt was like the one in that *I Love Lucy* episode in the candy factory. As a child, I thought life would be one sugar-coated thrill after another. Too much to do, but still I *had* to do it all, have it all, experience it all, shove it all in, even if it made me sick. And somehow the thing would keep moving forever.

Now it isn't the experiences I think about. I see the conveyor belt as overloaded with other things. Compromises. Negotiations. Navigations around all the things I've done that I wish I hadn't and through the empty spaces where I didn't do what I wish I had.

I'm starting a job that isn't my heart's desire so that I can marry a man who isn't either.

I don't know, Mom. It feels more like a maze. You spend all your time trying to figure out where you're going, like a lab rat trying to get its reward, but you keep running into dead ends. If you're lucky enough to figure it all out, your big reward at the end is falling into the abyss anyway.

But I don't say that. Instead, I just twirl the ends of my hair in silence, a habit I've had as long as I've had hair. Feeling the fine strands gliding between my fingertips provides a helpful counterpoint to contemplating thorny subjects.

After our spa day, Mom and I part ways, she to Santa Barbara and her husband John, I to my apartment and Seth. In a few days, I start my new job, and if the maze leads me to stick with my end of the bargain, I'll marry Seth three hundred and thirteen days from today.

"We're heading for troubled times."

Yuko, my old friend, said that a few days earlier on a visit from her new home in South Africa. We're walking arm in arm around the perimeter of our elementary school, Yuko's other hand resting on her newly pregnant belly. A misty fog has rolled in, covering us with a sheen of fine droplets.

The tall chain-link fence barricades us from the nooks and corners where our girlhoods had intersected and then become entwined. From the stairwell under the library steps, where we hid from the taunting, sing-song voice of Yvette Cate in fifth grade. And from the crunching of the dead, curling maple leaves outside Room Twelve in sixth grade, which had concealed our whispered confessions of my love for Kenny Fredericks and Yuko's for Billy Martin.

The first time I heard Yuko foretell was in fourth grade when she kept talking about the new school principal, who would be much nicer than the one we had. No one listened, but then the unsmiling Miss Fitz dropped dead in her office on a Friday afternoon and was replaced Monday morning by the young, funny Mr. Zane. Sporting a fuzzy beard and earth shoes, he promptly removed the frightening life-size bust of George Washington from the principal's desk and replaced it with a large jar of Tootsie Pops.

Then, in high school, long after we had both moved away, I drove down to visit Yuko in Palos Verdes for a weekend right after getting my driver's license. We lay on her bed getting high and listening to Pink Floyd. I was worried about getting into college because of bad grades in algebra and geometry and would probably blow the math part of the SAT. But Yuko had said not to worry. She saw I would be going to school near Boston.

What now, I wonder, but Yuko refuses to say. Adventurous Yuko, flying bush planes in Africa, married to a kind, bearded man that reminds me of Mr. Zane, and on the precipice of motherhood. A Japanese American cross between Amelia Earhart and Yoda. Heartbreak might darken her doorstep, but she'll always figure out how to call it something better.

I had thought I was over the hump, having learned to manage both Seth's and my wayward natures, to keep a balance, to give in without giving up, to keep moving forward. That it gets easier. But maybe it doesn't, and that's just what life is supposed to be—staying tethered to difficult people and burdensome responsibilities. Not drifting away, ever in search of, leaving debt and heartbreak in one's wake.

Basically, just holding on.

THIRTY-SEVEN

Tall buildings comfort me, as they have since the days of my father's apartment high above Sunset Boulevard. And his high-up law office I visited as a child, looking down at cars and endlessly changing traffic lights and people that all looked like tiny little dolls. I realize that I'm just like that when I'm at ground level—a little scurrying being like all the other scurrying little beings. Still, when I'm above it, I feel rarefied, really and truly at a higher, purer altitude.

The craziness, I once thought, was all down there. But now I know that it isn't. It can come from above, in planes commandeered by screeching zealots and filled with helpless human cargo.

I'm woozy with sleep when the apartment door opens and Seth walks in. He had gone to the DMV to renew his driver's license, but I thought he was going directly to work after that.

"The DMV was empty. No one there. The TV was on. Someone took planes and knocked over the World Trade Center."

I don't understand him for a minute; English is his third language, so something may be getting lost in translation. But then he turns on the television and I see it's true, witnessing for the first time what will become the endless visual news loop of one building and then the other disintegrating into the ground.

I work the swing shift in the word processing department of a law firm in Century City, high up in one of another set of twin towers, from 4:30 pm to 12:30 am. They close the buildings on the day of the attacks, but everyone is expected to report back for work the following day.

I return to work nervous and unsettled and do what I always do— stop at the lobby Starbucks for a venti black coffee with three packets of Splenda and then ride the elevator up to the thirty-second floor. Except now I try not to think about the people who died the day before while taking that same ride three thousand miles away, assuming they would be starting just another workday.

But I do think about it. My fellow word processors and I sit, quiet and listless, throughout a shift that seems endless. Few attorneys come in to hand us work. Those who do are brisk and businesslike, acting as if it's just another night with briefs to prepare for filing and deposition transcripts to summarize—as if the world hasn't just gone off the rails. I'm reminded once again that while I may have the intellect for the practice of law, I don't have the required single-minded nature that would require me to block out the persistent, crippling screech of reality.

The editing and transcribing work that does come in I perform in an absent-minded fashion, which I can do because it doesn't require much brain power. My mind instead is in those towers, not as I've seen them on CNN, vomiting flames and smoke and people from their innards, but as I imagine them in the minutes before Armageddon hit.

Who, I wonder, occupies the thirty-second floors in those towers? I picture a woman, thirty-seven years old like me, sitting down at her desk in Tower Two with a large coffee, logging in to her computer and glancing at the framed wedding photo she recently placed next to it. Like me, she's a newlywed.

Is this her dream job, being an administrative assistant, a word processor, an investment banker or publicist or sales rep or whatever she is, or has she just settled for the first job she could get in order to appease an impatient, ambitious husband? Is the smiling groom in the photo The One, the love of her life, or was it just a matter of pledging herself to a broken man she was used to rather than taking a chance on a potentially worse one—or worse yet, being alone? Does she have children, and if not, does she plan to? Has she just gotten her navel pierced, absent-mindedly keeping the fresh wound clear of her waistband as she checks her email?

I wonder what happens when she hears the explosion in Tower One and rushes to the window to see the devastation before her.

Does she heed her intuition, the faint but insistent voice that tells her to get out *now*, or does she choose instead to listen to the disembodied voices on the building-wide public announcement speakers assuring her that her tower is safe and secure? I wonder whether the corporate citizen, the model employee, wins out over the wife who knows in her heart that the Devil isn't quite done yet. Or perhaps she sticks around because she sees in Satan's fiery hand the possibility of a golden parachute, an opportunity for an epic do-over without the need to tie up messy loose ends. A chance to disappear herself in the chaos, to walk away and let everyone assume her to be vaporized, leaving behind only the ghost of a woman who chose wrong.

I imagine myself in the place of this imaginary woman and wonder whether anything would crystallize for me in the seconds following the first explosion. And if not, whether it would in those following the one that happened seventeen minutes later and forty-eight floors above me as I sat, undecided, taking nervous sips of my coffee.

Would I think of my wedding four months ago, standing there in my long-sleeved lace dress and mantilla veil at my mother's bedroom window, looking at the guests in their white chairs on the lawn who awaited my grand entrance? Would I remember that I wondered at that moment how it had all gotten that far, how it was that I was about to make a huge mistake—yet felt utterly powerless to avert it?

I made that long walk anyway toward the jacaranda tree under which Seth stood, toward the cementing of a troubled nine-year relationship.

I did it even though we'd been intimate only a couple of times in the last six years.

I did it even though he hit me, mostly with words but sometimes with his hands or objects.

I did it because he controls the money. I can't have my own bank account, or anything the creditors can grab.

I did it because I thought I painted myself into a corner.

I did it because I didn't know what else to do.

THIRTY-EIGHT

I stand on the newly tiled patio of our condo looking at the potted gardenia plant I bought at Home Depot. It doesn't look happy; its leaves are turning yellow, and there are no flower buds. I wonder if it's getting enough water or sun or too much of either. I know nothing about gardening and never managed to keep anything green alive. But I love gardenias, Grama Lopez' favorite. Having something of her in my new home feels right and hopeful. And it's something to replace the snow globe.

Grama Lopez held on long enough to see me married. Three months after that, when her failing heart made living too uncomfortable, she decided to go to bed permanently. She tended to her death in the quiet and gentle way in which she tended to her life, slipping away in self-contained, calm silence when no one was looking.

Above the fireplace sits my last photo with her, a silver-framed snapshot of me kissing her as she sits in her wheelchair, a gardenia corsage pinned to the turquoise chiffon dress she wears because it's my favorite color. Mom probably chose the dress because by then the long goodbye was well underway and Grama Lopez was no longer able to form preferences or desires or even converse much. Her gaze shifted continually from her hands to some distant point, as if trying to reconcile the fact of her own existence with that of other things apparently real to her but invisible to everyone else.

Also, on our patio, between the bedroom and the living room, is a little fountain made of concrete molded into rock formations. In the happy flush of first-time homeownership, Seth and I decide to create a grotto. The patio overlooks a long carport; the soothing white noise of a gurgling fountain will help blunt the sound of cars pulling in and out.

Other things are not so easy to blunt:

The sound of the snow globe breaking on the bathroom floor of our apartment a week after escrow closed on the new place when we'd already begun packing for the move.

The sight of liquid, flecked with glittering snowflakes, disappearing behind the toilet. A tiny blue dragon lying on the floor, rudely released from his protective dome, black crystal eyes staring at nothing.

Puff the Magic Dragon. Grama Lopez taught me that song, and when I was old enough to be careful, she gave me the snow globe for my birthday.

"What the fuck is the matter with you?"

Seth's voice, yelling the words he always yells when he comes at me or my stuff. No preamble. Just that opening riff that tells me I'm in deep trouble.

This time, it's because I want the bedroom closet in the new condo re-done by one of those companies that specializes in putting in shelves and drawers to maximize space. Seth is against spending the money. I hold my ground, getting annoyed when he doesn't see things my way.

It's always my annoyance that triggers him. I can't get mad at him and show it.

I learn, after he hits me the first time, that I need to leave, to walk out the door when I start to sense coming anger. Because once he gets to that place, he checks out and someone else checks in—someone that doesn't know how to stop until after fist has met flesh. I have to be ready.

This time, I get cornered in the bathroom. I can't get away before his eyes glaze over in that first rush of rage that keeps him from seeing me as separate from it. Trying to get to me in the tiny apartment bathroom, he flings aside a white wicker shelf stand that holds the snow globe.

The shattering glass snaps him back into the reality of what he's doing, allowing me to rush past him and out the door. I don't talk to him the rest of that day, or most of the next, when we drive in silence to the condo to meet Mom and her husband John, who haven't yet seen the new place.

The stress of the upcoming move and my tiredness make it hard to keep the mask in place, the bland cheer I'm generally able to hide behind after these episodes. Something in my face must be at odds with how I think I'm presenting, because Mom almost immediately walks me around the corner, away from the unit.

"What is it?"

The strangeness of this suburban location I've only been to a handful of times disorients me into an uncharacteristic transparency, accompanied by uncharacteristic tears. I'm not quite sure of my footing on this manicured green belt around the corner from a home whose title is solely in Seth's name. So, under the protective canopy of a sycamore tree in full summer leaf I unburden myself to my mother, feeling a cascade of relief bittered by shame. Now she knows. And she'll tell John, and then he'll know. And they'll both look at me and see a disappointment. Someone not smart enough, not confident enough, not financially or emotionally viable enough to sidestep a life with a guy like Seth in favor of a life where I don't have to disappear myself.

Mom is kind after this. She mercifully doesn't say much except that she wants me to be happy.

After we show them the condo, we drive separately to a nearby restaurant for lunch. I know when we arrive that Mom has told John on the way because when I get out of the car, he gives me a long, silent hug. I manage to keep from crying again, but all through lunch I feel his pity and the awkwardness that comes from not being able to talk about what everyone is thinking about. I see the sadness hidden behind Mom's subdued conversation and hear Seth's strained, overly polite responses that make him sound like a little boy trying to redeem himself after a pointedly bad transgression. It all feels as if someone has died. Not at all like a celebration of a new beginning—which this is supposed to be.

It's almost more than I can bear. Again, I think about our wedding last year, when I found myself staring out Mom's bedroom window at all the guests, knowing I was doing the opposite of the right thing yet feeling compelled anyway to hurl myself with frightening precision toward the wrong thing.

And now the condo. Another mistake, another tie that binds me to him. My greatest skill seems to be in making the best out of my own bad judgment, which occurs to me isn't a skill at all but simply a delaying tactic that somehow guarantees the making of more mistakes later.

And then I excuse myself and go cry again in the bathroom. I don't know why. It's not like this hasn't happened before and I haven't just shaken it off after a couple of days of lying low. But this time, I can't shake it. The thought of the snow globe on the floor stabs at me more than if he'd actually hit me again. I was going to bring it with me to my new home, to live alongside my last photo with Grama Lopez. This time, Seth had hurt something deeper than just me.

He fractured my hope. I'm trying to repair it with a grotto and new tile and the closet remodel Seth ended up agreeing to out of guilt and the teacher credentialing program I'm starting shortly. But it all feels as futile as trying to glue the snow globe back together and filling it with water and glitter, only to watch it all leak out again.

THIRTY-NINE

"Hi, sweetie. That was fantastic. I mean, really. They've never seen the likes of you around here before, I can tell you that."

My father greets me at the doors of an elementary school in Northridge, where I've just given the valedictory speech at the graduation of this year's crop of teaching credential candidates. He's the only family member available to witness my ceremonial propulsion into Career Number Three.

"An anomaly?" I start the banter as we hug. I'm a nervous kid again in my immense pleasure that he came.

"That's about right." I laugh, and he laughs—delighting together in wordplay, the hidden but effortless genetic magnet that we know will always connect us.

He takes me to lunch. Leaving my car in the school lot, we ride together in his silver Corvette. He's always favored two-seaters. "Less baggage," he says. I feel myself low to the ground, skimming the pavement of Ventura Boulevard on a carbon nano-composite magic carpet. The undercarriage is so fragile that he can't visit me at the condo because the lip of our driveway is too high and scrapes the bottom of the car.

I'm sitting low but riding high. The last time I was in the car I had slunk down, wanting to sink through to its bottom and flatten out on the pavement as my head turned to the passenger window in embarrassment. I had called my father to rescue me after Seth's and my dirty laundry was once again flung out in public.

That time, it was over a broken-down car in which Seth left me stranded just before we bought the condo. Another day, another drama, another effort to avoid involving anyone else in what's squarely my own problem. I called my father because he seems more available since he and Honey have split up, and he moved down the hill closer to where I live.

He doesn't push me to do one thing or another. He did, after all, stay with Honey long after their love story petered out and has been separated from her for six years with no talk of divorce—so he certainly is one to understand dithering. He took me out for coffee, and we took turns bashing Seth, the creative and gratifying verbal dismemberment making me feel utterly smart and superior—for a minute. Then he took me back to the apartment where Seth was waiting to begin another of our countless make-up dances.

I remember my nine-year-old self flying through the canyons with my dashing father in his Aston Martin. The long-ago magic carpet ride that transported me into a world where I was cooler and smarter and more carefree than I actually was.

The Aston Martin went away after Christopher was born, leaving behind my secret wish to be something better. I kept waiting for the return of possibility, just as I waited for my father to visit on the days he didn't quite get around to me.

It seems today that possibility may have returned. I'm satisfied just to be glad, united with my father in the simple joy of my achievement. He never knows quite what to do when I'm not doing well but is an easy companion when I am. My ever-present other concerns—Seth, debt, the niggling certainty that I'm not going to be able to stick to this path either—all of that recedes as the Corvette picks up speed.

I close my eyes and lean back, hoping this zooming metal carpet ride is delivering me to another, more sustainable cusp.

FORTY

It's New Year's Day, I'm in Paris, and tomorrow I turn forty. *Forty.*

I'm relieved to arrive here after the long Air France flight, to feel the plane make its wobbly but unmistakable contact with firm, unshaking ground. There has been the uncovering of a terrorist plan, something involving the same airline that was to have taken place a day or two prior to our flight. Getting through security was an epic hassle.

It doesn't help that Seth is Iranian and looks decidedly Middle Eastern. He's been an American citizen for almost ten years, yet they hardly look at his passport before the closer inspection begins. The peering into his eyes, and mine, for more than the few beats devoted to other passengers in line. Looks exchanged between various personnel as they place our checked luggage into a big pile and again as we place our carry-on bags on the conveyor belt. A compact man in plain clothes, whom we first glimpse standing next to the uniformed operators of the x-ray machines, re-appears at the gate area and sits by us, saying nothing until we board the plane. A different man who also says nothing sits next to us on the flight, and it all feels very uncomfortable.

We arrive a little after 10:00 pm and by 11:45 pm, I'm sitting in the back seat of my father-in-law's Renault on the Champ de Mars looking out the window at the Eiffel Tower and waiting for the start of 2005. We can't get out of the car because there's nowhere to park. The streets are glutted with cars and Parisians—a less organized, European version of Times Square. I have to be satisfied to sit in traffic and hope that it moves slowly enough that I can see the Tower light up at midnight.

I try to focus on what should be somewhat of a monumental moment, because how often am I going to get the chance to be in Paris at midnight on New Year's Eve—or ever? But as with so many such moments that I wish I could fully be *in,* I instead find myself awkwardly hovering outside of it. I look at a couple on the sidewalk with their fat, spiky-haired son. He seems to be about eight and is having an absolute fit over something. His loud yelling and wild gesticulating cow his parents, who try to shush him. And then I look across the street at two women standing arm-in-arm. I know that men and women in Europe are like that, touchy with friends of both genders in a way that's affectionate without being sexual. I wonder if they're friends or sisters or mother and daughter.

Seth and his dad, whose reunions are rare and brief, talk to each other in a mixture of Farsi, French and English, their heads silhouetted in close communion by the diffuse city lights. Members of a tribe I don't really understand and that I'll never be a member of. Neither of them appears to be particularly caught up in the surrounding festivities. I'm glad that Seth spent his childhood here and hope his fluency means that the locals will be somewhat less rude than people claim. I was in this city once before, almost twenty years ago with my mother, and what I remember most about that is the honking cars and people cheering late into the night because France had advanced into the World Cup soccer quarterfinals.

I'm here now to celebrate my birthday, visit with my father-in-law and get a glimpse of my husband's childhood—the apartments and schools and playgrounds. The place markers of memory that now for him glow pleasurably through a hazy gauze of passed time, just as my old neighborhoods do for me. Except those places are close enough for me to drive to whenever the urge overtakes me. Seth hasn't been back to Paris since leaving here at age twelve.

We haven't arranged any specific activities for this trip. We'll only be here for five days; I'm happy enough that we can afford the airfare and the hotel, a Best Western that actually turns out to be a pleasing little inn in the Latin Quarter that had been the home of Napoleon's chief physician. Our room is small; we have to climb over the bed to get to the bathroom, but it's clean and comes with breakfast.

There are no birthday plans either, although I'll of course go along with whatever Seth's father and girlfriend, whom I haven't met yet, want to do. They're saying something about a dinner, which is fine. Really, it's enough that Seth has brought me here, and I'll just go along with…whatever.

That's the thing: I'm not much of a planner. I just go along. Not like my mother, who choreographed our entire trip here together when I was twenty-two—the narrated city bus tour, the trip to Monet's house at Giverny, the Louvre, the Tuileries, the Champs-Élysées. She has long supposed that to be the best way, under the theory that the more experiences you plan, the more meaningful becomes the whole, in terms of the photos you're guaranteed to take and the memories you're guaranteed to make. And then you don't miss out. But I've always resisted that.

Sitting in the car, I realize the foolishness of my laissez-faire approach. Had I been more organized, more assertive, I could have had Seth book an earlier flight and figured out a New Year's Eve celebration more noteworthy than a congested Eiffel Tower drive-by. I could have established and articulated some sort of preference for actual birthday plans instead of leaving it to people I barely know.

And these are just the smallish things. Three months before this, Mom took me for an early birthday treat—a trip to a spa in Arizona where we reveled in massages, yoga and gourmet lean cuisine. Every night after our evening treatments, we hung our plush white robes on hooks and slid into the steaming hot tub, the kind of experience that among women invites the intimacy of hushed, revelatory heart-to-hearts.

It was the third night that it finally happened. The Talk. I knew it was coming, and I was prepared—but not *really* ready. I felt gauzy and sleepy after a hot stone massage and almost felt the need to grip the sides of the hot tub to avoid slipping entirely beneath the steaming water.

The two of us were quiet for a few moments, savoring the silence of the room that was deserted but for us. Mom took a deep breath and, as she exhaled, she tipped her head back. Tendrils of her hair, still shiny and black except for a few strands of gray, skimmed the water and I remembered how her thick, coarse hair always curled when it got wet. Lopez hair. Not the fine, brown, straight hair that my Uncle Rafe and I inherited from Grandma May.

"So delicious. Can we just stay here forever?" She closed her eyes. I smiled, happy as I always am when it's just the two of us in quiet companionship. But the stillness was temporary. Mom likes to be on the move, and when she can't be on the move, she can at least be in conversation.

"You're going to be forty. Forty! I can't believe it, Moon. Do you realize when I was forty, you were a senior in high school? Remember that trip back East to look at colleges?"

I remembered that trip, and how, after getting accepted to both Smith and Wellesley, I couldn't decide between them. She and I sat on my bed flipping a coin, and when heads for Smith came up, I kept flipping until tails for Wellesley appeared, and that's how I figured out where I really wanted to go to school.

Mom sat up out of her reverie, looked at me and sighed in the way that she does before a pronouncement.

"You know, with everything I went through, with Dad, with Landon, and even with John sometimes, I don't know what I would have done, what my life would have been like, without you and Greg." I smile as I squeeze her hand, but I imagine, no—I *know*—that she would have been fine. Amy Lopez May Hathaway Riordan doesn't survive. She thrives, no matter what life throws at her or what she sometimes inadvisably reaches for on her own.

"Moon, I want that for you, too. I do. I know you're happy with your life with Seth now, just the two of you, but I'm really afraid there's going to come a time when you're going to be, I don't know, sorry. What if you and Seth, God forbid, don't work out? What will you have? You won't be able to start over with anyone else at your age, not in that way, the way that having a child ties you to someone. And I think Seth, being Middle Eastern, might really need that.

"I mean, I think about my poor friend Andrea," she continued, taking another tack to cover her bases by referring to her longtime friend who was cursed with "never having been a wife and mother."

"Now she has Alzheimer's and no one to take care of her!"

I let Mom say her piece and give me the whole full-court press. At the end of it, once she lost steam and trailed off into the conciliatory boilerplate of the *well, it's your life and I'm sure you know what's best* variety, I sat there in silence, not quite knowing how to answer. I eventually respond with the first riposte I can come up with. Something along the lines that if the purpose of having kids is to ensure that Kaiser Permanente doesn't drop me and my doddering mind off on Skid Row wearing nothing but a hospital gown, I'll adopt a responsible adult while I still have my wits about me rather than have a kid now and hope they'll stick around to handle that kind of ordeal.

So that's the end of that. It's far from what I wanted to say, although I really do believe that the whole kids-as-eventual-nursemaids thing doesn't fly as a major justification for reproducing.

The whole truth, simple but not tellable, at least not to her, is that I'm just too far gone down the wrong path for all that. For the purpose of establishing myself as she envisions, I chose the wrong education, which I financed in the wrong way. I chose the wrong career—a couple of them in fact—and I married the wrong guy. Simply put, I'm just not…*sustainable*. At least not in the way I need to be in order to be somebody's mom.

A consistent and absolute lack of proper planning has been the road that led me here, today, into the middle of the Latin Quarter, with all these French people eddying around me. I feel weird, tired and disoriented after hurtling through the troposphere at five hundred miles per hour.

Yet I'm exhilarated, too, with a slightly unhinged feeling that excites me. It sinks in that, for the moment anyway, I'm free from teaching schedules and lesson plans and working out and my small, unremarkable condo, from the consequences of a whole host of choices that over time have irrevocably and unfortunately cemented me into *me.* I'm a continent and an ocean and several time zones away from all that. I sense, with a little carbonated hope and not a little relief, that there's some give left after all. That even in the middle of being the polite guest of my in-laws and in the void created by having no real plan,

I can abandon myself to the pleasing randomness of being a stranger in a strange land. I can wander the *animaleries* of Quai de la Mégisserie and commune with the prairie dogs and squirrels who seem as restless and bewildered in their cages as I am in mine.

Twenty-four hours later, I slip, with minimal fanfare, into my fifth decade.

FORTY-ONE

Oh, the places you'll go…

    I fumble with the airplane seatbelt until I feel its satisfying *click*, thinking of my favorite childhood author's ode to optimism that still perches on my bookshelf.

    "Congratulations! Today is your day. You're off to Great Places! You're off and away!"

    I look at the tarmac and then beyond it at the Los Angeles Airport Hilton, where I took the bar exam fifteen years ago. I think about how exhausted and disoriented I was at the end of those three days. I even lost myself on three different freeways before my brain regained the equilibrium necessary to shepherd me home.

    In the seat next to me, Mom busies herself arranging reading material. She's been talking about this trip for weeks as if it's the Concorde to Paris. I find this ironic and annoying because she travels pretty much more than anyone I know and always manages to be very high-end about it. So, this short trip to New York really shouldn't be that big of a deal for her.

    I should be the excited one because I don't get away that much. We did go to Tahiti for our honeymoon five years ago. And last year, Seth took me to Paris for my birthday. Granted, we were mostly visiting Seth's dad and spent my actual birthday having a pretty bland Shabbat dinner at his apartment. Still, it was Paris, and everything there was run-down anyway, which seemed to be the whole point of the place. All the dilapidation somehow seemed both intentional and desirable.

    That's where we've gone in our twelve years together, other than on weekend trips. Seth is the sole owner and operator of a retail shop that's open six or seven days a week, which doesn't allow him to get away much.

Still, I feel a private embarrassment thinking about a kindergartener's book. I'm too old for wide-eyed wonder at this point, and to be honest, I feel kind of *meh*, anyway.

For one thing, we're going to be houseguests in my childhood friend Alicia's apartment, along with her mom, who was my mom's best friend, and Alicia's brother, who was my brother Greg's best friend. I hate being a houseguest almost as much as I hate having a houseguest. It's all so awkward, having to mold myself to someone else's routines and rhythms and somehow be able to sense if I'm getting on my host's nerves or making the bed right. Or if the expensive full bottle of Jo Malone bath gel is for show or general use, whether I should have just brought my own, but I forgot to, so now I have to use the one that I probably shouldn't. It's exhausting.

On top of that, I haven't seen any of these people in years. So, I can't be sure whether my pleasant memories of them from the seventies will survive this trip now that everyone's old or well on their way and about to be thrown into nonstop togetherness for four days.

And then there's Greg, who was supposed to occupy the middle seat between Mom and me. Just thinking about him is making me itch with annoyance. The three of us together, finally coordinating schedules so that we can retrieve a little sliver of the past. But then Greg wrecks what's supposed to happen by pissing off his current girlfriend, who decides to decamp to Hawaii by herself in a fit of retributive pique. So, he has to cancel his plans with us in order to undertake the crucial getting-her-back-right-now project instead of just letting her cool her heels for a week.

As I look at the empty seat, the anger dissipates into sadness. Greg makes me laugh, and I need to laugh. I just finished my first year of teaching in a program at a new school in a teaching partnership that had seemed to hold promise. But after a matter of months, my needy, space-invading teaching partner, and for that matter, the entire staff and pointless meetings, did little more than suck the life out of me.

The plane speeds down the runway, and in that initial moment of weightlessness as it leaves the ground I'm left wondering whether, again, I've made yet another wrong turn.

FORTY-TWO

I like certainty. In fact, I need it. I have no use for words like *maybe, hopefully or perhaps.* I want to know for sure.

Something has felt off for a while. I quit my teaching job to return to my father's law firm because it offers more flexibility and more money—and because I sense something is coming where I may need those things. Fortunately, I've been getting along with him, so he's glad to have me back.

Seth spends his days at the optical store he's owned and managed for ten years and his nights playing video games at his brother's apartment. I spend my mornings in dance class, my afternoons at the law office and my nights at home with the cat, the computer and the television.

My husband has been very kind lately but in an off-hand, impersonal way. Offering to stop by the Christmas tree lot, which he usually can't stand doing, buying me the suede ankle boots I admired at Macy's, giving me the credit card without me asking so that I can do the marketing even though he doesn't have time to join me.

Usually, I love doing the shopping, going from store to store until all the items on the list are checked off, putting my purchases away and then saving the bags in a pile in the broom closet for when I need to scoop out the cat box.

On a Friday night just before Christmas, I find myself over the hill in Malibu, milling around CVS because I need a new hair dryer. Seth is at his brother's again, in the midst of yet another video soccer tournament.

It occurs to me as I peruse the aisles filled with the random drugstore offerings that I love looking at, that I'm lonely. I mean, I'm grateful that we're doing well enough to have the money so I can shop, that we have a condo in a pretty community and that I don't have to work full-time. With all of this, I should feel better than I do.

Disheartened, I cut the shopping trip short after treating myself to a new curling iron along with the hair dryer. Half an hour later finds me sitting at my computer. I've been scanning Craigslist lately—the Men Seeking Women Section. Never would I respond to one; I just like reading the hopeful words of lonely or sometimes just horny guys. *Pilot seeks co-pilot to navigate adventures together. Could you, would you, take a chance?* There are lots of raunchy ones too, but I like to read the sweeter, hopeful posts.

I know there's a reason I'm doing this, why I feel at loose ends, why I sit here, an envious Peeping Tom sneaking peeks at the lives of others. Something not terribly well-made to begin with is unraveling at an accelerated rate. For years, I've allowed myself to be nourished by the idea of what my marriage is or at least by the possibility of what it can be if I do things right. It's better than being slowly starved by the reality of everything that it isn't and can't be despite my efforts.

In a moment of sudden clarity, I realize that if I pick up the phone now, I'll find out and that it's time to ask questions, to know, to begin to re-occupy the certainty I need and love and that there will be no more *maybe, perhaps* or *hopefully.*

I swivel my desk chair around to look at the phone sitting in its cradle on the white tile countertop.

I walk over to it, pick it up, and dial.

"Hey."

"Hey."

In the silence that follows, there is awkwardness and expectation. I've asked no questions for weeks, allowing the space between us to marinate in a covert deception that's been fueled by my own willful ignorance. I haven't wanted to know, even though the constant stomach ache I've had for weeks tells me I already do. Seth has probably been waiting for this moment.

"Where are you?"

"At Sam's."

"Can I talk to him?"

Silence. I know he's weighing whether to tell me, knowing as I do that what's said now could create something that will inevitably take on a life of its own which will be beyond the control of either of us. Finally, I hear him take a breath.

"I'm not at Sam's."

"Where are you?"

"I'm at Houston's in Hermosa Beach." My favorite restaurant. Really?

"Who are you with?"

"A girl."

I can't quite believe how easy it is to smoke him out, or that I can be having this conversation in a normal voice. Shouldn't I be hysterical?

"I think you should come home."

"Okay."

It takes him three hours to show up. In that time, I do find myself becoming unglued. Not because he's cheating on me. We've had sex exactly twice during five years of marriage, and hardly more than that in the years prior. We're essentially roommates and buddies. I have no idea where my own sex drive went, but I know his has been raging, even though he never approaches me for that. Marriage vows notwithstanding, I can hardly expect him to live as a celibate.

I'm unglued because I'm not prepared for the sudden collapse of the whole house of cards. I rely on Seth financially; I can't even have a bank account in my own name. He's in control of the accounts, credit cards and mortgage.

I hold nothing. And now the frayed bonds that have barely held the two of us together are likely to get severed. The material goals that substituted for intimacy, the plan to buy a house, upgrade our cars and take vacations, will also go away. I don't know what's supposed to take their place.

These are the things that spin around and around in my head until Seth finally arrives and stands over me while I sit rooted to the sofa. Her name is Sunny, which rhymes with the name of my former stepmother, Honey, who my father left my mother for. I doubt there's much hope for me in the world populated by Honeys and Sunnys.

Sunny is an optical sales rep because of course she is. I imagine her in a tight pencil skirt and heels, a silk blouse unbuttoned just enough to reveal a lacy black bra. She strolls into the store carrying her bag of tricks, the Tom Ford sunglasses in their velvet cases. She leans over the counter so that Seth gets a proper view of the goods. And then ten minutes later, or on her next visit after she makes him take her out for sushi, she's on her knees in the little room behind the store, bringing my husband back to the life that I sucked out of him in a different way.

I imagine this is how it all went down until I realize it isn't my imagination. He is actually telling me this and not sparing the details.

"Come on, you knew this was coming." He's relieved now. Words tumble out of him, the relentless truth pummeling me. I ask questions. When? How long? I listen to myself interrogating him and hate the sound of it. None of his answers matter because, like he said, I knew this was coming. How it had arrived, the packaging of the details— none of that's important.

I eventually stand up and rage at him anyway because it's all I can think to do right now. I should have asked questions last month when I tried to order a movie on Pay Per View but got locked out because of all the movies that had already been ordered. When the customer service guy had the unenviable task of disclosing to me the assorted porn titles. I should have wondered what else I didn't know. Instead, I had tried to offer my unwilling body to my disinterested husband, thinking that might solve the problem.

Eventually, I run out of steam. I'm yelling because I'm scared, not because I want him. I'm also yelling because I'm not enough to hold his interest, or maybe anyone's. I know it's too late; his impassive eyes and emotionless tone tell me he's already gone. And yelling isn't going to get me anywhere.

The two of us stand there, looking at each other. He's getting antsy, probably wanting to go back to her. What is there for him here with me?

"I think I should go."

And then he does, and I'm alone in the small nest we created. Its only other inhabitant, Sheba the tortoiseshell cat, blinks at me from under the glass coffee table. The black leather sofa that we purchased four years ago utters a soft belch as I sink into it, there to remain for minutes or maybe hours.

Great. Now what?

Some days later, after my unsuccessful attempts to reignite Seth's interest in me, the *what* turns out to be Seth's move to a motel near his business and my move to the computer screen. There, from the ethers of the Internet, appears a man named Jake with salt and pepper hair and brown eyes with a hint of irreverence, eight years my senior, seeking a hiking buddy.

This time, I do more than just look.

FORTY-THREE

I can imagine what the kid is thinking:

Great. I have to meet another one of the girlfriends, AND I have to deal with Grandma and Uncle Josh.

I picture Mark huddling deep into the dirty beige leather back seat of his father's Lexus, having given up the front seat so I can sit there. His dad probably told him my name, but I'm sure he's already forgotten it.

They drive out the back gate of the apartment complex. It's a creepy place, really, with its dark hallways that always smell like weed and the tattooed guys who wear their t-shirts in the swimming pool. Mark probably wishes that his dad lived in a nicer place, but at least no one here knows him, and he doesn't have to worry about standing out or looking weird—which I remember was a constant fear in my own adolescence.

I can tell Jake is nervous about me meeting his son. The day before, he has a fit when his computer stops working in the middle of his attempt to buy Foo Fighters tickets for his nineteen-year-old daughter Jeannie, and he nearly rips the cord right out of it—which isn't anything unusual. Even in this first bloom of our romance, I've become used to Jake's benign fits of anger—benign because he directs them only at things. Never at people. His tantrums are predictable and brief, like a Fourth of July sparkler that spits its bright darts of light everywhere and yet nowhere, flaming out as suddenly as it ignites.

Then, as it gets closer to the time for me to arrive, I picture Jake becoming fake-cheerful. Pasting on a smile, his voice louder than usual as he tells Mark how much he's going to like me, as if his son's obvious lack of enthusiasm has made him hard of hearing.

The car zooms the short distance up the boulevard to pull up in front of the apartment complex where I wait. Mark sees a blonde wearing jeans and a pink jacket, holding a bakery box and hunching her shoulders, shifting back and forth from left to right as if cold or nervous.

I peer into the backseat window, removing my sunglasses so he can see my eyes.

Jake gets out of the car and takes the box from me, giving me a quick, self-conscious kiss before opening the front passenger side door for me.

"Hi, Mark. I'm Marty." I reach out to shake his hand.

"Hi."

He glances at me but quickly averts his eyes. He already thinks I'm trying to draw something from him, to find something out that he's not ready to tell. I'm eager for him to like me, and he knows it. He seems weary, old for his thirteen years.

I'm the latest in a long list since Jake and his ex-wife Anne split up ten years ago. Mark probably supposes that my eagerness will last only until I realize that no matter how much his dad likes me, Friday nights and sometimes Saturdays are theirs, his and his dad's. That after a while, I'll get sick of his dad's "priorities," which is basically just a code word for him. That he'll lie in his dad's bed listening to me argue with him on the sofa in the living room, as all the others eventually do, late on a Friday night. That we'll all eat dinner together in the apartment, awkward and silent over Mark's favorite takeout "broasted" chicken. He imagines I'll get annoyed at having to sit there with him, and sigh repeatedly as I pick all the skin off the chicken and brush it to the edge of my plate. He won't understand why I'd do that, because to him, the skin is the best part, and the chicken doesn't really taste like anything without it.

And he assumes that at some point, he won't see or hear about me anymore. Then another lady, the next one, will be getting into the car and acting all eager to meet him for the first time.

All us girls have just wanted his dad to themselves, it seems. I suppose Mark's been sharing his dad for almost as long as he can remember, with his girlfriends, with his own sister Jeannie, with the television jobs that take Jake out of town, sometimes for days at a time.

We stop at a deli on the way to visit Jake's mom, Mark's grandma. While Jake orders a bagel assortment, Mark stands in front of the glass case underneath the cash register and looks at the assortment of candy. Life Savers, Mentos, Fruit Stripe gum.

"I love all that stuff too," I say. I don't expect him to reply, and he doesn't.

"Want some Mentos, buddy?" Without waiting for an answer, Jake asks the cashier to ring up the candy.

Grandma Ruth puts the whole family on edge, from what I can gather. She asks how much everything costs and makes disapproving sounds when she doesn't like the answers to her endless questions. She starts out a lot with, "Shouldn't you…" or "Wouldn't it be better if…" when what she really means to do is not to ask a question at all but to tell people what to do. Whenever I've heard Jake on the phone with his mother, his responses are generally a tight, "Sure, Mom" or "Whatever you say, Mom," although it's obvious he really doesn't want to do whatever it is she's asking.

Mark sits on the loveseat in his grandmother's tiny apartment. He's quiet and well-behaved. I imagine he has nothing to say, anyway. I look at him watch his grandma set the table, putting out the bagels and cream cheese and lox, and spending a lot of time rearranging the plates and silverware.

I feel him watching me as I sit at the small, round dining table. There's a lot going on. I don't sit with him on the loveseat, or try to make myself busy, or ask a lot of questions, or demonstrate any physical affection toward Jake.

Jake's brother Josh sits on an armchair across from Mark. His eyes are open, but he isn't looking anywhere in particular. He moves his lips like he's talking to someone, but no words come out of his mouth.

Grandma Ruth looks at Josh and makes an exaggerated, sad face.

"I just don't know what to do about him anymore," she says to me in a low voice that would be loud enough for Josh to hear if he were paying attention.

I tell Ruth about my brother Mikey, not because he was at all like Josh, but because it might distract her. Ruth asks what happened to him.

"He died," I say. "But not from drugs." I say this matter-of-factly, the same way I told her what kind of pastry I brought. But Ruth makes a small noise when she hears it, as if someone had pricked her with a needle.

Josh emits a loud snort, and we all turn to look at him. Asleep now, his head lolls to one side, mouth gaping.

"Joshua, honey, wake UP!" Grandma Ruth says in a loud voice. "It's time to EAT!"

Josh jerks awake and stands up, unsteady. We all crowd around the table, which is only three steps from the sofa. Mark eyes the platter of bagels, cream cheese and fish. He plucks a plain bagel from the dish and begins tearing tiny pieces from it. He pops tiny pieces into his mouth, as if forcing himself to eat for everyone else's benefit.

I remember that. I found, in the early days of being shuttled between my father and Honey and my mother and Daddy Landon, that the best way to force myself to eat without throwing up was in tiny bites so that I could hardly taste what I was eating yet still manage to satisfy any adult who might be watching.

Mark keeps his eyes down while Ruth and Jake talk in loud voices about the lovely Viktor Benes alligator pastry I brought. Josh eats one slice of salmon and nods off again.

Josh doesn't drive, so after lunch we give him a ride to the bus stop. No one is really sure where he lives. Walking to the car, Josh is unsteady, shuffling and muttering. Mark watches him stepping on the dirty cuffs of the pants that are too long for him and is careful to keep his distance. I see the deep distaste bordering on fear of this person who looks like a homeless guy, yet who is his uncle. He's probably afraid that if everyone else in his family were to die, he might actually have to live with this man who wouldn't know how to take care of him, and how embarrassing it would be to have anyone know they were related.

"Wanna go to Universal CityWalk?" Jake has pulled up alongside his apartment building.

"Sure," says Mark.

Jake has told me how Mark loves CityWalk. The candy store there has Razzles and giant Pixy Stix, things that they can never find at Rite Aid or CVS. There's also the zero-gravity machine where they look at people who seem to be flying suspended in mid-air, and giant billboards of *The Simpsons,* their favorite show to watch together.

Yet Mark doesn't seem too excited by the proposed activity. I guess that's because a lot of times the activity never winds up happening when you only have Friday nights with Dad. And I'm also learning that my Jake is happiest when there isn't too much excitement about things, in either a good or a bad way. I'm sure Mark also knows that by now.

"Do you want to join us?" Jake asks me.

I'm sure Mark hopes I won't. He must be too used to it, Jake and the girlfriend *du jour* walking ahead of him holding hands, the woman pretending to enjoy herself for a few minutes or an hour—and then all of a sudden wanting to leave. And Jake, who's very considerate, won't want to spend a half hour looking around Magnet Max or GameStop like he would if it were just the two of them.

"No thanks. You guys go have your guy time, and I'll see you again soon." I smile at Mark and give Jake a quick goodbye kiss on the cheek.

A week later, I'm with the two of them again. We're going to watch my brother Greg race his car out in the Mojave desert.

After Daddy Landon was gone and Greg and I fell headlong into the messiness of full-time adulting, we each must have realized that at some point we would be the only ones left. Significant others would come and go, Mom wouldn't always be around and our father and half-brothers were not destined to be major players in our lives. I guess we just tacitly concluded that the burden of our disagreement about my errors and omissions and his choices would be preferable to the pain of not having each other to remember with. So we stumbled our way back to each other, paving over the initial awkwardness with our old private jokes that eventually cemented us into good again.

Jake tells me Mark likes cars and long car rides. Whether he really wants this outing, I don't know—but it's something. He's a quiet kid. Probably unsure about most places aside from his mom's house and

Jake's apartment, and the electronics stores where he can get lost in the gleam and the shine of computers and cell phones and all the things that go with them.

But he'll go along with it because he wants to spend time with his dad. He understands that I'm part of that package, at least for now, and that his understanding makes his father happy.

"Hey, guys. Come on in and sit your asses down!"

Greg reaches out a muscled arm and pulls Mark inside the trailer. The arm is tattooed from wrist to shoulder with a cobra. Its head rears up on Greg's forearm, and the snake's blue and yellow body coils around the rest of his arm, and around his neck. My brother's head is buzzed nearly bald, and he has three piercings in each ear—three silver hoops in one, and three diamond studs in the other.

Greg puts a *Family Guy* DVD in the player for Mark while we wait for the race to begin, and they talk about the race car. Greg swears a lot and so do I, especially when we get together. Almost every other word is *fuck* or *shit* and has been since he was old enough for me to teach him to both say the words and not say them in front of adults. I guess it's just become our thing.

When we were kids, it was our secret, letting us be different together in private. And maybe not so split up inside as I imagine we both felt with four parents and two vastly disparate households and three half siblings and two step-siblings. Neither of us were entirely whole outside of that world we made solely with each other.

And now I find I want to invite Mark into that, to hear him utter words like *motherfucker* or *dickhole* or whatever kids say now so that he can say something that he thinks ought to be said and then maybe feel a little more whole, too.

Mark's cheeks are pink now from laughing with Greg. Jake and I slip out for a walk along the dirt trail leading to the track. Jake is hunched over with his hands in his pockets, and I walk a short distance behind him.

Jake is someone who needs taking care of. He's had a hard life, and its vestiges seem to have taken up permanent residence somewhere between those bowed shoulders. The divorce from Anne on the heels of a near-fatal car accident, her drinking, the ups and downs of the television business he works in, teenage kids, his querulous mother and addict brother. And those are just the things I've learned of in the couple of months I've known him.

Jake has a roof over his head, a modest apartment on a busy boulevard. Even with his alimony and child support obligations, he can afford the electronics he and Mark love and concert tickets for the bands he and Jeannie love. So, he's getting by all right.

But in him is an aloneness that seems more than just that of a divorced dad. It's an aloneness that makes him stay in the car when he picks Mark up from Anne's house, even when she's not there. It's an aloneness that I recognize, that I feel late at night during these hot summers, when I walk out the door of the condo Seth and I shared just months ago and into the parking lot. And then I wander down to the end of the complex where there's one bright streetlight that flickers on and off, bugs buzzing high up in the air around it. I lean against the pole underneath the light, breathing in the warm air sticky with the smell of sage, and wonder how it would feel to just keep walking down my street, and then the next one, and then on to somewhere else. But unlike Seth and my own dad I never do go somewhere else; the pole becomes uncomfortable against my back after a while, and then I feel my feet steer me back to the dark quiet of my empty home.

Outside Greg's trailer, the hot desert wind blows sand around Jake's feet. I catch up to him, interlocking my arm with his and we walk, stopping at each of the race cars lined up along the entrance to the raceway. Mark catches up to us just as Greg roars by in his souped-up Miata, giving us the thumbs-up sign. We all stop and watch. I feel in that moment as if I've been here before, and that this hot, barren desert, which had seemed a moment ago boring and lifeless, suddenly is filled with things waiting to happen.

"Having a good time, buddy?"

Mark nods at his dad's question. He's trying to be a good kid. *The right thing is always the nice thing*, is what Jake says he tells the kids. I guess Mark's interpretation is that it's always best to go along with what other people want, even if it means not having a very good time.

He's got it in him, though, to buck his dad's urgings. Jake told me they all still tease Mark about how when he was little he could be counted upon to ruin any trip or outing. They called him the "Black Cloud." Like the time he was so excited to go whale-watching but then for some mysterious reason cried so hard after the boat left the dock that he made himself sick and alarmed the rest of the people on the boat. Jake made the captain turn the boat around and take them back so they wouldn't ruin the trip for everyone else. Jeannie wouldn't talk to him for a week.

Later, Mark will tell me that he hates not remembering things that he says or does—especially embarrassing things like ruining a family trip. He will also tell me that at the same time he often feels like ruining things. Sometimes he looks at his carefully polished collection of cars and trucks and wants to smash them with a hammer.

I used to feel that way about my tiny glass horses, the ones I collected during elementary school. Even though they were so pretty, or because of that, I would visualize the cold metal coming down upon all of them, the things that my family or friends gave to me or that I bought with my allowance. And while for a moment I felt a rush of excitement at that thought, the feeling was always replaced with a sharp pain, as if I was the one being hammered—pain at the thought of destroying the things that I loved and shame for even thinking it.

Greg wins the race, but there's no prize. The drivers all get together in the desert from time to time to race, and that's it. But after the race, everyone acts as if Greg won a million dollars. The other drivers slap him on the back, sharp "thwacks" of skin on leather, and Greg puffs out his chest and smokes a cigar. A brief discussion of where to eat ends as Greg decides he wants Indian food.

I see Mark look at Jake for guidance. Jake won't actually make him eat Indian food, but there's worry on his face that he'll have to do the nice thing and go along and just not eat until after when his dad will pick up something from KFC or Burger King.

"I think we'll take a pass," I tell my brother. "It's not really Mark's thing. Some other time, bro."

"Okey dokey. That's cool." Greg and I hug each other tight. We've spent the afternoon laughing and joking, talking to each other in our intimate, fragmented language that no one else understands. I'm aware of Mark studying us. I hope someday he and Jeannie get to have this between them. I'm sure that at this stage his sister mostly rolls her eyes at him and slams the door in his face when he wants to come into her room.

On the ride home, I glance at Mark in the rearview mirror. The heat has made him sleepy, and he drifts in and out of consciousness. I, too, am lulled by the sound of the engine and the slight rattle of the interior. It seems as if the car is moving in one long, straight line down a road that goes on forever.

Jake and I start to giggle when we come up behind a semi. He had showed me a YouTube video he'd seen with Mark, where some guy in a wheelchair somehow got stuck onto the front of a truck and was then pushed down the street for miles before the driver realized the guy was stuck there. I again find myself laughing for a long time at that image—even though I know I shouldn't.

Mark wakes up and hears us laughing, and when Jake tells him what we're laughing at, he joins in. Then he says he can show me a bunch of other videos when we get back.

Jake picks up broasted chicken on the way home. I devour my share, noticing the approval in Mark's eyes as I relish the crispy skin.

We watch the videos—the talking cats, the cat getting stuck on the ceiling fan and then all the fail videos of people wrecking cars in stupid ways. Mark shows me the video he made. He calls it "Ferrari Crash Test" and a million people viewed it, thinking they were going to see an actual Ferrari get totaled. But it was only a remote-controlled, ramshackle model Ferrari that Mark filmed as he maneuvered it into the wall. Some people were pissed off, but most loved it.

We watch one talking cat video three times—the one where someone inserts translations of a cat's weird growls: "Oh Long Johnson… Oh Don Piaaano…All the live long day…" I love animals, and I borrow Mark's laptop to show him my favorite pictures.

I had read a story about a family who found a random owl on the side of a road. It was just sitting there, hurt or sick. But it was alive and didn't try to fly away when they approached it. So, they put it into a cardboard box and took it to a wildlife rehabilitation center.

I show Mark the pictures. One is of the owl sitting in the car, looking at the camera with huge yellow eyes and giant pupils. Tufts of hair angle sharply upward from his eyes, making him look mad. Another shows only the two expressive eyes peering through the opening of the box. Others show the owl just sitting there in the box, like he had sat in the car. Not scared, exactly, but definitely annoyed.

"I wonder what he felt like, being rounded up and put into that box," I say.

Mark shrugs. "Maybe he knew the people were trying to help him, or maybe he was too sick to care."

"Well," I muse, "He wasn't going to be scared into making a scene. No flapping, no screeching or whatever it is owls do when they're upset."

Mark half-smiles. "Yeah, but still—he was probably pissed off, sitting in a strange box in a strange car."

I tell him I would have kept that owl, that I have a veterinarian friend who would have been able to treat him. I would have kept him in an open cage in my condo, so he could fly around if he wanted.

Mark looks over at his dad, who had dozed off on the sofa in the glow of the television.

"I think we need candy," I say. "Let's go to Rite Aid." I fish around for my car keys, and the jangling wakes Jake up.

"Whatcha up to?" he asks, dazed. He doesn't want to come along, because Rite Aid is just down the street.

"You guys don't need me," he says.

"An adventure," I say, as we walk down the dark, skunky-smelling hallway and out onto the boulevard.

At the store, I take a small plastic basket and start picking candy packages off the shelves and hangers: Sour Patch Kids, Sour Skittles, Warheads, a giant bin of Sour Straws.

"Go for it. You like Red Vines, right?" I grab a package.

"They're okay." I see Mark eyeing a pack of Pez candy, ten rolls of refills with no dispenser. I put the entire pack in the basket.

"No dispenser needed. Why waste money on some retarded plastic head?" At that, I get another half-smile.

I spend that night at Jake's after Mark confirms that he's okay with being on the air mattress in the living room.

The next morning, it's still dark when Jake leaves for work at the TV studio. I hear the front door open and then shut with a gentle squeak but find I can't get back to sleep. I tiptoe into the living room to check on Mark, which I'm not sure I need to do, but it's his first night here not sleeping in his dad's room, so it might be weird for him.

He wakes up for a moment when, in the darkness, I accidentally stumble against the coffee table. But then I hear a long sigh and sense him settle back into a warm cocoon of unconsciousness. I'm jealous of that pubescent sleep—the sleep that grabs at you and doesn't want to let go, that blessed cascade of deep rest that feels especially distant in these early days of change since Seth exited and Jake entered.

Heading back toward the bedroom, I see Mark's school backpack next to the front door. A folder with the haphazardly scrawled words "Language Arts" sticks up out of it.

I take the folder out, interested as a former educator to see what Mark's seventh grade teacher is up to. When I see the handwritten pages inside the folder, I take the whole thing into the bedroom and shut the door.

I hate writing, Mrs. Guthrie. You gave us this autobiography assignment and said we could write anything in our first draft as long as we write at least two pages a day. So, besides telling you that I think this whole assignment is kind of lame, what I want to say is, (a) I don't have enough of a life to write about, and (b) even if I did, why would I want to? I mean, don't you hear the same stuff year after year from every seventh grader you've ever had? We're all basically the same Oak Park kids, right? You already had all our brothers and sisters in your class, so you know all about us because you had them write their autobiographies, too.

So, you must know I was born in 1994 because you had my sister in your class when she was in seventh grade and did the autobiography assignment. I know you do because Jeannie showed me her autobiography last night, and she told all about me. I can't believe she still has it, but she said it's special to her because it was part of her English portfolio for Open House, which was the only Open House that our dad ever went to. She said she kept everything from that night, even the chopsticks from Yamato where we had dinner afterward and the little umbrella they put in her Shirley Temple. It still opens and closes. But I don't remember the dinner.

My dad left when I was two. I don't really remember him living here or leaving. I know that he almost died in a car accident around that time and broke his pelvis and some other bones. I visited him in the hospital, but all I remember is a weird smell and the apple juice he gave me. He had already taken a sip, so I didn't want any because I thought I would get sick, too.

I've lived in the same house on Blackbird Lane my whole life. I live there with my mom, her boyfriend, Rob, and Jeannie. But like I said, you already know all this. I'll also say that I really like cars and electronics which you probably don't know because when Jeannie wrote about me, I was only six. I wasn't as good with computers as I am now, but I did like cars back then and also magnets. I used to like the sound they make when they find each other and click. That sound drove my mom crazy though. So, I had to stay in my room with the door closed whenever I wanted to take them out. My stepdad likes cars, too, and golf. I call him my stepdad even though he's not married to my mom, because they're engaged. They've been engaged for a long time, and Rob keeps asking her when she'll make him an honest man. I don't know why he says that or why he keeps asking because she never answers him.

My mom is an artist. She paints pictures of kittens that she sells to people, mostly to old people or moms. The kittens in her pictures are always dressed up like ballet dancers or clowns. I guess people think they're cute.

My dad works on TV shows. Sometimes he goes out of town for work. When he's here, I spend Friday nights with him at his place or he picks me up and takes me out to dinner. He's not married, but he has girlfriends. So that's why I can't spend Saturday nights over. His apartment only has one bedroom, so when I'm there I sleep with him, although he says he can set up his air mattress in the living room if I like that better. I'm still thinking about it, but…

The story suddenly stops. But what? Maybe Mark's homework was interrupted when he heard his mother Anne coming down the hall. I picture him hastily closing his notebook, maybe taking *Flowers for Algernon* out of his backpack and pretending to read as she walks into his room.

"Hey there, Jellybean."

Jake has told me what the house is like after 5:00 pm. Anne's sing-song voice lets everyone know she's become her other self for the night. The crashing sound of ice cubes coming out of the automatic dispenser, the sharp crack of the Diet Squirt can being opened and the fizzy sound of the soda being poured echo through the air. Just after 5:00 pm, the vodka goes on top.

Anne maybe sits on the edge of his bed, slow and deliberate so she won't fall, and looks around the room like she's never seen it before.

"This is so nice."

I imagine Mark pressing his lips together and nodding, trying to see whatever it is that she sees. I bet his room is simple. Just his bed, a desk, his magnets and a few favorite cars from his Hot Wheels collection.

"Come downstairs and watch TV with me, baby."

Dancing with the Stars, American Idol—those are probably Anne's favorites. I see her curled and blanketed on the sofa, third or fourth or fifth drink in hand, Mark sitting at her feet with his laptop. I don't imagine he'd really care much for the shows, but I can see him criti-cizing the contestants' stupid song choices and cheesy outfits to amuse himself until his mother passes out and Rob comes downstairs to put a blanket over her.

Mark probably stays up late enough to hear Jeannie and her boyfriend come home, listening to their laughter and their conversation, trying to hear their words, wanting to know what's so funny.

"Oh nothing," they'll say, exchanging looks that tell him that he's not in their world, that they belong somewhere forbidden to him. Her door is likely always closed, with only that skunky smell coming from under the door to let him know she's there. Does he know what the smell is? Does he want to be invited in to find out for himself, to look at her lava lamp and poster of a dripping peace sign?

Does he feel himself splitting a little at his mother's house? Does it happen too on Fridays when he's at Jake's and then all over again when he goes back to Anne on Saturday or Sunday? I think about atoms, and how I once learned that splitting such a small thing can destroy huge cities just as those bombs did in Japan at the end of the Second World War.

I know that feeling. I knew it every time I went to my father and Honey and then back to my mother and Daddy Landon. I knew it at night when whatever house I was in was quiet and dark and I was blessedly alone. I knew it again when people swirled around me with their laughing and their conversations that didn't include me. Half of me in one place, half of me in another. Even though nothing ever exploded, the splitting did not feel good.

My cell phone rings, waking me up. Mark's pages are strewn across the bed. Somehow, it's noon, but Jake just laughs at my groggy voice when I answer. He tells me to go check on Mark and that I can take him home whenever I want.

Feeling sheepish, I walk into the living room.

"Hey, buddy. How ya doin'?"

Mark's watching an episode of *South Park* and eating Pop-Tarts, so he seems to be doing okay. I remind him that his dad had to leave early for work.

Alone together for the first time in Jake's small apartment, we both feel shy and strange without Jake there. I don't know what their morning routine is, and he's probably unsure whether I know when he needs to go home, whether it's okay for him to just sit there and keep watching TV, or whether he needs to be polite and make conversation.

I sit next to him on the sofa, and we finish watching the show together, relaxing a little because we both find it funny.

"Wanna head out soon?"

I know that's probably what Jake says to him when it's time to take him back to Anne's. I help him pack his few things. While he's in the bathroom, I tuck the candy we bought into his backpack along with the school folder.

On the drive, we talk about school. I tell Mark that I used to be a teacher and ask him how he liked the middle school camp, Outdoor Ed, that all sixth graders attend in the early spring. I tell him that my students went but that I wouldn't have liked it because the food seemed gross, and I can't stand the thought of sleeping in a cabin with a bunch of people.

Mark says he hated Outdoor Ed and shows me the one photo he let his mom take when he was about to board the bus there. I'm driving so I can't look for too long, but I see him standing next to two other boys who are standing close together, big, isn't-this-awesome smiles, wearing their parkas, totally into it. In the photo Mark stands aside, a good three or four feet away, sinking into the comfort of his hoodie, hands jammed into pockets, not smiling. He looks as if he belongs somewhere else, that he isn't having the same experience as the other two.

And clearly, he didn't.

"Yeah, the minute that bus started going up the canyon, I got sick to my stomach, and it didn't go away the whole weekend." I imagine his classmates thrilling over hikes and pond exploration and the dance party thrown by the counselors on their last night, and Mark just waiting for it all to end so he could return home to his magnets and his thoughts.

After that, there's silence. I look out the window at the familiar landscape of oak trees and bristly hilltops that hug the freeway. Although it's still early afternoon, the sun seems ready to set. Sad September light, Jake calls it. Mark closes his eyes. I imagine he feels himself swaying along with the car, sinking along with the sun.

And then we arrive at Anne's house. I feel myself look at Mark the same way I did the first time I met him because once again I'm unsure what to do. Another weird moment.

"I guess I'll see you later," he says.

I sense Anne's presence at the window peeping through the space between the living room curtains, but I avoid looking at her. We haven't been introduced yet, and I think it's better right now that we're not.

"Okay."

I lean over and kiss Mark on the cheek. He gets out of the car, hoisting his backpack over his shoulder, and as he passes the window, I notice him avoid his mother's eyes.

FORTY-FOUR

It seems I really don't understand God at all—although honestly, I haven't considered the concept for a while. But now I have to, having walked into a Twelve Step meeting for people who love those who do the drinking and/or the drugging. Toastmasters for the tormented, people with hard lives sitting in hard chairs telling hard stories of their loved ones' afflictions and addictions. They all look desiccated, sucked dry.

I'm not that way. Yes, there's been an intermittent though consistent pattern. Daddy Landon. Jimmy. Honey, maybe. Seth, probably. And now Jake, his two children, and his anxious though well-meaning ex-wife Anne. An undeniable parade of players whose BFFs have been some sort of substance.

But I'm most certainly *not* at the end of my rope; I'm at the beginning of a new story. My perfectly imperfect love carried me over the threshold into a new home and a new life. To paraphrase the song, our house is a very fine house with three cats in a sort-of yard. And life definitely has been less hard since Jake came along and rebooted me, so now everything feels easier.

I'm about to become the stepmom of a fourteen-year-old and an eighteen-year-old. In the mix is also their mother Anne, with whom I vow to stay cordial and drama-free. I don't want to be Honey, who was a disturbing revisionist when it came to the existence and significance of my own mother. Yet I'm finding it hard to manage Anne's drunk texts, late-night phone calls and cloying friendliness that in an instant can bitter into sarcasm and insults.

Jake's daughter Jeannie, whose initial goodwill began to fray at the edges once Jake and I moved into the new condo, is also proving to be her mother's clinging and emotionally rickety daughter. And then there's sweet misfit Mark, whom I call Serious Cat, a mini-Jake in both looks and his growing love for weed, which I have started seeing in his red eyes and long naps when he's with us on weekends.

So, if I'm to be the not-Honey, if I'm going to be the sort who faces things straight up instead of sweeping inconvenient truths under the carpet, I'm going to need to get everyone squared away. Jake came to one meeting with me, but no more after that. I'm learning that my sensitive, pot-loving fiancé is not much for confrontation or dialogue concerning touchy subjects.

There is hope for Mark. I've started taking him to the teen meetings, but he's gravitating toward kids I hope are just loaning him rather than giving him his present stoner identity. I get it; you have to be identifiable in middle and high school to avoid inhabiting one long, friendless hell. So, you have to be a jock, nerd, emo or stoner. Unfortunately, it seems Mark has gone over to the devil he knows rather than take a chance on one he doesn't.

Jeannie likes nothing more than to sit around and smoke weed with her dad. Together the two of them alternate between denying and ignoring Mark's addiction, while keeping their own to themselves and between one another. I wish there were another basis for their bond. Or maybe I don't. It's easier to feel excluded from a drug den than from a more enduring connection I wish I'd shared with my own father.

I'm okay with the weed, for a while. When I met Jake, there was a certain, pleasurable jolt I got from feeling drop-kicked back into high school, into those hazy afternoons of my senior year when I'd ditch chemistry class for an afternoon at the beach getting high with a couple of friends. I also enjoy the novelty of this new family I'm marrying into and their initially interesting ways. But I find them over time becoming confusing and increasingly irritating.

Now I experience a certain level of chaos within the space I occupy with my husband-to-be. We're supposed to be a unit now, not occupants of separate though porous spheres of influence. When it was happening solely in Jake's old apartment, I could indulge as I cared to, but there was always the option to go home and take a break—although I didn't often avail myself of that as I couldn't bear to be away from him for too long.

Stepmonster that I'm apparently becoming, I feel the need to draw a line. So, I now find myself once a week coming to the depressing back room of a church. Whiteboards display bible references and sayings like *Jesus loves me, this I know, for the Bible tells me so.* And in this musty room that seems to ask for blind acceptance of doctrine I personally don't buy, I sit here contemplating the concept of a Higher Power.

My childhood playmate Daniela, terrifying me into becoming a Jehovah's Witness. That particular God is a mean badass demanding homage in the form of fear and restrictive ritual.

Then there was Peter and Paul and the garden at God's House. We later found out that the garden wasn't even on the property of the vacant home. It belonged to a lonely old lady in the house next door who watched us dig and plant and secretly provided us with materials and encouragement. That God delights in mystery and pleasant surprises. It's too bad that he turned out to be a fraud.

My father found his God after he married Honey and started his new family. For him, God is a tiny, orange-robed man in India he visits several times a year. Shanti Ram was my God, too—for a while. I went to his ashram four times during my twenties, casting over and over for the next shiny thing. Shanti Ram told me to become a lawyer the first time I was there, which was the direction I was already headed despite my own insistent inner *No!* That's the only time he spoke to me. During my other three visits, I sat cross-legged at daily worship, as the tiny orange-clad figure walked among the throngs of devotees, using his hands and forearms to gently stir the air around him as if conducting some invisible, divine orchestra. Still searching, I failed to find. And then sometime after that, it came to light that Shanti Ram spent a lot of alone time with young boys, who are asked to pull their pants down so they may receive the honor of Swami's special anointment. So that God turned out to be a pedophile who, on top of that, gave crappy advice.

And there's Honey and the Church of The Good Shepherd in Beverly Hills, where she presided over the Altar Society and where her sons, my half-brothers, served as altar boys. I was confirmed there when I was twenty-seven so I could take communion with the rest of the family when we attended Mass. An emaciated, beaten-down Jesus hung his head on a cross under the stained-glass skylight, eyes closed in pain and resignation. The God of that place was elitist and sadly misinformed if in fact He did send His only son to wither away and die for the sake of the bejeweled and fur-clad ladies who kneeled in dutiful reverence before an altar adorned with hothouse flower arrangements.

Finally, when Seth and I were together, we went to a Kabbalah Centre for a while before getting married. That's one thing we did have in common: We're both seekers. We wanted to understand the larger scheme of things to make sense of Hutus killing Tutsis and Serbians killing Croatians, which falls on the tragic end of the spectrum. Closer to home, we wanted to understand how others were making it while we just were treading water, which felt more disheartening than anything, along with a whole host of other happenings large and small that made no sense. I found myself sitting in a cramped upstairs mezzanine with dowdy women while their men got preferential orchestra seating and the right to talk and to carry the Torah. They were a little standoffish because I wasn't Jewish. Seth nearly moved into the place before we met, so they probably saw me as the *shiksa* who lured him from the faith. So, the God of that place turned out to be a misogynist and a bigot.

It's as if I've been on a spiritual Grand Tour, with nothing to show for it other than a persistent sense of being had, so sure that the hidden coin was under one cup and then another until I had nothing left to play with.

But I'm not like this either, not like these women who surround me, chewed up and spit out by drunk husbands. Or heartbroken after having spent their wombs and their best years on children who now lie to them and steal from them. Kids who fly in the face of all the hopes once held when today's sullen, tattooed drug addicts were rosy newborns in pink and blue caps, little blank slates empty of everything but their mothers' dreams. I feel sorry for them. From my safer, child-less vantage point, it's easy to be magnanimous and wish them well on their search for something to help them make sense of what doesn't—although I still don't quite get what all the angst is about. I've always thought that people set themselves up for disappointment by having kids, and this belief is in the process of confirmation as I become inter-twined with Jake and his children.

Besides all that: If God is Love, then I've got God—because I've found Love. Love that is all-encompassing from a real, flesh-and-blood man who tends me like a garden with his devotion to my body and spirit, shaking open long buried and dormant seeds of possibility. I am feeling, pulsing, thrumming, pushing up through cold, hard soil toward the sun, watered by deep, wet kisses, this pleasing new growth gently scaffolded by hands that know how to love and a heart that knows how to touch. Jake is in me and with me, and Jake is mine.

That love, for want of anything else, has become my Higher Power. And, finally, it's enough.

FORTY-FIVE

We're on the road in the sad, soft light of an early September morning. I feel as if I'm in the belly of a dolphin, Jake's blue BMW with the white leather interior gliding through the shimmer of dawn, bearing me off to the safety and comfort of Something New and Different.

Jake finally got the call in late August on a stifling afternoon as we lay by the pool in our complex. That was one of the few things we could do for free outside our four walls. Our stomachs had been roiling for weeks with the strain of Jake's unemployment. We had our summer of love, followed by our summer of nesting and then, apparently, a summer of stress.

So now we're en route to Vegas, where Jake will begin work on a television show of indefinite duration. We'll be living at the Tropicana on the production company's dime, which is my idea of heaven. Not necessarily the Tropicana, but hotel living in general, where I don't have to worry about cooking, cleaning, making beds or picking up towels. Or about Anne and the kids. It'll be just Jake and me, two little peas in a pod, as we often refer to ourselves. A space that, if not strictly ours, will at least contain strictly us.

The day before we leave is Jeannie's twenty-first birthday. We all sit in the bar of a local chain restaurant, audience to a girl now legally doing what she's already been doing excessively for years. A beer sampler is brought to the table, except it seems like all the glasses aren't samplers but full-size—the bar's welcome into full adulthood in the eyes of the law. Anne and her boyfriend, Rob, are here with Jake and me. I watch them all watching her, wondering what they think of this little girl, brassy and annoying in her overconfidence that masks something else.

I wonder if Jake sees Anne all over again when she was young and just starting to discover the Long Island Iced Teas that she eventually chose over their marriage. And Anne herself, sitting there with a straw jutting up from her plain iced tea toward grim lips pressed together. All edges and lines, she seems neither happy nor sad nor sentimental about her baby girl's milestone. Maybe she wants to escape having to watch the start of another sad repetitive cycle of family history and instead longs for the sanctuary of her home where she can drink her fully loaded iced teas in private while Rob watches the golf channel.

I give Jeannie her birthday gift just before the beer arrives. Not momentous timing, but it won't get any better once the drinking starts. I present her with the blue velvet box containing the gold and diamond necklace and matching earrings that my father and Honey had given me for my own twenty-first birthday. It feels like an odd thing to do in a bar, or even at all. I had envisioned a cozy tête-à-tête over tea and cake, something girly and meaningful, and that I'd have the appropriate feelings to match. But I don't. I feel only as if I'm among strangers, passing along some fussy jewelry that I had never worn because it wasn't me. It feels equally alien to sit as a parental figure of sorts, silently watching the official beginning of what might very well turn out to be a sorrowful story.

And now, the morning after, I'm on the I-15 to Vegas, zipping away from the awkward, the alien and the tragic. Away, again, from my father's law firm, which I intend to be for the last time. I had become the degreed beck-and-call girl to yet another of his partners, a stubby, sausage-fingered woman who proved to be both unpleasant and demanding. It had been extremely satisfying to inform her, with three days' notice, that I would be leaving the office for an indefinite period and then witness her blustering about who would handle this or that in my absence. My father, used to my vagaries by now and also softened by his regard for Jake and the happiness I've finally found with him, wished me well and this time seemed to mean it.

I'm also escaping the triumvirate of Anne, Jeannie and Mark, and the day-to-day constellation of our lives around them. We're all like constantly shifting pieces of a complex puzzle. I bit off more than I could chew, at least when thinking that my transition from girlfriend to wife and stepmom would be altogether easy or pleasant. There have been rifts that only widened when I realized that I neither could nor wanted to match Jake or Jeannie bong hit for bong hit, or sanction Mark's journey down that same path. Jake loves me completely, whether I smoke or not, whether I approve of his doing so or not. The same may not necessarily be true for the kids.

The desert highway stretches before us in the morning sun. It cuts a straight and pleasing line through dead terrain and lifeless scrub. In the middle of all that is a city that buzzes with life, lights, come-hither ads and every form of sensory pleasure and vice possible. We'll be in the thick of it for months or more, with only intermittent hiatus weeks at home. Jeannie will mind the condo and the cats for the time being, and Mark will continue to run the gauntlet of high school. Anne will send incessant worried-mom texts that after 5:00 pm morph into drunken monologues that veer from angry to maudlin and back again.

We arrive at the hotel and are assaulted by a cacophony—people wandering the casino floor in various states of excitement and/or drunkenness, machines belting out their robotic victory tunes, brides-to-be advertising their status with tiaras and sashes, flanked by miniskirted entourages. I sit at a penny slot machine and stare at the jewel-themed display. Diamonds, rubies and emeralds invite me to stick a bill into the slot and try my luck. So I do. I put in a dollar, and feeling optimistic, bet a hundred credits. Nothing.

I sit for quite a while. There's been some confusion or miscommunication, which I'm learning is usual when Jake and I travel together. This is the flip side of marriage to a pothead, the yang of languorous thinking and planning to the yin of languorous loving. Jake had assumed our room was being paid for, but the production company had hired him on as a local, which meant he'd be responsible for all travel expenses. Eventually, they iron it all out in Jake's favor. My sweet husband always manages, somehow.

We finally settle in a room on the twentieth floor overlooking The Strip. I'm excited, relieved, free. We love each other in the big king bed with fresh sheets that will be changed daily. And then, after Jake falls asleep, sated by the drive, the unpacking and the sex, I lie on my side looking out the window. The MGM Grand across the street beams its eternal emerald light into our room, bathing it and us in an eerie green glow.

In the morning, Jake will go to work via elevator down to the grand ballroom where the show is taped. I wonder what exactly I'll do. I've quit my job to follow my love, and so I currently have no income. Jake doesn't care; he just wants me with him.

Finding myself unable to sleep my first night in this insomniac city, I wander over to the window and look down at the boulevard. It's just after Labor Day; a thinned-out tourist crowd trudges the Strip by night with their grain liquor frozen drinks and shopping bags from the M&M'S Store. It seems that nothing ever closes here.

I watch the crowd and wonder what I'll do besides walk the Strip in a trance. Maybe I'll write. Maybe I'll sit by the pool. Maybe I'll play penny slots while tired cocktail waitresses in ill-fitting polyester short-shorts bring me free rum and Diet Coke. I'm hesitant to do anything that costs money that I'm not making, mindful that a sizeable chunk of Jake's take-home pay goes toward alimony and child support.

I stand for a long time at the window, content as I always am to observe remotely. I watch people scurrying up and down the boulevard like ants in shorts and tank tops, industrious in their pursuit of stimulation. And then out at the lights scattered beyond the Strip, the bedroom community of Summerlin and beyond that the darkness which I know to be the mountains of Red Rock Canyon rising in the distance. And then up at the blankness of the desert night sky, its stars obliterated by the artifice of city lights.

FORTY-SIX

Mark doesn't make eye contact anymore—at least not when I ask him the loaded questions, like who he's hanging out with, why he's so tired all the time and why his eyes are always so red.

"I'm with people."

"I stay up late at night."

"It's my allergies."

And then he's gone, upstairs to his room with the door closed, always closed, or out the front door to meet his *people*.

Just two years ago, he was bright and sharp and open and looked forward to our Burger King, candy and movie nights, followed by endless *Guitar Hero* tournaments when Jake worked late. He loved being by my side then, my devoted shadow.

Now we're mainly in Vegas, where Jake has a job that he needs to hang onto. When Mark comes down to spend the night while we're at home, he has no interest in burger and movie nights. Instead, he asks me to drop him off at the mall—in the parking lot far from his fellow teenagers so that no one will see him with me. Are his friends supposed to assume that he just materialized there? And then I pick him up at ten, again at a safe distance.

I wonder if he's upset that his dad and I aren't around much.

I wonder if I should be making the trip home alone every weekend so that Mark can get a reprieve from his mother, and I can nurse us back to how we were.

On New Year's Day, during our holiday break at home, I search Mark's backpack while he's in the shower and find a prescription pill bottle. I note the irony of the child-proof cap as I wrestle with it, finally getting it open and seeing the weed inside.

I sit downstairs at the dining room table with the bottle in front of me, spinning it around. I had thought it was enough that I don't much drink, that I keep an ordered home, and that I walk a resolute and straight path amidst the chaos of Jake and Anne and Jeannie's habits. I know that once Mark starts, there might not be anyone else around who can make him stop.

When Mark comes down and sees me with the weed, he smiles, embarrassed. I had expected anger that I'd intruded or denial that it's his, but instead, he seems relieved to have been exposed.

"I love it," he confesses. "The first time, it was like a lightbulb went on. I saw how things really were, and they didn't bug me. I can eat. I can deal with Mom. I have friends now because I'm with the stoners."

I didn't expect to hear truth spurt out like hot water from a pent-up geyser, more words in one minute than he's spoken in the five months we've been away. It makes sense, and it's also what his father says about weed, plus or minus a few words. But I don't know where, on this awkward pseudo-parenting spectrum, understanding should end, and consequences begin.

We sit there together, awaiting Jake's imminent return from his golf game. The pill bottle sits between us, at once a fifteen-year-old's new best friend and a potential doomsday device.

Jake arrives, glances at us and heads directly upstairs to our bedroom. I don't know how he does that deeply dissatisfying thing where he somehow registers what's going on without looking directly at anyone or anything.

Leaving Mark at the table, I follow my husband upstairs.

"I found weed in his backpack. I think you need to talk to him about it."

"I don't want to discuss it." Jake keeps his back to me as he drops change on the bedside table.

"With him? Or with me?"

"I don't want to discuss it." He avoids looking at me as he goes back downstairs, and I hear him leave the house. I drive Mark up the hill to his Mom's because he has plans with friends. Neither of us says anything on the ride there; Jake's abrupt departure took the wind from us so that we're adrift and disconnected once again. I give the weed back to him as he exits the car. If I keep it, he'll just get it from somewhere else.

When Jake comes home hours later, I'm in bed watching television. I don't ask where he went or why, and he doesn't tell me; we seem tacitly to have agreed that what happened today will be dealt with, if it's dealt with, between father and son. How we are together right now feels heavy and uncomfortable, and words can't provide relief because he won't speak them. Instead, we use our bodies to find our way back to each other.

Minutes or maybe hours later, we awaken, disoriented. Jake unspools himself from me to grope for his phone.

"What is it, Anne?" Long silence.

"Where is he?" Short silence.

"I'm leaving now." Jake fumbles in the dark for his clothes and tells me he's going to the hospital. Mark and two of his friends are there after having intentionally consumed an entire package of Benadryl between them. Jake doesn't ask me to come along, and I don't offer.

I lie awake, the predawn darkness heavy with a silence that feels accusatory. I picture Jake and Anne and Rob and Jeannie at the hospital, hovering over a hallucinating Mark who, at least according to Dr. Google, may also be having seizures. They are there. I am not.

I fall asleep or sort of fall asleep and wake up mid-morning. I glance at my phone; there's been no call or text.

I wander downstairs, and on the dining room table where I had sat last night with Mark and his weed, I find two dozen yellow roses in a beribboned, cut-glass vase alongside a bouquet of birthday balloons. Jake must have brought them home before coming up to bed last night.

Next to the flowers is a birthday card that features two cartoon dogs riding together on a roller coaster.

To my wife
My partner in fun
Another birthday—what a year
It's been a fun-filled ride

Monster hills and loop-de-loops
We've faced 'em side by side…

Through ups and downs and turnarounds,
You know what's always true?

I couldn't be more glad to share
This thrilling life with YOU!

Happy Birthday!

I try hard to will my heart to melt at my husband's thoughtfulness. He wanted to give me a happy birthday; it's not his fault it isn't turning out that way.

It's not?

I try hard to will myself to go to the hospital or at least call Jake to find out how my stepson is. Mark could be dead for all I know.

And what if he is?

I sit down among the balloons and flowers, feeling mocked by the empty chair across from me. I wonder how it is that I wound up here, adrift in a family not of my making and ashamed of my apparent inability to navigate even the basics of caring for them.

I should call my sponsor, but I don't want to. For a couple of years now, I've sat staunchly alone in the bleachers of the Program, high above the real work while Mark sits in the adjacent teen meeting and finds comfort among his similarly afflicted peers, the kids with the parents who booze or blaze or shoot up. That was my job, I thought, to fuss over and fix or at least de-clutter my love and his life.

A month ago, I let someone else in when I came to the grudging realization that the mess I thought I could leave when we left for Vegas never left me. Jake was still high all the time, Jeannie still called multiple times per day with her incessant drama, and half of Jake's paycheck still went to Anne for alimony and child support. My head still spun, surrounded by slot machines and souvenir stores instead of soccer moms and sport utility vehicles. Geography made no difference.

When I got sick of thinking about it all, l called my sponsor so I could start talking about it all. Or at least some of it.

"Don't just do something. Sit there. He'll call when there's something to report and when he does, all you need to do is be kind." This is what she says when I do call her. And that whatever happens, I will be all right. It's a short conversation.

I find that I crave the sun, and so I walk outside, a little way down the path that leads from our home. I sit at the top of the steep concrete staircase that leads down to the street.

Two years ago, just before my marriage, I sat here with Jake and Mark on a muggy summer night, watching a rare electrical storm traverse the ridges of the hills across from us. My arms around them, I felt as sharp and kinetic as the brilliant forks dancing before me. My fiancé and his boy leaned into me, and I into them—a new little family pulsing with love and promise. We all felt that and felt ourselves feeling it. Later that night, in bed with Jake, I wrapped myself around him and felt a spasm of happiness so acute and alien that it frightened me.

I notice I'm holding a balloon that I don't remember taking from the house, a yellow happy face bobbing in the crisp January wind.

I don't want to let go of this sweet balloon, part of Jake's gift; I think I should hold onto it for a while. The string jerks against my fingers, the helium urging its host toward the sky. For a moment, I feel as if I'm restraining a leashed, restless animal.

By accident or not, the string slips from my hand. The happy face bobs and smiles as it ascends into the sun. I watch as it recedes from me, becoming a tiny dot, until my eyes smart from the effort of looking.

Standing up, I turn toward the home I created and the life that tethers me to it.

FORTY-SEVEN

Why are all these people in my house? A moving mosaic of Jake's relatives fills our home in celebration of his birthday.

Fifty-four isn't a milestone. But we've only been married for a little under three years, so I still feel the need to bring it, to be the perky, confident hostess entertaining my husband's well-to-do cousin Nana from Long Island as well as his mother, who lives in senior housing nearby. Jake's ex-wife Anne is here too, a fixture at any family gathering even when, strictly speaking, they're not really her family anymore. I've come to expect her presence at these events regardless of whether she's invited. At least she isn't drinking—yet.

I feel myself start to fray at the edges as the women crowd the small kitchen, offering well-meant suggestions and assistance with the middle eastern birthday meal I'm preparing at home to be economical. It hasn't been a pleasant year. Jake's been laid off twice in two years; whether it has to do with his constant pot smoking or the ever-shifting loyalties within the television production world, I don't know. He's found a day of work here and there, subbing for an absent stage manager or associate director; that and unemployment are keeping us afloat, barely.

My own career aspirations are nonexistent. The perfect excuse to abort my second attempt at lawyering alongside my father came along when Jake got hired for a long-term job in Vegas a year after we married. What new wife lets her husband loose in Vegas while she languishes in an office in another state? Not this one, although really it wasn't him I was worried about. It was me. Or, to be more accurate, my penchant for chaining myself to the wrong thing. I should have realized after my first go-round with the practice of law, and after the costly consequences of quitting, that I'm not a head-before-heart kind of girl, at least in the way that's necessary to get and keep a full-time, respectable job.

So, in keeping with that, I've just started teaching Pilates, which is kind of ironic because the concept of rows of barefoot, Lululemon-clad women lying on reformers in Westlake Village is somewhat at odds with the unpolished life that Jake and I have fallen into together. I don't buy hundred-dollar leggings these days, and Jake would sooner fly to Mars as waste money taking us to some overpriced wine bar or gastro-whatever.

Maybe it's the whirlwind of divorce from Seth followed immediately by my all-consuming romance with Jake. Or the fact that I've been going through a pretty gnarly early menopause for the past three years. But I feel out of the loop. I don't know what's going on "out there." Movies, music, television, the news—I'm not dialed into any of it. The clients at the Pilates studio, where pop music is always playing on Pandora, talk about Adele or Bruno Mars, or the royal wedding between Prince William and Kate Middleton, and all I can think is: *What? Who?* And that feels strange because I used to know. And care.

A similar disconnect simmers tonight. I'm embarrassed, even though I'm smiling and doing my best to channel my mother's effortless social effervescence. We don't even have a trash can in our small kitchen—just a garbage bag that we hang by its plastic drawstrings from one of the cabinet drawer handles. Cousin Nana lives in a mansion on Long Island. When Jake and I visited her family a year after we married, dazed, broke and more than a little stressed out after his first layoff, we would stumble down their spiral staircase each morning to find the granite kitchen center island laden with a catered deli breakfast, and then a lavish lunch a couple of hours later. Come evening, we'd find ourselves at some expensive steakhouse for dinner, still struggling to digest the day's previous offerings.

Nana looks at me with an exaggerated, raised-eyebrow expression, when Anne asks me to refrigerate the elaborate birthday cake she baked for Jake. *Why is she even here,* Nana stage-whispers. I shrug and just keep smiling, even though I imagine that I must look like a crazed lunatic by now. Silent smiling is an easy alternative to figuring out a proper response

Yeah, it *is* odd to have an ex-wife orbiting me with a persistence that would be flattering if it wasn't so *weird*. She's sweet, sending cards and candy bags on holidays and cakes for birthdays, but she's also sort of desperate in her constant angling for inclusion. I eventually learned to ignore the post-5:00 pm drunk dialing and loopy texting.

I step up my determined bustle in the kitchen, putting water on to boil for the rice and then chopping parsley and onion for the tabouli. I wonder whether it's possible to run toward something at the same time as fleeing something else—or whether it even matters since all of it's just a form of running anyway.

As I run with my love and his kids and the eventual promise of a secure, pension-funded retirement, I dodge defaulted student loans that have metastasized into six-figure debt, as well as a tax mess from my first marriage. Of course, true love can't save me from myself. But at least I'm sweating less about my messy financial misdeeds.

Four years ago, I ran toward this life that thrummed and buzzed like a hillside awakening into spring. Tall, untamed grasses to lose myself in, mustard flowers and blue lupine growing wild. Occasional thorny ceanothus plants or yellow jackets in the mix added a little challenge to keep me on my toes. Mad love, sexual love, awakened a fierce and unapologetic female energy that had lain dormant for years. Kids to guide. Clattering in the kitchen, making salad and potatoes to compliment Jake's flawless barbecue. Boisterous *Guitar Hero* tournaments on Friday nights. An eighth-grade boy who refused to shower and wanted to stay up all night glued to his X-box. A barely-out-of-her-teens girl with perpetual "frenemy" and boy *du jour* dramas. All of it intense, unpredictable and constant. A life I had fantasized about not so long ago while I sat home alone watching romantic comedies while Seth placated me with increasingly implausible excuses for his extended absences.

Summertime now. The hillsides have browned under an intense sun that arcs high and lingers on its journey. The mustard flowers withered weeks ago, leaving in their wake tall, dry grasses where coyotes lie in wait, hoping to waylay an unwary rabbit. I hear them at night, the distant, frenzied yipping that I imagine signals a kill. Just to make sure, I feel around to Jake's side of the bed when that happens to make sure both our cats are safe and accounted for.

The birthday party has disbanded. The dishwasher whirs, a clean stovetop gleams beneath the light of the microwave, and the refrigerator is filled with leftover rice pilaf and the remainder of the birthday cake. Jake has trundled upstairs, there to slide into his nightly weed-induced slumber.

He has left me, so I slip out for a night wander. Up and down the residential streets of our neighborhood, ambling the capillaries that branch up and off the main suburban boulevard, connecting with one another or just abbreviating into cul-de-sacs punctuated by driveway basketball hoops.

I take comfort in the silence of the streets and the darkness that separates me from the people inside the homes I pass, eating or playing or laughing or fighting in the lighted rooms and sleeping or crying or dying in the darker recesses. I'm shrouded, invisibly wandering alongside the manicured lawns and flower beds tended in the daytime by men in wide-brimmed hats. The gardeners dig and pull and plant, creating rows of vibrant flowers encircled by tidy brick borders and dewy lawns. The houses and yards all back up against dried-out summer hillsides; the gardeners must remain ever vigilant against the encroaching bushy, disorderly chaparral that yearns to take back its territory.

My favorite street has houses on only one side. There is nothing but hill on the other side, above a retaining wall and culverts that have been taken over by wild rosemary. When I walk that street, I stay on the hill side of it so I can strip the leaves off a small branch. I crumble them between my fingers, releasing their aroma. I cup my palm around my nose and inhale.

Dried grasses rustle on the hillside, stirred by a tepid breeze. Wind chimes tinkle from someone's yard across the street. I spy a rabbit, still and wary. It blends in with the brown scrub, invisible but for the white underside of its tail that flashes briefly as it darts away. The day's heat still rises from the ground, wrapped in smells of sage, rosemary and earth. Even though I'm starting to sweat a little and it's cooler across the street where timed sprinklers make sure that lawns remain lush and that green belts stay green, I stick to the wild side.

Somewhere above me, a coyote bays into the musky night. I feel an urge to dash up the hill toward that sound, to find out whether she's calling her mate or attempting to lure some unsuspecting dog to its death. I've heard they do that.

Instead, I turn toward home to take my place in bed alongside my husband and the cats who huddle close and comforting beside us.

FORTY-EIGHT

They're playing that one song over and over again as family and friends gather in the bleachers to watch Oak Park High School's Class of 2012 graduate. I sit on the hard metal bench, uncomfortable in a dress that feels too tight, alongside Jake, Jeannie, Anne and Rob. When I lean over to ask her, Jeannie informs me that the song is by a pop group called f.u.n. It stopped sounding fun several repetitions ago, but I don't say that.

We crane our necks and shade our eyes, looking for my stepson Mark among the sea of blue-robed, soon-to-be graduates milling around at the edge of the football field, waiting for the ceremony to begin. Anne spots him and stands up, waving and yelling. A jumbo screen above the stage runs a slideshow of the year's happy highlights—homecoming, senior retreat, prom night—interspersed with pictures of the kids as babies. It all looks so flawlessly produced.

The song starts again, blaring from the loudspeakers. I suppose that's the sort of anthem they're obliged to play on a milestone occasion like tonight—one that reflects infinite optimism that this year's crop of high school graduates is going to rush out and change everything for the better, bounding out of this night and into perfectly self-actualized lives.

I think of the years following my own high school graduation. Shot out like a pinball at seventeen, I bounced over the course of five years between Santa Barbara, Boston, Los Angeles, Maryland and London before finally settling in L.A. I didn't set the world on fire; I burned bright, for a little while, until getting snuffed out by time, circumstance and a fickle nature that stubbornly persisted in not staying any particular course. They say Mark's generation, with its smartphones, texting and strange, abbreviated conversations, is the height of instant gratification-driven attentional deficit. But I was no different. Even though phones were stuck into walls and there were no distractions other than books, music and a handful of television channels, I still couldn't manage to hold on to any one experience for long before discarding it and flitting off to the next.

Will it be different for Mark? He isn't going to school three thousand miles away; he's driving over the hill to a local community college. From there, who knows? But this is good for him, I think—a slower start out the gate. He doesn't have to set the world on fire or burn brighter than the sun right now. Or ever. Maybe that will give him a chance, even though I see the odds as stacked against him because of who he came from, disloyal to Jake as that thought is. Even so, I hope he will choose some things more wisely than his parents or I did.

I hear the opening strains of *Pomp and Circumstance*. The kids start their slow procession across the field to their seats. There are remarks by the principal, various faculty and by the valedictorian. All of them exhorting this year's class to get out there and make a difference.

The ceremony settles into a rhythmic drone of individual names being named and diplomas being awarded. My attention wanders. I look at the other families sitting in the stands and wonder about the stories that bind them. There are, I'm sure, a fair number of stepparents in the bunch. While I feel qualified to be sitting here, I don't share Anne's fevered obsession with her son. But I'm pleased and proud to have watched Mark navigate his teenage years successfully enough to emerge a tentative but solid young adult—at least in the ways he's chosen to show us after a couple of stumbles. I know there are shadows, too. I hope he eventually finds the courage to examine them.

I can make these assessments, all high-up and wise, because my own life has a settledness to it that makes me think, at age forty-eight, that I finally, maybe, have the adult thing down. I'm teaching enough to contribute to the running of our household, and Jake has kept a steady gig that keeps us in our condo and our cars in the garage. Mark spends his weekends with us and has a part-time job which he'll continue when he starts college in the fall. Jeannie works for a bank that likes and promotes her. The boyfriends she allows us to meet now seem less alarming than they used to.

The wild, carefree love I bounded into has gelled into contentment. There are cracks, to be sure; the pot smoking and drinking continue unabated, but all that somehow manages to live at the periphery of our cozy tableau. Jake will partially retire in a couple of years, and we'll be able to coast into a future of travel and home improvement.

I find myself in this moment, this *now*, and not standing outside of it anymore. Awkward and uncomfortable as it still feels, I'm somehow able to manage as a second wife, a pseudo-mom, and a participant in the social contract of suburbia where I get to watch a boy I've grown to love grow up and then grow out of here.

The ceremony below me ends, and three hundred blue mortarboards shoot up into the air.

FORTY-NINE

Day One

A rough start to my pre-fiftieth birthday trip
The inn is locked when we arrive
And Jake loses it
because he's already frazzled
from work and from putting on Thanksgiving
and from talking himself into readiness for the headache
that is modern travel
I don't do well with rage
although I can handle it
But not without the sacrifice
of sanity for discombobulation
Which happens when I go a long time
without asking myself
How *you* doin'?

Day Two

Decompression begins
Finally
There isn't much that rum punch won't ease
Especially when served by people
who don't know and probably don't care
about the silly things that plague the minds

of non-islanders
The band plays on
And the waves roll in
And the clouds float by
And we somehow make it to our room
And pass out
And after that…
The start of renewal

Day Three

I'm tempted to think of all my tropical experiences
Tahiti
Fiji
Maui
Kauai
And a little Mazatlán and Puerto Vallarta
thrown in between
And now Anguilla
Why must I categorize,
compare and contrast?
There is no place like this right now
Where my feet are
So that's all that matters
And the rum in front of me
And the sunset behind me
And the conch chowder on its way
So who cares about South Pacific
versus the Caribbean
versus Mexico
Or then
versus now
It's all good

Day Four

I awaken to rain
and hope for lightning
It comes, but not nearly as frequently
As I'd like
Stranger as I am in a familiar land
of palms and turquoise
and indifferent time
that neither passes nor stands still
and won't be pushed
Much as I try

Day Five

It's still cloudy after last night's rain
We tell ourselves *it will pass*
Although I'm not sure why we need that to be so
There's construction going on anyway
Jackhammers that drown out the surf
A waiter sings and cleans
next to us
As we sit in a restaurant
that hasn't yet opened
And dig our toes into sand
that until a minute ago
Had no footprints

Day Six

I see a chicken and a goat
Actually, a few of each
in overgrown, verdant yards
The rain slants into us

and a toothless, wizened man
invites us in from the rain
I've had a few tropical drinks
mind you
And their sugary sharp nectar rushes through me
and mixes with sweaty, salty sea air
so that I feel a sort of ecstasy
where all the islands and their people
seem the same
And all the world, in fact,
is a sweet paradise
when I run through the rain
straight into the milky pearl water

Day Seven

I walk out onto the patio naked
and cast furtive glances at the driveway
In case the maid has arrived
The ocean still looks pissed off and the wind is searing
Why didn't we just go to Kauai instead?
But I wanted it to be *different* this year
So maybe it's not about calm waters
or a sunny day
Or about doing *it* better
whatever *it* is.
I promise
No Facebook
No Likes
No Comments

Day Eight

The rain shoves off across the sea
so we turn our faces to the sun

and resume holiday making
Vindicated again.
The wind still howls, though,
and makes the screen clatter and the door thump
A rooster Somewhere Over There
doesn't know the time
and so we listen to his inopportune shrieks
Reminding us that time
is just a mental construct
anyway

Day Nine

The perfect storm I seek finds me
on another beach in another bay on another day
A glossy bold rooster eats fries from my hand
and we lie in a cove where I find a necklace
and a tank top
Random but delightful.
I meet some women from New York
who bring me just enough conversation
We paddle about in the blue swells
and discuss love.
Dear husband sits on a berm
because he thinks we may get swept away
Well, I certainly do
And it's awesome.

Day Ten

It's going to end soon, this
I want to say *too bad, I've just gotten settled*
But that feels like something everyone says at vacation's end
So I'll just say that I've recovered a little me-ness
and gotten rid of a little meanness

or just nourished something that only grows
in leisure, sun and sand
And I hope this hothouse variety blooms
for at least the plane ride home

Day Eleven

We walk The Point at sunset, hesitant to leave the beach
He puts some sand in plastic bottles, and I collect shells
Something to remember it by….
But we can't take those things on the plane
and they confiscate the hot sauce we bought
So now all I have is a conch shell bracelet
the color of the water we swam in
And a t-shirt from the bar
where we sat, breathless and sandy
Ruddy-faced drinkers of sun
And warmed by rum

Day Twelve

The flight is delayed
for several hours
We passengers sit slumped in cracked black seats
in a holding pattern
Sunburned faces glum
This isn't how we wanted it to end
I can see a sliver of ocean outside the terminal
and a palm tree
And I think of last night's sunset
I like who I was, then

FIFTY

Adecade ago today, I wandered Paris, a disoriented foreigner suspended in the murk of turning forty.

How is it that now I'm fifty?

Faces surround me in an outdoor grotto at the top of Topanga
Canyon, at a restaurant called Inn of the Seventh Ray. I've never
come here before but have always wanted to, so Jake, ever my beloved
wish-fulfiller, organizes a surprise birthday brunch for me.

My family and I pick at the gourmet bird food that is the specialty
of this place. They're all good sports for showing up; early January is a
time for feeling bloated, hungover, broke and just generally over it in
terms of socializing. For that reason, I've always insisted that no one
ever throw me a birthday party. It's just too painful to watch all the
trying.

This has been a protracted milestone celebration. First, the trip to
Anguilla after Thanksgiving, then Vegas for my actual birthday a few
days ago, and now this. Every step of the way, Jake has treated, pam-
pered and gifted me. Queen, not for a day but a good six weeks at least.

I don't feel or look particularly great today, the lingering effects of
an inconvenient and nasty flu I acquired just after Christmas. I'm not
going to let it spoil things, so I don't allow Jake to cancel the Vegas trip
or my birthday dinner at the restaurant atop the hotel. I dutifully make
it through the pan-seared scallops and pistachio-crusted lamb loin *bor-
delaise* before collapsing, exhausted, back in our room.

Still tired from the trip, I'm not in the mood for brunch today, but
drag myself out of bed and into the shower because Jake insists that his
mother wants to celebrate me.

And then I walk into the restaurant and see my mother-in-law and then my stepkids, Jeannie and Mark. Then my mother, her third husband John, my father, his third wife Barbara and her son, my brother Greg, his third wife Hayley, Greg's son Harrison that he had with the wife before Hayley, and my half-brother Christopher.

And Sofia, the scourge of my girlhood who had suddenly and without explanation turned on me with her chewed-up hair and manic eyes, the woman that, with the blind instinct of a prey animal, I had learned to avoid. My mother told me when I was young that Sofia had fled to our home to escape a bad boyfriend, and then when I was older that Sofia's lover was actually a rapist who also happened to be her father. This information allows me space for compassion, although that compassion sleeps uneasily alongside the more forward-leaning resentment that my childhood tormentor somehow is allowed to remain an adjunct family member. Especially here today. That I've found and maintained the connections responsible for this celebration is not because of her brand of care but in spite of it.

I find myself in the center of a circle where everyone yells *Surprise!* I stand there uncertainly, as always, not quite sure how to receive a celebration of myself. I focus instead on my nephew Harrison, who jolts me into the moment, with his six-year-old inability to be anything other than present. I'm then able to break out of that circle, careening with him down the pebbled pathways of the restaurant's herb garden before we all sit down to eat.

The art of aging well. That's what the new thing is now, probably because most of the country's population is getting old and the elders want to be at the forefront of that just like they were at the forefront of sex, drugs and rock 'n' roll.

They tell me to eat this and not that, to push and stretch and contort my body in varying but precise order of movements in yoga, spinning or HIIT regimens that I espouse to my fitness clients before casting them off in favor of the next thing.

And then there are all the social media sayings and slogans intended to make the inexorable march toward mortality feel somewhat manageable. Like, *Bloom Where You're Planted.* Purple cursive writing on a pink background. One of the zillion Facebook directives I scroll through daily, but that's the one that comes to mind as I look around at the faces bent over their brown rice breakfast bowls and gluten-free scones.

Suspension is something I've finally given up in favor of rootedness because not many can bloom while suspended. It doesn't come naturally to me, this business of hunkering down among people who are actually paying attention. But I do it. I take root for Jake, his children and the network of parents and stepparents, full-blood and half-blood and step-siblings and friends that curl around the years like the tendrils of my white jasmine on its trellis. I'm now a part of something larger than myself that somehow keeps me staying the course, although the conditions are not always ideal or even easy.

Can a human being blossom in spite of themselves? The things I see growing in the pavement cracks on sidewalks are just weeds, ordinary unbidden things that flourish with no care or intention. And then I look around at the lushness surrounding my family at my birthday brunch—hothouse flowers, vine-canopied archways, and well-manicured fruit-bearing trees studded with strategically placed ponds and waterfalls. Not just intended but planned, landscaped and cared for with big-budget expertise and an eye for studied, casual elegance.

My own planting falls somewhere in between the accidental and the orchestrated. I know I have chosen, not always with wisdom or expertise, but I've landed in a more or less indigenous zone, learning to surround myself more or less with what grows naturally. In my actual little plot, I grow geraniums, beloved by my mother, who no doubt values their stubborn insistence on thriving despite spotty tending. Also, succulents—jade and ice plant and donkey tail plucked from behind the condo complex swimming pool or from the bushes next to the staircase leading down to the street. I re-pot the cuttings, arranging all of it in ways that please me but undoubtedly look haphazard to others.

Mismatched pots sitting in corners and teetering on railings. No planning. Hardy greenery in funky containers—life that tolerates heat, drought and poor soil, having been yanked from somewhere else by a hopeful but realistic woman with empty window boxes to fill.

FIFTY-ONE

I don't want any more pets. It gets harder every time I have to comfort a sick, frightened creature as the vet administers the lethal cocktail.

I think of the two blue starfish I long ago shepherded across a Fijian reef with childish concentration, intent on bending them to my will. But that initial undertaking of pet ownership, despite its rapid and upsetting end, did not dissuade me.

This is the unmanageability of love, of attachment. Jake and I holding our big boy, the black cat with a white spot on his right paw, who trembles in fear and pain between us as we stare at each other with tear-glossed faces. Talking to Whiskey in reassuring, parental voices, telling him he's going to feel well again and that he's going to be reunited with his original mommy, Aunt Luisa.

The thing is, I don't *know* that. I used to, before a glut of actual death challenged my certainty. Aunt Luisa, Daddy Landon, my brother Mikey, my grandparents—all of them departed without a whisper of where they were going, there to remain without providing any follow-up information. Once I thought I had a visitation from Papa, his presence so vivid that I awoke to the smell of wood, an olfactory calling card from a man of few words who loved to work with his hands. Sadly, I know my own mind and its propensity to play tricks on its gullible, needy host. So now I hesitate to cling to such ephemeral evidence of a world beyond this.

"They're just dumb creatures. They rely on us to do the right thing." Jake said this when we inherited the black cat, Whiskey, and his tuxedo-coated sister, Charlie, from Aunt Luisa after she suddenly and unexpectedly died in her sleep, which is what we felt we had to do since there was no other provision for their care.

The two cats huddled in our closet for a week, tormenting us. It was impossible to avoid hearing, in their piteous, nonstop meowing, grief for their home and the woman who doted on them, and impossible to do anything about it but wait until they decided to trust us to do right by them.

This is the unmanageability of love, of attachment.

And now I'm gutted by the death of the gentle black cat whose trust and love I eventually did win. I wear his tag on a chain around my neck. I lie in bed at night craving the reassuring nightly protocol of his silent, balletic leap onto the bed followed by a walk in two circles followed by a contented settling down, the soft plush of his backside pressing against my cheek. Jake, usually the emotional one, holds me when I awaken suddenly and randomly, finding myself sobbing and gasping. That an animal is what breaches the imposing levee around my heart is embarrassing. I wish I could carry on this way when I lose people.

The pain eventually ebbs over the weeks that follow. I emerge from the trance of it to realize that I've become tribe-less. My passion for my husband, and his for me, simmers always. My life is with him and, to a lesser extent, his children. But they're not my tribe, so I find myself tiptoeing away more often than I should, leaving them to the sort of parallel play I've learned is a hallmark of stoners. I'm the classic dog-in-a-manger. I don't want the disjointed conversation, the red eyes, the perfect presence during long stretches of nothing, but I don't want them to have it, either.

We've been a family for seven years. Perhaps we all feel the itch of that. Shrugging and scratching sometimes at what doesn't always fit. Jeannie seeing me now more or less as an inconvenience, diverting her father's attention and largesse away from her. I'm a police figure in Mark's eyes now that I've banned weed in the house—even though I can't control who smokes it elsewhere or with whom. And my beloved Jake, desperately trying and failing at being all things to all of us. His motto is that the *right* thing is the *nice* thing. He undoubtedly came up with that before finding himself living alongside people harboring extremely different definitions of both those words.

This is the unmanageability of love, of attachment.

I make a date with my sponsor, who I've not spoken to in weeks or months—I can't remember. She'll no doubt tell me something necessary that I don't want to hear. Probably about the impossibility of managing love and attachment.

Eventually, I go to the animal shelter and adopt a black boy cat named Einstein.

FIFTY-TWO

Drip, drip, drip. July. The faucet is leaking. Why am I even hearing it or thinking about that? Why am I looking at the paisley pattern on the bedspread and counting the little dots around the leaves while the doctor on speaker phone says the word *adenocarcinoma*, matter-of-factly as if it's a weather phenomenon we're experiencing instead of a death sentence we're likely getting? Why am I thinking about what the doctor is thinking as he gives us this news, and whether he's just going to hang up the phone and go to lunch or on vacation while we find ourselves suddenly teetering at the edge of an abyss?

Drip, drip, drip. August. A small fountain gurgles gently in the snug massage therapy room while I lay face down on the table, trying to empty my mind and enjoy the Stress Relief Special, hot stones and essential oils gliding over my skin.

My mother has brought me to the refuge of the Ojai Valley Inn for a short respite before the real onslaught begins. Jake will start chemo next week, so I have left him in the care of his mother so that I can seek momentary sanctuary with mine.

I'm comforted in the bosom of this quiet place and of my mother's love. I'm taken aback by her boundless and fierce protection of me—a lioness with her cub. I've probably likewise surprised her with my willingness to receive it. I find my prickliness to be dissolving, revealing something soft, pliable, encompassing and in need of kindness. Surprisingly, this doesn't shame me; I lean into it and allow this mother's milk, which I had resisted or thought was something else, into my veins.

Drip, drip, drip. October. Poison inches its way from the bag attached to the pole, through an IV line and into the port under the skin of my husband's chest. That poison will invade him here at the oncology clinic and then a different kind will be delivered to our doorstep for a continuous at-home infusion.

I sit in the straight-backed chair next to his recliner, wondering if this slow-moving army of toxins will kill the thing that's killing my husband or whether they'll just combine forces into an evil axis that kills him. I've lost track of time already, barely a month into this. It's autumn—at least in the world outside of this room. It's been a season of ceaseless sunny skies and hot days, a numbing sameness that has started to feel tiresome and almost sinister. My breath rises and falls in my chest. I think of our summer of love, and then the one of nesting, and then the one of fear, and then this past one, of raging at cancer's cruel ripping away of our dreams and schemes. I know this current season will also, at some point, shape-shift into something else. Maybe better, maybe worse. Notwithstanding the weather, our lives will not remain the same.

Drip, drip, drip. December. I think of the blood of Christ, and the delicate pale body on the cross at Church of the Good Shepherd, where long ago I kneeled with my stepmother for midnight Mass. I sit alone in the back pew of a different church this Christmas Eve, stealing an hour away while Jake safely rests in an opioid slumber, praying to Whom, I don't know, for a miracle I do know won't happen. The Christ on this cross is still a Savior of someone else's understanding, eyes sorrowful and disappointed, no doubt let down by the sorry lot for whom He was sacrificed. I also think of the slow ebbing away of my husband's life force, which I try to combat with IV fluids, prayer and whatever supplement the Internet tells me I should give him. I lie most nights in the spare room so I don't disturb him, watching tornado porn on YouTube, footage of mile-long F5 storms carrying away entire towns. I wish some force of nature more noble than cancer would be the thing that carries us both away. Sudden and apocalyptic death by a great funnel cloud from above is preferable to the indignity of a hospital bed, diapers and morphine.

Drip, drip, drip. Time. I think of my stepfather's towering grandfather clock and the orderly ticking that reverberated through our home, culminating in a chimed tune every fifteen minutes. And all the clocks in my best friend Yuko's house that weren't synchronized but still incremental. Still chronological. Today, time doesn't tick, and it doesn't feel either incremental or chronological. Instead, it melts, like the clock in Salvador Dali's painting, the seconds, minutes and hours gathering as one teardrop after another, each a murky chrysalis of possibility.

The only thing I believe to be true is that my husband is dying.

Perhaps no longer nourished by his care and feeding, I'll dry up and blow away like a cocoon whose inhabitant never evolves enough to emerge. Or perhaps I actually *will* emerge from this, broken but not so much that I can't somehow flutter above the ashes of dashed dreams and a story that veered horribly off script.

Perhaps. It's a magical, powerful, maddening word, containing every possibility and lacking any certainty. I have had to learn to live and love in the world of Perhaps. Sooner than later, I suspect, I'll have to grieve there as well. Perhaps isn't an entirely bad place, though. I find there to be something comforting about existing in a long, dark gravity-less rabbit hole where there's no knowable destination, where at least for now no one expects anything of me and where getting through the damn day feels like achievement enough.

I'm starting to wonder whether my Higher Power, Jehovah, God, Whatever or Whoever, is no more and no less than a whispering presence named *Perhaps*.

EPILOGUE

You, the one who gathered me up when I washed ashore limp and loveless, are gone.

I am here.

She, the one who took you and loved you for better and for worse, in health and then in sickness, until death did us part, is gone too. Another survives her.

I am here.

There's a little sandbar off Poipu Beach on Kauai that used to be easily accessible by foot. Over the years, storms have remodeled the shoreline so that you either have to swim there or gingerly navigate the surrounding rock beds leading to it. Sometimes both.

Seven years ago, Jake introduced me to this island on what became a belated honeymoon. The mild, leeward south side of Kauai was his favorite. We spent a lot of time meandering that beach, but found ourselves mostly on the isthmus, exploring tide pools and peering at their slithering, sideways-crawling inhabitants, or photographing the indifferent, solitary monk seals that lumbered ashore for naps. From that vantage point, we could see waves lashing the rocky coastline to the northeast, and in the opposite direction, ribbons of placid beach.

Jake dug holes in the sand, and I searched for shells and sea glass while we made a Plan—the first we'd ever had the courage to make. To come back here for good after he retired in ten years and rent some little shack in Kapa'a a couple of blocks from the beach. He'd buy a boat, run sunset excursions, do a little handyman work. I'd tutor kids during the school year and then teach fitness classes at resorts during the high season. We'd be frugal locovores, feasting on fish and island-grown produce. The isthmus served as a protective cradle for our furtive weaving, a place of pleasing separation and distance from mainland complications and from the persistent sense of never being able to achieve quite enough back there.

Last summer, we came back for the second time. Except there hung in the air the question marks around Jake's health. The tests had started. By that time, we knew there was a shadow on his pancreas and that, along with his increasing physical pain, cast a huge pall over what should have been a celebratory pre-retirement trip and the beginning of some long-awaited financial security.

Instead, we sat quietly on the isthmus, Jake dulled by OxyContin, and me dulled by the shock of what was uncontrollably and tragically unfolding. In the space between us lay The Plan, disappearing into the abyss of a jarring new reality. I had started down the rabbit hole of researching his symptoms, so I was beginning the awful process of knowing—and of knowing that he knew as well.

Today I stand on Poipu beach, shading my face with my hand, looking across the water at the isthmus. A snorkel, fins, and a small, sealed plastic bag are at my feet. Mark, Jeannie and Jeannie's boyfriend are lolling under a striped umbrella up the beach a ways, no doubt taking the opportunity for a quick vape while I'm off on my walk. Which is fine—the kids already got their vote on where to scatter the ashes: Waimea Canyon yesterday, Ke'e Beach the day before. Now it's my turn.

I grab the baggie and paddle out to the sandbar before peeling off the fins and picking my way across the surrounding rocks.

Plopping down onto the sand where we last sat together next to the rock that we had decided looked like a cat's head, I open the baggie.

First, the bracelet I had made for Jake when he started chemo, black and white lettered beads on a maroon string. S-U-R-V-I-V-O-R. His body faltered, but the beautiful heart that beat within it never hardened, even though it had every right to, given the hand he was dealt. A heart that stayed golden, right until his last breath, in our bedroom, in my arms.

Then, the stones engraved with the words *Strength* and *Healing*, stones that he carried in his pocket to every treatment. He showed up and let them wreck his body, gambling for more time despite the dismal odds. He sucked it up for Thanksgiving and Christmas and worked when he could through nausea, diarrhea and crushing fatigue. That was his strength.

And though he couldn't overcome what was pretty much the worst draw in the cancer lotto, his legacy to me was an unconditional and healing love. That gift will endure. Perhaps one day it will turn me toward the sun again.

And then the necklace, the palm-shaped Hamsa amulet my mother gave me for protection after Jake's diagnosis. I recognize that I mostly did my best to manage the unmanageable. And the clashing armies of sadness and guilt and regret and anxiety and anger thus far haven't figured out how to join forces and take me down. I suppose all that seems to be good enough evidence of protection.

I dig a hole next to Cat's Head Rock, place the four items in it, and fill the hole with wet sand.

Then I put the fins and mask on and paddle back toward the living. *I am here.*

ACKNOWLEDGEMENTS

Special thanks to:

My family, for providing a fertile ground for growth.

Jodi Gaines, for unconditionally loving and supporting all the versions of me it took to get here.

Gregory Copploe, for lighting the path and keeping me on it.

Julie Vogel, for being the best friend, stylist and unofficial therapist a girl could ask for.

Don Cromwell, for helping me find my way to good again.

And, all who supported me on this journey. You know who you are, and I appreciate you.

www.ingramcontent.com/pod-product-compliance
Lightning Source LLC
Chambersburg PA
CBHW071553120726
48009CB00001B/31